Teaching and Learning in a Multilingual School

Choices, Risks, and Dilemmas

Language, Culture, and Teaching
Sonia Nieto, Series Editor

Teaching and Learning in a Multilingual School

Choices, Risks, and Dilemmas

Tara Goldstein
*Ontario Institute for Studies in Education
of the University of Toronto*

With written contributions by
Gordon Pon
Timothy Chiu
Judith Ngan

LAWRENCE ERLBAUM ASSOCIATES, PUBLISHERS
2003   Mahwah, New Jersey   London

Lawrence Erlbaum Associates, Inc., Publishers
10 Industrial Avenue
Mahwah, NJ 07430

Cover design by Kathryn Houghtaling Lacey

Library of Congress Cataloging-in-Publication Data

Goldstein, Tara, 1957– .
Teaching and learning in a multilingual school : choices, risks, and
dilemmas / Tara Goldstein.
        p. cm. — (Language, culture, and teaching)
    Includes bibliographical references and index.
ISBN 0-8058-4016-8 (p : alk. paper)
1. Linguistic minorities—Education (Secondary)—Ontario—
Toronto—Case studies.   2. Education, Bilingual—Ontario—
Toronto—Case studies.   3. Educational anthropology—Ontario—
Toronto—Case studies.   I. Title.   II. Series.
LC3734.3.T67 G65   2002
370.117'09713'541 —dc21   2002023159
                                                                 CIP

Printed in the United States of America
10   9   8   7   6   5   4   3   2   1

To the students, teachers,
principals and administrative staff
at Northside Secondary School

Contents

Part II   Dilemmas of Discrimination

Series Foreword

Sonia Nieto
University of Massachusetts, Amherst

What does it take to be an effective educator today? It is becoming increasingly clear that the answer to this question lies not only in knowing subject matter content or learning specific strategies. Teachers today also need to know more about the students who currently occupy U.S. classrooms and, even more important, they need to challenge the conventional wisdom concerning the abilities and skills of these students. The goal of the textbooks in the *Language, Culture, and Teaching* series is to help teachers accomplish these things.

At the dawn of the 21st century, the United States is more ethnically, racially, and linguistically diverse than it has ever been. The 2000 Census, for instance, found that whereas Whites decreased from 80% to 75% of the total population in the 10-year period from 1990–2000, the African American population increased slightly (from 12.1% to 12.3%), as did the American Indian population (0.8 to 0.9 percent). Even more dramatic, the Asian population increased from 2.8 to 3.6 percent and the Latino population grew by more than one quarter, from 9% to 12.5% of the total (U.S. Bureau of the Census, 2002).

A striking indication of this growing diversity can be found in the current number of foreign-born or first-generation U.S. residents, which in 2000 reached 56 million, the highest level in U.S. history, or triple the number in 1970 (Schmidley, 2002). Unlike previous immigrants, who were principally from Europe, over half of the new immigrants came from Latin America and a quarter are from Asia (U.S. Bureau of the Census, 2000). The growing immigration has been accompanied by an increasing linguistic diversity: Nearly 18% of the total U.S. population now speak a language other than English at home, with over half of these speaking Spanish (U.S. Bureau of the Census, 2000).

The impact of the growing cultural and linguistic diversity is nowhere more visible than in our schools. Over 3 million students, or 7.4% of all those enrolled in both public and private schools in the United States, are limited in their English proficiency (Macías & Kelly, 1996). Moreover, of the 47 million students enrolled in public elementary and secondary schools, nearly 40% are Hispanic, Black, Asian, or American Indian (National Center for Education Statistics, 2002). This percentage is misleadingly low, however, because most students of color are enrolled in urban schools, which are far more diverse: By 2000, the 100 largest school districts in the country had a so-called "minority" enrollment of 68%. These 100 school districts alone serve fully 40% of all students of color in our nation's schools (National Center for Education Statistics, 2001). It is in these schools that most prospective teachers will work.

Diversity is certainly not limited to urban centers; many suburban and rural schools are also experiencing tremendous changes in student diversity, and every school in the nation will soon be characterized by similar cultural, racial, and language diversity. But in spite of the growing diversity in schools around the country, racial and ethnic segregation in schools has been on the rise. Indeed, much of the progress made in integrating the nation's schools during the past several decades was wiped out by the end of the 1990s. For Blacks, the 1990s witnessed the largest backward movement toward segregation since the *Brown v. Board of Education* decision (Orfield, 2001). For Latinos, the situation has been damaging as well: Currently, Latinos are the most segregated of *all* ethnic groups not only in terms of race and ethnicity, but also poverty (Orfield, 2001).

Poverty in the United States as a whole, which had grown to 14.5% of the total population from 1970 through the mid-1990s, improved somewhat during the 1990s because of the booming U.S. economy (U.S. Bureau of the Census, 2000). Nevertheless, African Americans and Latinos, among other groups, are still over-represented among the poor: Whereas Whites represent just over 9% of the poor, Blacks make up over 22% and Hispanics over 21% of those living in poverty (U.S. Bureau of the Census, 2000). The connection between poverty and poor academic achievement is very high, for reasons ranging from ill-equipped schools to poorly prepared teachers, to the mismatch between how families prepare their children for school and the expectations that schools have of families.

Along with the changing complexion of U.S. schools, notions of how best to educate students of different backgrounds have also changed over the years. Although the common school movement of the late 19th century provided educational access to a much broader segment of the population than had been the case previously, a time-honored function of the public schools was to assimilate young people to be more like the "mainstream." Spring (1997) has made a compelling case that rather than a noble effort to provide all students with an equal education, the common school movement was primarily "an attempt to halt the drift towards a multicultural society" (p. 4). Indeed, U.S. educational history is replete with examples of racist and exclusionary policies that served to segregate or remove from school, Native American, African American, Asian, and Latino students, and that discriminated against children of Southern and Eastern European backgrounds (Kaestle, 1983; Spring, 1997; Takaki, 1993; Weinberg, 1977).

Assumptions about cultural and racial superiority and inferiority have a long and deep-seated history in our educational history, and these notions have often found their way into teacher education texts. For much of our educational history, the conventional wisdom was that students whose cultures and languages differed from the majority were functioning with a deficiency rooted in their very identities. Consequently, the thinking was that the sooner students assimilated to become more like the majority—in culture, language, appearance, experience, and values—the easier their transition to the mainstream and middle class would be. In the latter part of the 20th century, these ideas began to be repudiated, largely by people from the very backgrounds whose identities were being disparaged. It is no accident that educational movements in favor of ethnic studies, bilingual and multicultural education, and affirmative action all emerged around the same time. These movements represented a denouncement of ideologies that had heretofore excluded large segments of the population from achieving educational success.

Continuing in that tradition, the books in the *Language, Culture, and Teaching* series challenge traditional biases about cultural, linguistic, racial, social class, and other kinds of diversity, and about students who embody those differences. Written by a range of educators and researchers from a variety of cultural backgrounds and disciplines, these books attempt to fill the gap that currently exists in preparing teachers for the schools and class-rooms of the 21st century. Aimed primarily at teachers and prospective teachers, the books focus on the intersections of language, culture, and teaching—specifically, on how language and culture inform classroom practice. At the same time, the series reframes the conventional idea of the textbook by envisioning classroom practice as critical, creative, and liberatory. Rather than viewing the textbook as unquestioned authority, the *Language, Culture, and Teaching* series asks readers to reflect, question, critique, and respond to what they read through their thinking and practice. Using the "problem-posing" approach proposed by Freire (1970), the books in this series ask prospective and practicing teachers to think imaginatively and critically about teaching and learning, especially in terms of cultural and linguistic diversity.

The books in this series also support the Freirian idea that education is never neutral or objective. The role of teachers is likewise never neutral, but a *political project* on behalf of, or against, the interests of those they teach. The books in this series do not claim to have all the answers, but they encourage readers to question their beliefs and attitudes about their students, and to con-sider why and how they teach. By taking the intelligence of teachers seri-ously, these books remind teachers, in the words of Freire (1985), that "to study is not to consume ideas, but to create and re-create them" (p. 4).

REFERENCES

Freire, P. (1970). *Pedagogy of the oppressed.* New York: Seabury Press.

Freire, P. (1985). *The politics of education: Culture, power, and liberation.* South Hadley, MA: Bergin & Garvey.

Kaestle, C. F. (1983). *Pillars of the republic: Common schools and American society, 1780–1860.* New York: Hill and Wang.

Macías, R. F., & Kelly, C. (1996). *Summary report of the survey of the States' limited English proficient students and available educational programs and services 1994–1995.* Washington, DC: U.S. Department of Education, Office of Grants and Contracts Services, The George Washington University.

National Center for Education Statistics (NCES). (2001). *Characteristics of the 100 largest public elementary and secondary school districts in the United States: 1999–2000.* Washington, DC: Author.

National Center for Education Statistics (NCES). (2002). *Public school student, staff, and graduate counts by state: School year 2000–2001.* Washington, DC: Author.

Orfield, G. (2001). *Schools more separate: Consequences of a decade of resegregation.* Cambridge, MA: The Civil Rights Project, Harvard University.

Schmidley, D. (2002). *Profile of the foreign-born population in the United States: 2000.* Washington, DC: Bureau of the Census, U.S. Department of Commerce.

Spring, J. (1997). *Deculturalization and the struggle for equality: A brief history of the education of dominated cultures in the United States* (2nd ed). New York: McGraw-Hill.

Takaki, R. (1993). *A different mirror: A history of multicultural America.* Boston: Little, Brown and Company.

U.S. Bureau of the Census. (2000). *Poverty in the Untied States: 2000.* Washington, DC: U.S. Government Printing Office.

U.S. Bureau of the Census. (2002). *USA statistics in brief: Population and vital statistics.* Retrieved from http://www.census.gov/statab/www/poppart.html

Weinberg, M. (1977). *A chance to learn: A history of race and education in the U.S.* Cambridge, UK: Cambridge University Press.

Preface

This book is for teachers and teacher educators working in communities that educate adolescents who do not use the school's language of instruction as their primary language. At the center of the book are findings from a 4-year, critical, ethnographic case study (1996 to 2000) of Northside, an English-speaking Canadian high school (Grades 10 through 13) that had recently enrolled a large number of immigrant students from Hong Kong.[1] The arrival of these students, many of whom chose to speak Cantonese at the school, had an impact on the school's linguistic and cultural environment and the ways teachers and students traditionally worked together. A variety of new issues and dilemmas had to be thought through and negotiated.

In this book, I explore two different kinds of schooling dilemmas: dilemmas of speech and silence (chaps. 2, 3, and 4) and dilemmas of discrimination (chaps. 5 and 6). Although specific in many ways to their particular context, these issues and dilemmas are also general; they arise, in various forms, in all English-speaking schools that serve populations of students whose first language is not English. Thus, the relevance of this book extends far beyond the one school and community on which it focuses. Readers are actively encour-

[1]The ethnographic data on which the book is based has been collected with the assistance of a 3-year Social Sciences and Humanities Research Council of Canada (SSHRCC) grant (1996–1999). I wish to acknowledge and thank SSHRCC for its financial support. I also wish to acknowledge and thank my research collaborator, Cindy Lam, for her assistance and analytical insights during the first two years of the project. Northside, the name given to the school in this book, is a pseudonym.

aged to think about how the issues and dilemmas manifest themselves in other contexts and can be adapted and applied in their own settings.

For the teachers at Northside who worried about helping their students become more proficient in English, one set of dilemmas revolved around how to best encourage their students to speak and practice English. Other dilemmas included deciding how, if at all, to modify teaching and assessment practices to accommodate the large number of students who did not use English as their primary language. For Cantonese-speaking students, dilemmas included deciding whether to speak English or Cantonese at school and whether or not to "cross" linguistic, cultural, and racial boundaries when developing school friendships.[2] For students who did not speak Cantonese, there were challenges around how to most productively negotiate linguistic, cultural, and racial differences in group work and collaborative student projects.

Each chapter in the book includes four components: an excerpt from the ethnographic study of Northside, an analytic commentary on the ethnographic text, a pedagogical discussion, and suggestions for further reflection and discussion.

- *Ethnographic Excerpts From the Study.* The ethnographic texts that open each chapter have been selected from the research study at Northside for their potential to describe and illustrate the dilemmas under discussion.
- *Commentary.* The analytic commentaries following each ethnographic text are drawn from a variety of theoretical perspectives and cross a number of academic disciplines and fields. These include interactionist sociolinguistics, language minority education, English as a second language (ESL) education, critical literacy, antiracist education, and critical teacher education. By separating ethnographic description from ethnographic analysis, I hope to provide readers with room to undertake their own analysis of the dilemmas presented before reading mine.[3]

---

[2]The notion of "crossing" linguistic, cultural, and racial boundaries comes from Ben Rampton (1995). Working through such dilemmas and challenges was not easy. There were a number of ways to think about and respond to different issues and not all teachers and students agreed on what was the most effective way of moving forward. This book is about the multitude of ways teachers and students in one school thought about, responded to, and negotiated linguistic and academic dilemmas with each other. The insights they derived from their experiences of working across linguistic, cultural, and racial differences are valuable to educators everywhere who work in communities that have become home to large numbers of immigrant families.

[3]I was first introduced to this innovative writing practice in the work of Ruth Behar (1993).

- *Pedagogical Discussion.* In addition to analyzing and comparing findings from my own research study with those in other communities, I have tried to build on the ethnographic insights offered by the teachers and students at Northside by including a discussion of pedagogy in each chapter.
- *For Further Reflection and Discussion.* The inclusion of activities at the end of the Pedagogical Discussion sections provide readers with opportunities to think about their own schooling experiences and apply the insights they gain from the chapter to their own teaching and learning contexts.

Features of the Text

Play Reading for Critical Teacher Education.   One source for the activities at the end of each chapter comes from a play I have written based on some of the ethnographic data from the Northside study. The play, *Hong Kong, Canada,* is included in Appendix A. Although the characters and plot in *Hong Kong, Canada* are fictional, the linguistic and racial conflicts dramatized in the play actually occurred and were documented during my fieldwork. Parts of some of the monologues and dialogues have been taken verbatim from the study's interview transcripts. The first activity involving work with the play appears in chapter 1 and asks readers to read the entire play aloud so they will be familiar with its plot, characters, and conflicts. By "performing ethnography" and thinking about the play in terms of their own educational settings, readers can compare the characters' experiences in the Canadian city of Toronto with their own.

Critical Educational Ethnography: Methodology and Decisions. Readers who are interested in the methodological choices I made while designing, conducting, and writing up the critical ethnographic study at Northside can find a methodological discussion in Appendix B. In writing this book, I have come to think about the manuscript as a "hybrid ethnographic text" that combines insights from ethnographic study with pedagogical discussions for educators working in multilingual schools. Characterizing this book as a hybrid ethnographic text as well as teacher education text allows me (and perhaps other education professors) to use the book in graduate qualitative research methodology courses. Key to its use in such a course is a fully developed methodological discussion. Moreover, because a 4-year, critical, ethnographic study is at the center of the text, a detailed methodological discussion is expected.

Dilemmas of Curriculum and Assessment and Strategies for Developing Oral Presentation Skills. Although the book has been organized around dilemmas of speech, silence, and discrimination, readers will find that everyday dilemmas of curriculum and assessment are also discussed throughout the book. As well, in the last appendix, which is particularly related to the discussion in chapter 6 on oral presentations, I have included a set of activities that might be of interest to readers who need to teach their students the discourse of making English oral presentations at school. The activities in Appendix C were designed by teacher and research assistant Judith Ngan and were used in a workshop Judith gave at Northside.

Discussion of Other Immigrant Communities. As mentioned earlier, it is the ethnographic data from the Northside study that initiates the analytic and pedagogical discussions in this book. However, a discussion of other immigrant communities is taken up in each of the chapters. In some chapters, this discussion appears in the Commentaries. In others, it appears in the Pedagogical Discussions or Activities for Further Reflection.

Overview

The book begins with an introduction that provides readers with an ethnographic description of the linguistically diverse student body at Northside and bilingual Cantonese–English life at the school. It includes excerpts from student interviews and discusses how and why Cantonese- speaking students born in Hong Kong used Cantonese as well as English to achieve academic and social success at school.

As previously mentioned, I explore two different kinds of academic and linguistic dilemmas in this book. The chapters in Part I discuss the ways teachers and students negotiated dilemmas of speech and silence. Chapter 2, "Accepting and Legitimizing Multilingualism," begins with an excerpt from an interview with math teacher Evelyn Lo, who encouraged her students to use their primary languages when working on the math problems she assigned.[4] The Commentary examines the teaching and learning dilemmas associated with the use of languages other than English in the classroom and the Pedagogical Discussion suggests ways teachers might think about negotiating the politics of language use in their own classrooms.

---

[4]The names of all of the teachers and students in this book are pseudonyms except for student playwright Timothy Chiu, whose work appears in chapter 6.

Chapter 3, "Promoting and Legitimizing English," looks at the work of a teacher who promoted English monolingualism in her classrooms. The chapter begins with an excerpt from an interview with Hong Kong-born English teacher Anne Yee, who had implemented an English-only policy in her classroom as a way of providing her English as a second or other language (ESOL) students with more opportunities to practice English. The Commentary examines the dilemmas that arise from promoting English monolingualism in the classroom and includes a discussion of students' responses to Mrs. Yee's classroom English-only policy. The Pedagogical Discussion in chapter 3 continues to explore the strategy of promoting English monolingualism by looking at the lessons that can be learned from the American Ebonics Debate which took place during the 1996–1997 school year, the first year of the study at Northside.

In chapter 4, "Responding to Silence," antiracist educator and writer Gordon Pon and I explore the issue of student silence in multilingual classrooms. The chapter begins with two students' accounts of silences in Anne Yee's English classroom. Focusing on the finding that some of the students resented the Cantonese-speaking students' silences and found them burdensome, in the Commentary, Gordon and I make use of the theoretical work undertaken by Asian-American scholar King Kok Cheung, who provides us with alternative ways of understanding classroom silences.[5] The Pedagogical Discussion in chapter 4 explores how teachers and students might work with student silences in their own classrooms.

Teachers and students who work in multilingual, multicultural, and multiracial schools not only need to negotiate dilemmas of speech and silence, they also need to learn how to cope and challenge the everyday discrimination they face both inside and outside school. The chapters in Part II of the book discuss the ways different students at Northside experienced discrimination and the ways these experiences might be dealt with at school.

Chapter 5, "Resisting Anti-Immigrant Discourses and Linguicism," begins with excerpts from an art journal of a Canadian-born, Chinese art student named Evelyn Yeung. For Evelyn, the recent arrival of students from Hong Kong at Northside resulted in her being marked as a recent immigrant because she was Chinese. This marking meant that she was forced to deal with anti-immigrant discourses and prejudices on a daily basis. Although she was marked as a Chinese immigrant from Hong Kong, Evelyn was also marked as not being Chinese by her classmates from Hong Kong because she could not read and write in Chinese. In response to Evelyn's acute dis-

---

[5]See Cheung (1993).

comfort with both of these markings art teacher Leslie Edgars, suggested that she work on an art project that required her to learn how to write in Chinese, seeking help from some of her Hong Kong-born classmates. The Commentary analyzes Evelyn's artwork as a pedagogical project that challenged various discourses of discrimination and the Pedagogical Discussion focuses on what teachers and teacher educators can learn from the antiracist work that Ms. Edgars and Evelyn undertook together.

Chapter 6, "Oral Presentations, Accent Discrimination, and Linguistic Privilege," begins with a play written by one of the students at Northside entitled *No Pain, No Gain*. The play was produced in a summer playwriting workshop that involved 15 students from Anne Yee's English class. In his play, Timothy Chiu, who immigrated to Toronto as an adolescent, talks about the pain associated with having to give an oral presentation in his second language and the disappointment of a performance that does not live up to his own and his family's expectations of excellence. In the Commentary, Timothy's play is analyzed in terms of the pedagogical and assessment dilemmas that arise for teachers and students when not all members of a multilingual school community have the same kinds of linguistic capital and privilege. In the Pedagogical Discussion, the analysis moves from what Timothy says in his play to an analysis of how the playwriting workshop helped him develop the skills he needed to produce better classroom presentations.

The book concludes with a chapter entitled "Challenging Linguistic Inequities in Multilingual School Communities," which summarizes the different ways student multilingualism was received at Northside. The concluding chapter also discusses what kind of school language policy most effectively challenges educational linguistic inequities facing ESOL students enrolled in schools where English is the language of instruction.

In the following pages, then, readers are introduced to a variety of dilemmas that teachers and students working in multilingual, multiracial schools need to negotiate daily. It is my hope that this book's mix of ethnographic description, analysis, and pedagogical discussion will provide readers with insights that are useful in their own multilingual schooling contexts.

A Word About Language

Choosing the right words to write about linguistic, ethnic, and racial differences is a complex undertaking. Following sociolinguist and educational researcher Angel Lin and the students at Northside, I refer to Cantonese as a language even though I recognize there is debate on whether Cantonese is best described as a language or a variety or dialect of Chinese.[1]

In discussions of racial identities, I followed antiracist educator and writer Beverly Daniel Tatum and used the word *White* to refer to people of European descent. Following Sonia Nieto and Carol Mullen, I used the word *Anglo-Canadian* to describe White people in Canada who are British in origin and *Euro-Canadian* to describe White people in Canada who are European but not British in origin.[2] I have also followed Beverly Tatum in using the words *people of color* to refer to those groups in Canada and the United States that are and have been historically targeted by racism. Like Tatum, I recognize that the expression *people of color* is not perfect as it insinuates that White people have no color. I also recognize that working with White students to recognize their Whiteness and White privilege is key to antiracist teacher education practice.[3] When referring to people of color from various groups of color, I use the words that the people them-

---

[1]See Lin (1997b, 2001).

[2]See Tatum (1997), Nieto (2000) and Mullen (1999).

[3]For a short review of what such antiracist teacher education practice might look like see Goldstein (2001b), Mullen (1999); Olson (1999); Sleeter (1999); Lawrence and Tatum (1999).

selves have used to describe themselves and others. A particular comment about the word *Oriental*, which was sometimes used by students to describe Asians and Asian Canadians, is important here. Many people find the term Oriental, when used in reference to people, to be offensive. As writers Jeff Yang, Dina Gan, and Terry Hong explained, there are several reasons why:

"Oriental" brings up painful chapters in Asian global history. The terms *Orient* and *Oriental* were popularized during the height of Western colonialism, when nations to the south and east of Europe were subjugated and exploited. As a result, use of the term can be an automatic cue for references to the British Raj, the Opium War, the occupation of the Philippines, and other events and periods in which the inhabitants of Asian countries were enslaved, victimized, or otherwise mistreated by Europeans (and later, North Americans).

It has problematic racial and political connotations. Although *Orient* translates simply as *The East* for many people, over time, particular ideas have become associated with the term: The Orient was seen as the farthest point from civilization (i.e., Europe) and a region of barbarism, exotic custom, and strange delight. As discussed in chapter 2, Orientals were conceived as mysterious and inscrutable, with traditions and beliefs so different as to be inhuman—and thus requiring of either speculative study (e.g., by anthropologists or religious evangelism).[4] As social historian Edward Said detailed in his seminal book, *Orientalism*, the intent and result of orientalism was the objectification of cultures in Asia and the Middle East, providing a rationale for colonial subjugation, missionary conversion, and military adventure.[5] Later, it also created a context for domestic racism and xenophobia.

It's nonspecific. As perceived by western Europeans, The Orient included all of Turkey, the Middle East, Asia, and to a lesser extent the Pacific Islands. An Iranian was therefore just as Oriental as a Chinese person, though in contemporary times, the term is never used in that manner. While the term *Asian* is not much more specific, it is at least a term bounded by geography rather than a set of ideas.

It doesn't have an appropriate counterpart. The term *Oriental* stands alone: No one refers to Europeans or Americans as *Occidentals* (which is loaded with the same imagery and history as *Oriental*).

---

[4]The term "other people's children": was created by Lisa Delpit (1995).
[5]See Said (1994).

It's more appropriately used for inanimate objects. The establishment of trade routes linking the nations of Asia and the Middle East (which occurred long before the opening of Asia to the West) meant that commodities and other goods were regularly transmitted between cultures. As a result, when people refer to Oriental spices or rugs, they have a stable rationale from which to speak: Spices and rugs are among the only things that the group of peoples known as Orientals actually had in common. In general, Yan, Gan, and Hong believe that the use of the adjective in relation to inanimate objects or abstract concepts has largely been considered acceptable, if not embraced.[6]

Many of us teaching and learning in North American schools have never been taught that the word *Oriental* can cause offense. As a result, some of the participants in the study used the word to describe Asians and Asian Canadians. When writing this book, I decided not to replace the participants' use of the word Oriental with the words Asian or Asian Canadians. My intent in including the word in participants' quotations is to illustrate the continuing legacy of Orientalism, which students and teachers need to challenge in our classrooms.

---

[6]See Yang, Gan, and Hong (1997).

Acknowledgments

This book about choices, risks, and dilemmas in a multilingual high school was undertaken with the strong support of an important network of people. I owe them all a great deal of thanks.

First, I would like to thank the students, teachers, principals, and administrative staff at Northside Secondary School in Toronto, who opened up their school lives to the research team and me and allowed us to learn from them. Not only did they answer our countless questions, but they also shared their talk with us. I greatly appreciate their willingness to put up with the inconvenience of tape recorders and microphones in their classrooms and I want to thank them for their trust that we would use their words well. I also want to thank the staff from the Research Office at (what is now) the Toronto District School Board. They provided helpful feedback on the project, guided me through the Board's ethical review process, and introduced me to the principals at Northside, who gave me permission to conduct research at the school. I would also like to acknowledge the Social Sciences and Humanities Council of Canada for its financial support of the research study.

I must acknowledge the significant contribution made by Cindy Lam, who worked as co-investigator on the project. Cindy engaged in continual dialogue with me on the interpretation of the data collected in the first 2 years of the study and her insights have helped shaped the content of this book. In the third year of the project, when I began experimenting with the genre of playwriting as a way to disseminate some of the research findings, my playwriting instructor, Larry Carr, played a key role in helping me develop the dramatic writing skills I needed to create an ethnographic playscript. I very much appreciated his fine instruction. The nine graduate and undergraduate students who worked as research assistants on the project contributed to the quality of the data that was collected, the sense that was made of the data, and the ways we were able to "give something back" to the people participating in the study. I would like to thank and acknowledge research assistants Tammy Chan, Wing-Yee Chow, Veronica Hsueh, Judith Ngan, Gordon Pon, Victoria Shen, Edmund Tang, Noel Tsang, and Alice Yeung for their excellent work and commitment to the project.

Series Editor Sonia Nieto, Naomi Silverman from Lawrence Erlbaum Associates, and applied linguist Angel Lin from the City University of Hong Kong provided suggestions on earlier drafts of this book that were most helpful and I would like to thank them for the time they took to read and comment on my work. Their feedback helped me sharpen my analysis and clarify the points I wanted to make. I would like to acknowledge and thank similarly, Donald F. Hanes from the University of Wisconsin–Oshkosh and Suzanne Irujo at Boston University for their comments as reviewers of the book for Lawrence Erlbaum Associates. Many thanks also go to Margot Huycke, Kelly Allen, and Kathy Scornavacca for their expert copyediting, and to Lori Hawver for her administrative support during the publishing process.

Finally, I wrote this book during a sabbatical leave at the School of Education of the University of Queensland in Brisbane, Australia. I would like to thank Allan Luke, the Dean at the School of Education, for hosting me. Allan's vision, writing, activism, and mentorship in education have stimulated and inspired many of us. I was extremely fortunate to have had the opportunity to work with him and the other exciting faculty and staff at the University of Queensland. Philip Taylor at Griffith University and Susan Grieshaber at the Queensland University of Technology, both also located in Brisbane, and Kerry Robinson and Tania Ferfolja from the University of Western Sydney and the University of New South Wales were wonderful hosts as well. I learned much from engaging with their work.

At the end of these acknowledgments, my thoughts turn to my great Aunt Léa Roback, Québec unionist, political activist, and feminist who died in August, 2000. She and many others of the Roback family have inspired the generations that have followed them with their commitment to the ideals and practice of social justice. Their ideals live again within this book.

—*Tara Goldstein*
Toronto, Ontario

Contributors

Gordon Pon

Gordon Pon is an antiracism educator and social worker. He is currently working in the field of child protection and completing his PhD in education. His doctoral thesis examines the thoughts and feelings that Chinese Canadian students have towards antiracism, education, and globalization.

Timothy Chiu

Timothy Chiu is currently in his second year of an Honors Geography degree in Environmental Studies at the University of Waterloo, in Ontario, Canada. Timothy was born in Hong Kong and immigrated to Toronto at the age of 10. He enjoys playing sports, listening to music, and reading.

Tara Goldstein

Tara Goldstein is an Associate Professor working at the Ontario Institute for Studies in Education of the University of Toronto (OISE/UT). She teaches in both the pre-service teacher education and graduate education programs. Tara's teaching and research interests include working towards equity in education, the education of immigrant adolescents, schooling in multilingual communities, playwriting as critical ethnography, and applied theater research. These interests have all come together in her first ethnographic play,

Hong Kong, Canada, which was performed at the Robert Gil Theatre, University of Toronto, in July 2000. Tara is also the author of *Two Languages at Work: Bilingual Life on the Production Floor* (1997), published by Mouton de Gruyter and the co-editor with David Selby of *Weaving Connections: Educating for Peace, Social and Environmental Justice* (2000), published by Sumach Press.

Judith Ngan

Judith Ngan is a graduate student at the Ontario Institute for Studies in Education of the University of Toronto and was a research assistant at Northside during the first year of the study. Judith is currently working as an elementary school teacher in Ontario.

1

Introduction: Bilingual Life and Language Choice at Northside

Perhaps more than any other debate in education, the study of language grapples with questions of power and identity.

[From *The Real Ebonics Debate: Power, Language, and the Education of African-American Children*][1]

THE CASE OF NORTHSIDE

The four-year critical ethnographic study that instigated the writing of this book began with an investigation of how immigrant high-school students born in Hong Kong used Cantonese as well as English to achieve academic and social success in a Toronto school where English was the language of instruction. Much had been written on teaching strategies for accommodating English as a second or other language (ESOL) high school students in such schools, and setting them up for academic success. However, much less had been written about how students themselves used different lan-

---

[1]See Perry and Delpit (1998).

guages to achieve success.[2] The findings revealed that although the use of Cantonese contributed to academic and social success of in a number of ways, it also created different kinds of linguistic and academic dilemmas for teachers and students in the school. Influenced by contemporary Canadian discourses, beliefs, and policies around immigration and language use, these dilemmas and issues were complex and required skillful negotiation.[3] I learned a lot from watching and listening to the ways students and teachers negotiated academic and linguistic dilemmas at Northside, and I wanted to share what I had learned with other educators working in multilingual communities.

The reason I was interested in undertaking a study of bilingual life at a high school like Northside in the first place had to do with my work as a teacher educator at the Ontario Institute for Studies in Education of the University of Toronto. The conversations I had with students enrolled in the Initial (Pre-Service) Teacher Education program had revealed that their understandings around language learning and the use of languages other than English at school were often limited. As mostly monolingual speakers of English, very few of my students had any personal experience with the difficulties and dilemmas associated with learning and using English at school. I wanted to provide them with an opportunity to hear high-school students and teachers speak to these difficulties and dilemmas. As discussed in greater detail below, having recently enrolled a large number of Cantonese-speaking students from Hong Kong who were using English as a second language, Northside was an excellent school in which to undertake such a study.

---

[2]Educational theorists, educators and applied linguists who have written about ways of creating effective and equitable learning environments that respond to the needs of a linguistically diverse high-school student population include Coelho (1998); Corson (2001); Cummins (1996); Genesee (1994); González and Darling-Hammond (1997); Hernández (1995); Jaramillo and Olsen (1999); McGroarty and Faltis (1991); Nieto (2000); and Pennycook (2001).

[3]As explained by educational theorist Daniel Yon (2000), in popular usage, *discourse* refers simply to conversation and writing. In the field of discourse analysis and discourse theory, however, the term *discourse* is defined as a collection of statements and ideas that structure the way we understand the world around us. Discourse shapes how we come to think and produce new knowledge. To illustrate, different discourses around immigration shape whether or not people think Canada's immigration policies are too lenient or too harsh. Discourse can also facilitate shared understandings and engagements with others. For example, people who share similar ideas on the harshness of current immigration policies can work collectively to lobby for change to these policies. However, although discourse may facilitate thought and action, it may also work to constrain, because it sets up barriers and blind spots to thinking and acting. Anti-immigrant discourses, such as the discourse of invasion discussed in chapter 4, may constrain collective lobbying for more lenient immigration policies.

As a critical, ethnographic, teacher education text, the goal of this book is to reveal and question coercive and discriminatory schooling polices and practices. The lens through which I examine different ways of negotiating linguistic and academic dilemmas reflects this goal. In linking the data from the study with the critical literature in the fields of sociolinguistics and education, I learned that it is not always clear what kinds of practices are coercive and what kinds of practices are not. This uncertainty is reflected in the commentaries and it is my hope that readers will engage with the questions posed there and form their own understandings on how to create effective and equitable learning environments in English-speaking schools that serve multilingual students.

Over the 4 years of the study, I worked as the principal investigator and leader of a multilingual, multicultural, multiracial research team that was composed of a co-investigator, 10 graduate and undergraduate students from two universities in Toronto, as well as some of the high school students studying at Northside. One Chinese Cantonese-speaking parent born in Hong Kong also joined the team as a translator and transcriber for a short period of time. The co-investigator, research assistants, and I did not all work together at one time. There were a total of five research teams: one that was put together for the pilot study in the summer of 1994 and four different research teams that were put together over the 4 years of the project. The research teams and I spent the first 3 years conducting fieldwork at Northside and reading together in study groups.

The fourth year was spent transcribing and translating data, discussing different ways of understanding talk by Cantonese-speaking students, and examining both the bilingual and monolingual transcripts for important ideas and discourses. Further discussion of our fieldwork and the reading we did to enhance our fieldwork is taken up in Appendix B.

The decisions around which data to share with readers in this book rested solely with me. However, the transcribed ethnographic texts, the commentary, and the pedagogical discussion in each chapter have been "member checked" by those research participants who provided the data.[4] The task of member checking the data included verifying that the transcribed ethnographic texts in each chapter actually represented what the participants had wanted to say during their interviews. Any misrepresentation of ideas was corrected and then approved by the research partici-

---

[4]Readers should note that my goal was to have all data and analyses included in the book undergo a process of member checking by those participants whose words had been used. However, it was not possible to locate all of the students who originally participated in the study. As a result, almost all, rather than all, data and analyses have been member checked.

pants before being published here. Similarly, the analyses in the Commentary and Pedagogical Discussion sections were read by those research participants whose words have been analyzed. Any disagreements with my data analysis as well as any elaborations of my data analysis have been included in the book.

In the third summer of the project (July 1998), 15 students from Anne Yee's English class at Northside were hired as student researchers to participate in a 12-session playwriting workshop. As is explained in chapter 6, the goal of the workshop was to provide the students, most of whom did not use English as a first language, with an opportunity to develop their English language skills and write their own ethnographies through the genre of playwriting. As is discussed further in Appendix B, the idea to involve student researchers in ethnographic research through playwriting evolved from the need to negotiate the politics of researching "other people's children."[5] The student playwriting workshop also allowed the research team to work toward what ethnographer Patti Lather calls "catalytic validity," evidence that the research process had led to insight, and ideally, activism on the part of the research participants.[6] An example of one of the plays that was written in the summer playwriting workshop opens chapter 6. A discussion of the ways that the experience of participating in the workshop led to insight change also appears in chapter 6.

Having begun this Introduction with a brief discussion of the research we undertook at Northside, I continue the chapter with a description of the academic programming and linguistically diverse student body at Northside. It is my hope that such a description will provide readers with a set of contextual understandings they can use in thinking about the dilemmas and issues presented in the rest of book. The first ethnographic description is followed by a more specific discussion of bilingual Cantonese–English life at the school. In this second discussion, I look at some of the ways Cantonese-speaking students born in Hong Kong chose to use Cantonese and English in school and the decisions that lie behind their choices. My discussion here does not include a comprehensive analysis of language practices in the Cantonese-speaking community at Northside.[7] Rather, it includes a selected review of those practices that are particularly relevant to the discussion of academic, linguistic, and pedagogical dilemmas that are taken up in the rest of the book.

---

[5]The phrase "other people's children," was coined by Lisa Delpit (1995).
[6]See Lather (1986).
[7]See Heller (1994, 1999); Lin (2001); Rampton (1995).

ACADEMIC PROGRAMMING AND LINGUISTIC DIVERSITY AT NORTHSIDE

Since opening in a mostly middle and upper middle-class suburb north of Toronto in 1970, Northside Secondary School had established a reputation of academic excellence. During the first year of the study, Judith Ngan, one of the research assistants on the project, brought me a copy of the real estate section from one of Toronto's Chinese newspapers. An advertisement for one of the houses located close to the school used the property's proximity to Northside as a selling point. The community is still mostly composed of middle and upper middle-class families; most Northside students were working toward college or university admission, and the school's 1995–1996 *Quality Assurance School Review* reported that students identified high academic standards as a major strength of the school (North York Board of Education, 1996). The *School Review* also reported that students at Northside at 16 years of age achieved at levels above the system average in mathematics testing, literacy testing, and accumulated credits. Students taking mathematics, sciences, and computer sciences at Northside had an impressive record of success in national and international contests and competitions. The school also offered a strong arts program. According to Northside's School *Profile*, a school board publication written to help parents understand what the school had to offer students, about half of the student population took part in the school's visual arts, drama, or music programs. There were also opportunities for students to develop skills outside the classroom by joining programs in peer tutoring, peer counseling, and cooperative education.

According to *School Review*, 86% of the students at Northside were immigrants to Canada and 60% reported that their primary language was a language other than English. The top five primary languages spoken by students were English (38%), Cantonese (35%); Mandarin (6%) and Farsi and Korean (4%). The large percentage of bilingual and multilingual speakers at the school meant that although English was the language of instruction, everyday talk in classrooms, hallways, and the cafeteria took place in English as well as other languages. This was an issue for many people at the school.

The review team, who had interviewed individual teachers, department teams, students, student groups, office staff, caretaking staff, and administrators for the 1995–1996 *School Review*, reported that "all parties interviewed expressed concern about the amount of non-English spoken in both the hallways and classrooms of the school" (p. 3). The team also reported that the group of 10 parents they spoke to expressed "considerable concern about language and the strong feeling was that English should not only be the language of instruction, but also the only language spoken at school" (p. 7). Although the review team didn't explain the reasons behind this concern, one of the recommendations they made was that the school continue to work on the English literacy initiative it had already begun, but also include in this initiative a "major focus on oral [English] language development" (p. 10). I interpreted this recommendation as a direct response to the amount of "non-English" being spoken at school and the desire to make English the only language spoken. What the staff was being asked to do was this: Initiate a schoolwide, oral English development program in a multilingual school where students were already successfully using both English and languages other than English to conduct their academic and social lives.

After reading the *School Review*, the first question that was raised for me was why there was such concern that English be the only language spoken at the school when, overall, Northside students were achieving above the system average and successfully working toward admission to colleges and universities. I initially thought the answer to this question may lie in the linguistic make-up of the school and parent groups the review team spoke to when conducting the school review. Although the majority of students at Northside had a primary language other than English, most of the teachers and staff we spoke to were monolingual or primary speakers of English. And while the review team reported that the group of parents they met with were representative of the school community, it did not state whether the opinions of speakers of languages other than English were represented in the *School Review*. Yet, looking for answers in the linguistic make-up of the interviewees could not fully answer the question of why people were concerned about multilingual practices at Northside. I knew I could not assume that all English speakers believed that English was the only language that should be spoken at the school, and neither did many of my English-speaking colleagues who were public high-school teachers. Nor could I assume that all speakers of languages other than English believed that the use of languages other than English in the classroom was helpful to students studying in their second and third languages. In fact, findings from a 1995 survey study undertaken in Hong Kong, where many students at Northside had begun their secondary school education, revealed the opposite.[8] When asked about their beliefs about the use of English and Chinese as languages of instruction, parents said that English instruction brought about a better standard of English than did a

---

[8]See Tung, Tsang, and Lam (1997) for a full description of this survey research.

combination of English and Chinese instruction.[9] They also said they favored English instruction over Chinese instruction because of the socioeconomic importance of English in Hong Kong.

Importantly, the survey was undertaken before the implementation of the linguistic streaming policy adopted in Hong Kong in September, 1998. After September, 1998, only 114 secondary schools (around 30% of all secondary schools) were allowed to use English as the medium of instruction for their newly admitted (form 1 or grade 7) students. The rest of all publicly funded or subsidized secondary schools (around 70% of all secondary schools) were expected to use Chinese (that is, spoken Cantonese and written Standard Chinese) as the medium of instruction for all new form 1 students.

At the time the 1995 survey was taken, secondary school entrants in Hong Kong took tests that measured their Chinese and English language skills. Students were then classified into three groups according to their test scores in both languages. Students who were placed in group 1 were those whose test scores indicated that they were able to learn effectively in either English or Chinese. Students in group 2 were those whose test scores indicated that they would learn more effectively in Chinese. Students in group 3 were those whose test scores indicated that they would probably learn more effectively in Chinese, but were capable of learning in English. Interactionist sociolinguist Angel Lin, who conducted ethnographic research in Hong Kong secondary classrooms in the mid-1990s, tells us that the majority of secondary schools that had been advised to switch to Chinese as the language of instruction (on the basis of the language test scores of their incoming students) still continued to call themselves "English medium schools." They conducted classes in a Cantonese–English oral mode and English written mode. Lin saw this pedagogical practice as a local coping response in schools where students with limited access to English resources were struggling to acquire an English medium education.[10]

Returning to the findings of the Hong Kong survey, most of the children agreed with their parents' views on English medium instruction; however, they also supported a gradual transition from Chinese to English medium education, and were in favor of teachers using both English and Chinese in the same lesson. In contrast, both parents and teachers tended to believe that teachers should not teach the same lesson in both English and Chinese (even

---

[9]As explained by Lin (2001), Chinese in the Hong Kong context is often taken to mean Cantonese in its spoken form and Modern Standard Chinese in its written form.

[10]See Lin (1997b). As already mentioned, Lin's research was undertaken before the implementation of the 1998 linguistic streaming policy. The language situation in secondary school classrooms since the implementation of the 1998 policy has not been studied.

though many teachers were teaching bilingually in their own classrooms). In commenting about this contradiction, Lin suggested that the surveyed teachers experienced some conflict between what they believed was (officially) correct practice and what they found necessary to do in their own classrooms. She also suggested that the unfavorable attitude toward bilingual classroom practices expressed by parents and teachers in the survey might have been a result of the official, academic, and media discourses, which claimed that bilingual classroom practices have negative educational effects.[11]

Returning to the question of why there was such concern that English be the only language spoken at Northside, the answer seemed to lie in understanding the importance, value, and privileges English held for parents, teachers, and students. It also lay in understanding the kinds of difficulties, tensions, and dilemmas that students and teachers associated with the use of languages other than English at the school. These are discussed in the chapters that follow.

In discussions of the desire for English monolingualism, I have found that it is helpful to distinguish between the desire for a monolingual English classroom and the desire for a monolingual English school. Although the *School Review* reported that there was a strong feeling at Northside that English should not only be the language of instruction, but also the only language spoken at school, not one of the 10 teachers we interviewed had any objections to the use of Cantonese spoken for social interaction outside the classroom. Those who believed that their students' best interests were served by English monolingualism in the classroom did not call for English monolingualism in the hallways or cafeteria.

In August, 1995, very shortly after the *School Review* was submitted to the principal of the school, the school board to which Northside belonged adopted a new language policy. Entitled the *Language for Learning Policy*, the policy consisted of 10 "core assumptions" that administrators and teachers were to adopt as a basis for their planning around language initiatives. Four of the 10 assumptions are particularly relevant for the discussions I pursue in this book. They are the assumptions that:

1. Language, culture, and identity are closely linked. A program that recognizes, respects, and values students' racial, cultural, and linguistic backgrounds, as well as the varieties of language, helps them to develop a positive sense of self and motivates them to learn. All students need opportunities to think critically about the social values and status

---

[11]See Lin (1997a) for a critical analysis of these official, academic, and media discourses.

assigned to different languages by various groups in our society and to explore issues of bias and stereotyping related to language and culture.

2. First-language literacy is important for second-language learning. It helps students to grasp key concepts more easily and influences general academic achievement.

3. All languages and varieties of languages are equally valid forms of thought and communication. Canadian Standard English is the language of instruction in The Board's Schools and all children in The Board's District need to develop proficiency in this language.

4. Students' first languages play an important role in the classroom, in the school program as a whole, and in communication with the home. (*Language For Learning Policy*, pp. 7–8)

While the *Language for Learning Policy* explicitly named and legitimized English as the language of instruction in its schools, it also legitimized student use of languages other than English at school in several ways. First, it asserted that effective, "motivating," school programming was programming that recognized, respected, and valued students' linguistic backgrounds. Secondly, it asserted that first-language literacy was important for second-language learning. Third, it asserted that students' first languages had an important role to play in the classroom and the school program as a whole. The introduction of a language policy that legitimized student multilingualism at the same time the *School Review* acknowledged a local desire for English monolingualism and recommended a schoolwide oral English development initiative produced an extremely interesting moment in Northside's history. Teachers and administrators were being asked to respond to two contradictory desires: the desire for institutional English monolingualism and the desire for student multilingualism. They were also being asked to implement a schoolwide oral English development initiative while recognizing that students' primary languages played an important role in attaining academic success. This moment resulted in teachers experimenting with a variety of pedagogical practices in their classrooms that are at the center of the discussions that follow.

When several different school boards in the metropolitan Toronto area merged to form the new Toronto District School Board in January, 1998, the policies implemented in each school board were replaced with new policies. A new language policy for the new Toronto District School Board was adopted on May 27, 1998, after our classroom observation work had been completed. A discussion of the similarities and differences between the

Language for Learning Policy (North York Board of Education, 1995) and
the new *Literacy Foundation Policy* (Toronto District School Board, 1998)
is taken up in the Conclusion. The impact and implications that the implementation of both language policies have for critical educational practice is
also taken up in the Conclusion.

THE CANTONESE-SPEAKING STUDENTS
AT NORTHSIDE

Although other recent sociolinguistic ethnographies on adolescent language use have investigated the language practices of many of the different
linguistic groups in one school,[12] the study at Northside focused on the language practices of one group, the Cantonese-speaking students who were
born in Hong Kong. The reason behind my choice to limit the scope of the
research project in this way had to do with the recent high enrollment of students from Hong Kong who used Cantonese at school. The students' language practices brought issues of multilingualism into high relief for the
staff at Northside and they were hoping that the research project might bring
new insights.

   Between the years of 1991 and the first 4 months of 1996 (the most recent
statistics available), 48, 535 people, about 11% of the city's population, had
immigrated to Toronto from Hong Kong.[13] As explained by historian Paul
Yee, around the mid-1970s, Canada began making efforts to attract foreign
business immigrants who could bring in capital and entrepreneurial skills to
help the Canadian economy. These efforts were particularly successful with
Hong Kong Chinese who were beginning to worry about their future. When
the People's Republic of China was established in 1949, it was expected that
the Chinese Communists would invade Hong Kong. They had long de-
nounced the "unequal treaties" of the 19th century and never formally recognized Britain's control of Hong Kong. However, China made no military
advances toward the colony. In 1966, Chairman Mao Zedong started his cultural revolution because he thought China was slipping back toward capital-
ism. He purged the army and government of his opponents and established
the Red Guards, teenagers who attacked authority figures such as teachers,
professors, writers, and artists. In 1966, Red Guards invaded Macau, the
Portuguese territory across from Hong Kong, and plastered it with posters.

---

[12]See, for example, Monica Heller's (1999) study on the use of French, English, and Somali in a
French-language minority high school in Toronto and Ben Rampton's (1995) study on the use of
Creole, Panjabi, and Stylized Asian English in an English school in South Midlands, England.

   [13]See Statistics Canada: www.statcan.ca (search "Hong Kong immigration").

A few months later, violent demonstrations against British rule took place in Hong Kong, inspired by the Red Guards. There were strikes and bombings, and martial law was imposed. The economy came to a halt. In July, 300 Chinese soldiers crossed the border and killed five Hong Kong police officers. Property values dropped sharply and so did trade and tourism. But China needed the foreign currency channeled through Hong Kong's trade activities, and by the end of the year, order was established. However, the riots made Hong Kong residents worry about a Communist takeover. Many looked for ways to emigrate and Canada became a popular destination. Yee reports that Hong Kong lost 67,000 of its people to Canada in the period of 1972 to 1978, and 130,410 between 1988 and 1992. Direct investment from Hong Kong grew from $10 million in 1967, to $426 million in 1986, and to $2.3 billion in 1991.

In 1984, China and Britain reached an agreement to transfer Hong Kong back to Chinese rule in 1997. Under the agreement, it would become a "special administrative region" with much control over its government, except for foreign policy and defense. It is intended that Hong Kong retain its capitalist economy within China's socialist system for 50 years after 1997. However, uncertainty about the quality of life under Chinese rule have led many people of the educated middle class in Hong Kong, who have enjoyed high incomes and want to keep their freedom and lifestyle, to leave Hong Kong.[14] Many of the 48,500 middle class people who immigrated to Toronto from Hong Kong between 1991 and the beginning of 1996 settled in several suburbs outside the city and enrolled their children in suburban schools like Northside.

STUDYING LANGUAGE CHOICE

Language-choice research involves finding out what makes people in multilingual settings choose to use one language over another. The study of language choice has been undertaken by sociolinguists, sociologists, social psychologists, and anthropologists. My own work draws on the work undertaken by interactionist sociolinguists Monica Heller, Angel Lin, Marilyn Martin-Jones, Bonny Norton, and Mukul Saxena. These researchers have made use of anthropological research perspectives and traditions and have linked people's individual language choice decisions to their goals and roles in life and larger historical, economic, political, and educational events.[15]

---

[14]See Yee (1996).

[15]See, for example, Heller (1988a, 1988b, 1994, 1995, 1999, 2001); Heller and Martin-Jones (2001); Lin (2001); Martin Jones (1995); Martin-Jones (1995); Saxena (2001); Norton (2000); and Norton Peirce (1995).

As will be seen now and in the chapters that follow, in discussing the relationship between language choice, identity, and the political economy, I follow these researchers and draw upon the economic metaphors found in the work of French sociologist Pierre Bourdieu. Bourdieu has theorized that people make choices about what languages to use in particular kinds of "markets," which he defines as places where different kinds of resources or "capital" are distributed. Markets allow one form of capital to be converted into another. "Linguistic capital" can be cashed in for educational qualifications or "cultural capital," which, in turn, can be cashed in for lucrative jobs or "economic capital." Bourdieu sees markets as sites of struggle in which individuals seek to maintain or alter the distribution of the forms of capital specific to it. At Northside, the struggle was over what linguistic resources could or should be used to access cultural capital (school knowledge and educational qualifications). In order to maintain the forms of capital specific to a particular market (for example, the need to use English to obtain school knowledge and educational qualifications at Northside), Bourdieu suggests that all participants have to have a total and unconditional "investment" in the market and in the way different forms of capital are distributed. Bonny Norton has theorized that ESOL learners can experience ambivalence around their investment in English[16] and at Northside this ambivalence resulted in linguistic dilemmas for students and contributed to the school's struggle over language practices.

As discussed earlier in the discussion of the survey undertaken in Hong Kong, people assess the market conditions in which their linguistic products will be received and valued by others. This assessment can constrain the way they speak or the way the think they ought to speak. Some linguistic products are more highly valued than others and are endowed with what Bourdieu calls a "legitimacy" that other linguistic products are not. The official languages of Canada are French and English and, in Bourdieu's words, it is the role of Canadian schools to "legitimize" and "impose" these official languages on students. Although the *Language for Learning Policy* legitimized the use of languages other than English to help students access and produce school knowledge, English was the official language of instruction and assessment at Northside and there were a multitude of ways that teachers and students constructed its legitimacy. However, because markets are always the sites of struggle and places where people experience ambivalence around their in-

---

[16]See Norton (2000) and Norton Peirce (1995) for further discussion on ambivalence and Bourdieu's notion of investment. Also see Judith Butler (1999) for a discussion on ambivalence and Bourdieu's notion of "habitus," those "embodied rituals of everydayness" that motivate or incline [language] practices in the market.

vestment in English, there were also moments when the legitimacy of English was contested because of the value associated with the use of other languages. Critical education theorist Jim Cummins has talked about these moments as opportunities to challenge "coercive relations of power" in the classroom and work toward "collaborative relations of power."[17] Cummins's ideas are explored further in chapter 5.

CHOOSING TO USE CANTONESE AT SCHOOL[18]

Following the work of the interactionist sociolinguists just mentioned, I begin this analysis of language choice with the belief that people associate particular languages with membership in particular social groups. Put a little differently, I work with the idea that particular languages symbolize particular social identities. At Northside, most Cantonese-speaking students born in Hong Kong used Cantonese to speak to other students born in Hong Kong. The use of Cantonese was associated with membership in the Cantonese-speaking community at the school. It symbolized a Hong Kong Canadian identity. The choice to use Cantonese to seek and maintain membership in the Cantonese-speaking community was related to the students' goals of academic and social success at school. To illustrate, research in a finite mathematics class revealed that the use of Cantonese allowed students to gain access to friendship and assistance that helped them achieve good marks in the course. Having friends in the classroom (achieving social success and collecting social capital) was related to the goal of a getting high or passing mark (achieving academic success and collecting cultural capital) in several ways.

First, friends explained things you didn't understand, for example, an explanation the teacher had given of a math concept, or the reason an answer to a math problem was not correct. Second, friends encouraged you to contest a mark a teacher had given you on an assignment, quiz, or test if they thought the teacher had made a poor evaluation judgment. This is illustrated in the following exchange where one of the students, Lawrence, was trying to figure out why the math teacher, Mrs. Lo, had taken three marks off an answer he had given in one of the problems on a quiz. He didn't think his answer was completely wrong and wanted to ask Mrs. Lo to reconsider the mark she had given him. Eddy and Cindy were helping Lawrence figure out why his answer was not completely wrong when Cindy realized that Eddy

---

[17]See Cummins (1996).

[18]Some of the ideas in this section were first discussed in Goldstein (1997).

had also correctly answered one of the questions that had been evaluated as partly incorrect.

Translation and Transcription Notes

In this exchange, and the other exchanges in this book, each Cantonese speaker's original Cantonese utterances have been translated into English and appear in *italics*. Any additional information needed to make the meaning of the speaker's words clear to the readers appears in brackets within or right after the translated or English utterance. Nonverbal communication such as laughter is indicated in parentheses. Words that appear in **boldface** are words that were originally spoken in English. In the exchange that follows, the only English words uttered by the Cantonese-speaking students were words associated with the math problems the students were talking about and words associated with the English names of the math teachers teaching summer school.

Lawrence:	*I really don't understand it. I only have two parts wrong. How could someone take away three marks? I didn't think too lowly of her* [And I thought so highly of her].
Eddy:	*She thinks lowly of you.*
Lawrence:	*I don't know.*
Cindy:	*How come you have half a mark for your* **bonus question**?
Lawrence:	*Yeah, that's what I don't understand. It's not that I don't know* [the right way to do the problem]. *Where did I lose nine marks? There are only two parts here, that is the* **A** *and* **B relationship** *one.* **A** *and* **B** *are wrong, but* **C** *is correct.*
Cindy:	(Looking at Eddy's answer that was also evaluated as being partly incorrect) *Heh, heh, heh. Your last question should be right.*
Eddy:	*Me?* [Mine?]
Cindy:	*You.* [Yours.]
Eddy:	*I told her. She said she's not going to talk it over with me. I don't how to do it.* [how to explain why my answer is partly right and why she should change the way she marked the answer]. *Forget it.*
Lawrence:	*Never mind.* (Laughs).
Eddy:	*Yesterday, I asked the* **afternoon finite** [math] *teacher. He said I should have some marks, that I shouldn't have a lost a mark.*
Lawrence:	*Did you find it?* [Did you find a way to explain why your answer is partly right?] *Even you can't find it?* [Even you can't find a

way to explain why your answer is partly right?]. *I really don't know what to do.*

[*Translated Exchange*, July 20, 1994]

Negotiating a mark in a second language was not always easy for Cantonese-speaking students. As English was the legitimate language at Northside, those students who wanted Mrs. Lo to consider changing a mark she had given them on a test or assignment had to submit a written statement in English as to why they should receive more marks. Further discussion of this practice is taken up in the next chapter. This meant that students needed to be able to articulate exactly why their answers were (partly) right and why they should receive more marks. Talking with friends about your case (in Cantonese) sometimes helped make the task of negotiating a mark easier.

The third way that having friends was important to succeeding academically had to do with the way friends advocated for each other in the classroom. Students helped each other access the teacher's attention during "classroom practice" activities so that their classmates could ask Mrs. Lo to re-explain a math concept, find out why an answer to a math problem was incorrect, or contest a mark she had given them.

In interviews with research assistant, Veronica Hsueh and me, students also told us that finding friends who were intimate companions as well as classmates was important for reasons that were not linked to academic success. Intimate friends helped students with "problems," for example, family problems, problems with their girlfriends or boyfriends, and academic problems they couldn't tell their families about.

Initiating friendship (whether it was a collegial or intimate friendship) and developing or nurturing a friendship was related to the way people spoke to each other in the classroom. Once a friendship was established, the students were then able to ask each other for help and assistance. Talk that was associated with making friends in the math classroom took place in different languages that varied according to who was involved in the interaction. Such conversations between students who used Cantonese as their primary language were undertaken in Cantonese.

The use of Cantonese to seek and maintain friendships within the Cantonese-speaking community at Northside can be understood as a survival or coping strategy. Following Monica Heller, who talked about Franco–Ontarian resistance to English as having to do with "creating a francophone space from which to more easily enter the anglophone world." I understand the use of Cantonese as a way for students to create a Cantonese space from which they could move more easily into the anglophone world in their school.[19] This understanding mirrors Angel Lin's argument that bilingual Cantonese–English teaching practices in Hong Kong were a coping response to students' struggle to acquire English linguistic capital. The Cantonese-speaking students at Northside were using a coping strategy they had used in Hong Kong.

RISKS ASSOCIATED WITH USING ENGLISH

As linguistic capital was associated with achieving social and academic success at school, Cantonese was associated with social and academic benefits. These were benefits that were not associated with the use of English. In fact, the use of English was risky because its use could jeopardize the access to friendship and assistance that was so important to academic and social success in school. Cantonese-speaking students reported that other Cantonese students told them that they were "rude" if they spoke to them in English. When asked why it was rude to speak in English, one student told us that some people thought that you were trying to be "special" if you spoke English or that you liked to "show off your English abilities." In the following interview excerpt, student Victor Yu explains "showing off" this way:

> For the Hong Kong people, right? We will, we will rarely use English to speak to each other except for people who are born here or have been here for a long time. If that is not the case, right? We will speak Cantonese because if we like talk English with them, right? They do think you are really, like, showing off your skill in English.
>
> [Victor Yu, *Interview*, October 9, 1996]

To understand the reasons behind the association between the use of English and showing off, it is helpful to refer to the work undertaken by Angel Lin, who talks about English as the language of power and the language of educational and socioeconomic advancement in Hong Kong.[20] To illustrate her point, Lin writes that a student who wants to study medicine, architecture, and legal studies in Hong Kong must have adequate English resources (linguistic capital), in addition to subject knowledge and skills, to enter and succeed in English-medium, professional training programs (gain cultural capital). After graduating from these programs, students also need to have adequate English resources to earn the credentials to enter these professions that are accredited by the British-based or Brit-

---

[19]See Heller (2001).

[20]See Lin (2001) for a fuller discussion of English as *symbolic domination*, a term used by Pierre Bourdieu (1982/1991).

ish-associated professional bodies (Hong Kong was a British colony until July, 1997). Students' access to linguistic capital that provides them with the mastery of English needed to enter high-income professions in Hong Kong is uneven. Only a small elite group of Cantonese speakers has had the opportunity to obtain such mastery. The elite bilingual class in Hong Kong includes people who are wealthy enough to afford high-quality, private, English-medium secondary and tertiary education and a very small number of high-achieving students get access to such education via their high scores in public examinations. It is the association of English with membership in this elite bilingual class in Hong Kong that helps explain why Cantonese-speaking students at Northside associated speaking English with showing off. Back in the city of Toronto, English is also the language associated with educational and socioeconomic advancement. Students at Northside passed courses and acquired cultural capital by demonstrating what they had learned in English. Students from Hong Kong who were first-generation immigrants to Canada used English with varying levels of proficiency and mastery. This meant they had varying levels of linguistic capital at school. When Cantonese-speaking students used English with other Cantonese students, they demonstrated their proficiency or mastery and could be seen as showing off their linguistic capital and flexing their linguistic power. Students who depended on friends and classmates for assistance with academic activities and a social life at school did not want to risk being considered a show-off.

Bonny Norton, bringing feminist poststructuralist theory into current discussions on language, identity, and the political economy, has written that as well as being related to markets and different forms of capital, language is a place where people construct their sense of selves.[21] As mentioned earlier, Cantonese was associated with being part of the Hong Kong community at Northside. In addition to being associated with showing off, English was also associated with being "too Canadianized." Student Max Yeung told us that when a Cantonese speaker used English, it was a sign that most of his or her friends were "Canadians" (people who were born in Canada and were English speakers) and that "they [were] in their own group." Such speakers were considered outsiders to the Hong Kong community at Northside. Although the use of Cantonese was associated with social and academic resources, the use of English was associated with costs, and most

---

[21]See Norton (2000) for a discussion of what poststructualist feminist theory and the theory of subjectivity can contribute to current understandings about second language learning. For a discussion of other critical theories and the contribution they make to the field of second language acquisition see Pennycook (2001).

students in the Hong Kong community at Northside avoided using English with each other. This strategy, demonstrating ambivalence in students' investment in English, rubbed against the desire for students to only use English at school, it also created several dilemmas for the students.

DILEMMAS ASSOCIATED
WITH USING CANTONESE

Choosing to only use Cantonese with other Cantonese speakers at Northside was problematic for some of the students. These students told us that although working and socializing almost exclusively in Cantonese provided them with friends and helped them succeed in their courses, it did not provide them with many opportunities to "practice" English. Mirroring the results of the Hong Kong survey discussed earlier, these students talked about the educational and socioeconomic benefits, and the cultural and economic capital associated with being able to use English well. English was not only the legitimate language of instruction and evaluation at Northside, but the legitimate language at the universities they wanted to attend. Strong proficiency in English provided students with access to a wider range of programs and courses at a university. The students also suggested that strong English skills were required in many of the local labor markets and in such high-status and high-influence professions as law, politics, and upper management positions in both the private and public sector.[22] The dilemma for these students was how to find opportunities to practice English (which would benefit them in the long term) at the same time as they used Cantonese to achieve immediate social and academic success at Northside. One of the challenges for teachers at Northside, then, was finding ways to assist Cantonese-speaking students in developing their spoken English language skills without forcing them to assume the social and academic risks associated with showing off and breaking the sociocultural, sociolinguistic norms of their linguistic community. Several teachers at Northside took on this challenge, and their pedagogical approaches are discussed in a number of chapters that follow.

A second dilemma associated with using Cantonese at school was that many of the teachers and students didn't like hearing it in the classrooms and hallways. As is also discussed in the chapters that follow, the teachers who believed that students' academic success depended on English mono-

---

[22]See Maclear (1994) for a discussion on the need for the Canadian school system to ensure that the English language abilities of Asian high-school students are developed on an equal basis as other students.

lingualism in the classroom contested the school board's effort to legitimize student multilingualism and promoted the use of English in a number of ways. Some experimented with classroom English-only rules or policies while others discussed their preferences with students at the beginning of their courses and reminded them to "speak English, please" whenever they heard another language being used. Often, these teachers' preference for English was related to the fact that some students in their class reported that they felt excluded or "left out" when other students used languages they didn't understand; students also worried that others were talking negatively about them. These feelings of being excluded and talked about often reflected the teachers' own feelings.

Students who spoke Cantonese (or other languages) in classrooms where teachers had made their preference for English clear risked their teachers' displeasure and disapproval. Students overheard using Cantonese in classrooms with English-only rules or policies risked being punished or disciplined. In all classrooms, students who spoke Cantonese risked the anger and resentment of classmates who felt excluded from their conversation. Yet, as discussed earlier, using English with Cantonese speakers was also costly. In the following interview excerpt, Frank Li described the dilemma this way:

Tara: ... so is it correct to say you use both English and Cantonese during the day, here at Northside?

Frank: Well, mostly I use English, 'cause even though [I am] with Chinese people, I, I sort of avoid talking in Cantonese because most of the time I'm, I'm with some Chinese people and then around there's someone who cannot speak, couldn't understand Cantonese. I, I always think it's not nice, to, to, to speak Cantonese in front of people that don't understand it. That's why. But [when] I, I talk with some Chinese people I still use Can—English in [some cases], but if they don't understand English that's another story.

Tara: Okay, then you'll use Cantonese.

Frank: Yeah.

Tara: Let me ask you about teachers in Northside. Do you have any teachers who have rules about using Cantonese in the classroom?

Frank: Well, me, I don't, but I've heard of other people that have [teachers who have rules] ... [One teacher] says, a nickel or a dime, every time that you speak Chinese and, but, for me I think, well, I try my best not to speak Chinese in class .... But, you know, sometimes it's really hard because when my Chinese friends are talking in Chinese, you know, that, that's, it's not polite [to speak in English]. 'Cause

like, okay, [it's like] I was trying to show off or whatever. That, that,
you know, in that case, I'll, I will speak in Cantonese, but maybe just
a few words....Well, you know, trying my best not to [speak in Can-
tonese]. Sometimes it just happens. Okay, [if] they ask, they ask me
a question in Chinese, [then] I should answer in Chinese, that's what
I should do.
[Frank Li, *Interview*, February 19, 1997]

There were a number of ways Cantonese-speaking students tried to work
through this linguistic dilemma at Northside. Some, like Frank, tried to accommodate the language preferences of their English-speaking classmates
whenever it was possible, censoring their use of Cantonese. Others chose to
use Cantonese despite the anger of other students, while still others codeswitched from Cantonese to English and from English to Cantonese in an
effort to accommodate both English and Cantonese speakers and work
across linguistic differences in their classrooms. Further discussion of these
strategies is taken up in chapter 2.

In this introduction I have written about some of the ways students from
Hong Kong experienced Cantonese–English bilingual life at Northside and
the academic and linguistic dilemmas that emerged in their bilingual community. In the chapters that follow, I explore the ways teachers and students responded to and negotiated these dilemmas in their classrooms. As mentioned
in the Preface, the chapters in Part I look at dilemmas of speech and silence
whereas the chapters in Part II explore dilemmas of discrimination. The commentaries and pedagogical discussions in each chapter are not intended to
provide an authoritative reading or interpretation of the dilemmas being discussed. Rather, they are presented as ideas that may confirm, challenge, or
build on readers's own understandings of schooling in multilingual communities and create opportunities for further reflection and discussion.

TEACHING IN "NEW TIMES"

Before moving on to a description and analysis of the choices, risks, and dilemmas that come up for students and teachings in multilingual schools, a
brief word seems important about the broader relevance of the Northside
study. In discussing and sharing parts of the book with a number of people
living in different parts of the world, it became clear that the linguistic and
academic issues that have been raised at Northside have also been raised for
others who live and work in other multilingual communities. A playwriting
colleague from a small town in Wisconsin told me that my play, *Hong Kong,
Canada,* resonated with her experience of growing up in a town that hosted

a large number of families from Laos. Similarly, teachers and students in Brisbane, Sydney, and Toowoomba, Australia, who work with people from many different parts of Asia, found the issues raised at Northside were reflected in their own schools.

One of the reasons that the issues raised at Northside are familiar to those living in other parts of the world has to do with the impact of globalization. In the last 20 years, globalization has brought unprecedented economic, cultural, and technological changes. One of these changes is mass immigration, which is very different from the immigration of post-war times. Many immigrant elementary and secondary school students in our "New Times" are growing up with several cultures. They are living in more than one community and hear and speak more than one language.[23] For example, there are many Asian students attending Canadian and American schools who travel back and forth between North America and Hong Kong and Taiwan to visit parents and/or other close relatives who live and work there. They continue to access and consume Chinese pop culture from Hong Kong and Taiwan through the Internet, cable TV, CDs, and videos. I understand that this is also the case in some parts of Australia. Learning to work effectively with students who call more than one place home and have strong affiliations in more than one community is critical to good teaching of "New Times." We need to develop new understandings about the lives and needs of our immigrant students. In a small way, this book attempts to begin a discussion about what such an understanding entails.

---

[23]The term *New Times* has been to used by several writers to refer to the economic, cultural, and technological changes associated with globalization. See, for example, Hall (1996) and Luke (1999).

I

Dilemmas of Speech and Silence

My grandmother was very popular in Chinatown. While we shopped, we were stopped every few feet by her acquaintances. Everyone talked loudly and waved their arms. I couldn't understand why they had to be so loud. It seemed so uncivilized. She also took me to visit her friends and I occupied myself with extra game pieces while they played mah jongg. But as I started to grow up, I stopped going to Chinatown with her, where it was too loud, and then I stopped spending time with her altogether. I started to play with friends who weren't loud and weren't Chinese.

—From Anne Jew, *Everyone Talked Loudly in Chinatown*

It was when I found out I had to talk that school became a misery, that the silence became a misery. I did not speak and felt bad each time that I did not speak. I read aloud in first grade, though, and hear the barest whisper with little squeaks come out of my throat. "Louder," said the teacher, who scared the voice away again. The other Chinese girls did not talk either, so I knew the silence had to do with being a Chinese girl.

—From Maxine Hong Kingston, *Woman Warrior*

2

Accepting and Legitimizing Multilingualism

Sometimes for the problem solving or the probability stuff, you know, you know me, right? I think in Chinese. In English, I often have to spend, like, 15 minutes [to understand a problem], right? But in Chinese, I...like...6 minutes or 5 minutes, I can, I can figure out [the problem]. It's really easier.

[Rose Chan, a student in Evelyn Lo's summer finite math class, *Interview*, July 27, 1994]

As discussed in the Introduction and demonstrated once again in the quote above, the use of Cantonese contributed to the academic success of students from Hong Kong by helping them make links between their own knowledge and the knowledge of their classrooms and school. However, students like Rose Chan, who is quoted, were only able to use their linguistic resource of Cantonese when their teachers supported the use of languages other than English in their classrooms. This chapter explores the way student multilingualism was legitimized by Evelyn Lo, one of the math teachers at Northside. The chapter begins with excerpts from an interview with Mrs. Lo, who not only allowed her students to use languages other than English in the classroom, but also used Cantonese and Mandarin herself. Born in China, Evelyn Lo immigrated to Hong Kong as a child, and then immigrated to Canada as an adult. She was trilingual and her use of Mandarin, Cantonese, and English in the classroom were associated with the various roles she played there. The data used in the chapter comes from observa-

tions, tape recordings, and interviews that research assistant Veronica
Hsueh and I undertook in Mrs. Lo's summer finite math class. Excerpts
from two additional student interviews have been juxtaposed with the data
from this site. The interview excerpts, commentary, and pedagogical discussion that appear in this chapter have been member checked by Evelyn
Lo. The interview excerpt begins with me asking Evelyn about the different
roles she plays as a teacher.

"AT TIMES, PEOPLE LEARN BETTER
FROM THEIR PEERS"

Tara:	The next set of questions, Evelyn, asks about your role as a teacher. What different roles do you play as a teacher in this classroom?
Evelyn:	As a leader, I show them how to learn. I motivate them, make them learn not just from me but from their peers as well.
Tara:	Why is all that important?
Evelyn:	At times, people learn better from their peers, through discussions and conversations. Working in groups, working together they learn a lot more.
Tara:	What happens when kids work together that does not happen when they work with a teacher?
Evelyn:	One teacher has to cater to 30. A lot of the time they have a special need or special question. If they go to their friend, they talk it out and have a discussion. They learn a lot more. Then if they have any trouble, they come to me. I use myself as a resource person.
Tara:	Where did you first come to adopt this student-centered approach? You once told me that schooling in Hong Kong is very different and [that] your life as a teacher in Hong Kong was very different.
Evelyn:	Well, as you noticed, I always teach a lesson. I will spend 20 minutes explaining a concept in detail and then I get them to work on their own; in groups or in pairs … But all the basic concepts I've done in a very traditional way … But on top of that, I get them to work in groups.
Tara:	So you actually have a combined approach.
Evelyn:	Yes, so it is not that much of a difference in that way, because I do teach a lesson in the traditional way. But on top of it, I get them to learn from their peers and work together with their peers.
Tara:	This was an approach you did not take in Hong Kong?
Evelyn:	No. We do not allow or have the kind of facilities to do that, because of tradition, space, and time. Here things evolve and I find it better

	that way. So slowly, I just follow whatever is possible and use whatever method works.
Tara:	We have noticed that there are times that you use English, times that you use Mandarin, and times that you use Cantonese. What is your own sense of how you use those languages in this classroom?
Evelyn:	Basically as teaching goes, I always use English. To teach a class, when I give basic concepts, when I give instruction to the class, I always use English. When I talk to students, I always use English unless they are stuck. Then in private I will explain it to them in the language they prefer.
Tara:	So you basically make your choices based on the language they prefer.
Evelyn:	Yes, if we are just one-on-one.
Tara:	In the private space.
Evelyn:	Yes. To the class I will use English.
Tara:	So if you approach a table [students in Mrs. Lo's class sat at tables in groups of six or seven], and that table has both English-speaking and Cantonese or Mandarin-speaking students, and you think that the whole table is listening, you will use English?
Evelyn:	Definitely.
Tara:	So the only time you would use Cantonese or Mandarin is on one-on-one.
Evelyn:	Right and if they are stuck. Otherwise, I would prefer to use English because their textbooks are in English and they need to communicate in English. When they are writing a sentence [to conclude an answer to a math problem] or whatnot they have to use English. So it is better for them to learn the proper terms.
Tara:	In your classroom, the students are allowed to use their own languages. It is okay.
Evelyn:	That is for their academic improvement. Yes, English is important. They need to speak English for interactions with other people and all that. But when we get down to it, really it does not matter, like they can discuss and use whatever language they prefer to tackle a problem that is more difficult to understand.
Tara:	For you, if using your first language aids them in actually succeeding academically, that is fine?
Evelyn:	Sure, why not find a way to find out what they need? So they can use that to benefit whatever they need to do in the future. Some of the students find it very difficult to research in English. They can always read some of the materials in Chinese, find the information, and write it up in English. They can do that. That will help them to reach a better comprehension. For the initial stages, okay. As long as they

find the information. In that sense, they are encouraged to write in their own words, because they don't have the original to go by.

Tara: You have told us that often you do some counseling with students. Have you had the opportunity to do any counseling with students in this classroom?

Evelyn: I never initiate that, but whenever they come to me with problems, I always sit down and talk with them. Give them a chance to tell me what the problem is and we talk about options. I let them make a decision. They talk about boyfriends, girlfriends, family. Mom wants them to do well—they get punished if they don't get a 90% or whatnot. We talk about those things and how to handle those situations and what is the best way to tackle that and how to phrase the problem.

Tara: What language do you find you use when you're doing that kind of counseling?

Evelyn: A lot of the times it started out in English and it ended in Cantonese or Mandarin. When they want to pour their heart out, they feel more comfortable using their own language.

Tara: When students come to talk to you about their marks and their assignments and quizzes, I know you have a particular strategy in place. What language do you find that most students use, what language do you use, and why?

Evelyn: Basically I insist that if they have any contest with their marks, they have to write it down in writing. So when they write it down they write in English. And I always respond to it. Even if it is not a legitimate thing, I tell them why they should get that mark. I always respond to them. I always insist they write it in writing. So I seldom talk to them about marks. But if they do approach me again I say, "Well, if you are still not happy about it, write to me about it." They always write in English. They never write in Chinese.

Tara: Tell me a little about the importance of friendship for students in school. As a teacher, what have you noticed about the importance of friends and having friends in school for students?

Evelyn: I always insist in the first class, I tell them to find a friend and write down their phone number in case they need any lesson or assignment. They have to phone the friend to find out what they need. It is their responsibility to make it up. I actually encourage them to form a network. In case they are stuck, they can always phone whomever and find a friend to work with. So I do encourage that. Especially in summer school, it is 4 hours [long]. It can be very boring. So if they can sit in a group, if they have a couple of friends, while they work between groups they can talk a little bit. They can socialize; they can

still have a life here. To make activity more happy, to create an at-
mosphere to learn, to find a reason to come in the morning.
[*Interview*, August 3, 1994]

COMMENTARY: TEACHING AND LEARNING
IN CANTONESE AND MANDARIN

The Fluidity of Language Choice
and the Practice of Codeswitching

As discussed in the aforementioned interview, Evelyn Lo's uses of Mandarin,
Cantonese, and English were associated with three roles she played in the
classroom: teacher, "helper," and counselor.[1] Interactionist sociolinguists tell
us that language choice is fluid and that there is a range of choices open to
people in their use of language to symbolize various identities. For example,
Robert Le Page has explained that people create different ways of talking that
resemble those belonging to the groups or roles they wish, from time to time,
to be identified with.[2] People make different selections among the language
practices and roles and identities available to them at different times.

In her role as teacher and authority in the classroom, Mrs. Lo performed
particular tasks. She took attendance and sent students who were late to the
office to get a late slip. Mrs. Lo also formally presented the math concepts to
be studied each day, assigned classroom and homework tasks, designed
quizzes and tests, evaluated students' assignments, quizzes, and tests, and
dealt with students' questioning or contesting of the mark she had given
them on their work. In this role, Mrs. Lo only used English, which was the
language of instruction in the school and symbolic of her authority as the
class leader and evaluator of her students' work.

After her formal presentation of the math concepts to be studied each
day, Mrs. Lo assigned a set of "classroom practice" activities. Students
worked on these activities either individually, in pairs, or in small groups,
with others seated at their table. It was during these classroom practice activities that students used their primary languages. Mrs. Lo visited each student table and provided assistance to individual students who needed it.
Classroom practice was a time period that was clearly carved out of the
4-hour summer math class and always followed Mrs. Lo's introductory presentation. During classroom practice Mrs. Lo assumed a role that research

---

[1]See Lin (1988) for similar findings and a discussion of the use of language alternation as a
communicative resource to negotiate different roles in the classroom.

[2]See Le Page (1968).

assistant Veronica Hsueh and I called helper. As discussed in the interview, in this role, Mrs. Lo used Cantonese and Mandarin with students if they were "stuck," that is, having difficulty completing a problem.

In her role of counselor, Mrs. Lo provided academic and personal counseling to those students who needed support. The type of counseling she provided during the 5 weeks we visited her classroom included academic advice about working harder in school to a student whom she felt was not working to his or her full potential and career advice to a student trying to make a decision about when and where to go to university. Mrs. Lo also told us that she was speaking regularly to a student who was working on family issues at home. In this role of counselor, Mrs. Lo used English with students who did not speak Cantonese or Mandarin, but often used Cantonese with the Cantonese speakers and Mandarin with Mandarin speakers.

On Public and Private Spaces in the Classroom

As she explains in the interview excerpt above, Mrs. Lo only used Cantonese and Mandarin in spaces that were "private," off what Canadian and British sociolinguists Monica Heller, Marilyn Martin-Jones, and Mukul Saxena have called the "center stage" of the classroom floor.[3] Mrs. Lo created such spaces by scheduling time for classroom practice, which allowed her to transform center stage into what I call a "shared stage." On the shared stage, students solved math problems collaboratively, using whatever language was most helpful to them. For Mrs. Lo, center stage was a public space for whole-group instruction and therefore a space where she only used English, the language of instruction at Northside. However, a shared stage where students instructed each other provided her with private spaces that could legitimately (with the support of the *Language for Learning Policy* discussed in the Introduction) become multilingual if students were stuck on a problem. The Cantonese and Mandarin counseling Mrs. Lo undertook with individual students took place "off stage," during the daily break or after class was over for the day. Mrs. Lo's creative use of time to create private spaces of instruction and assistance in her classroom not only allowed her to accept student multilingualism, but also allowed her to use her own trilingual set of resources to support student learning.

---

[3]See Heller and Martin-Jones (2001) and Martin-Jones and Saxena (2001), where the concepts of *center stage* and *off stage* are introduced.

On Interethnic/Interracial Relations
in the Multilingual Classroom

Mrs. Lo's support of languages other than English in her classroom was tied to her vision of what it meant to work as a teacher in a multilingual community. In a presentation Mrs. Lo, Veronica Hsueh, and I gave at the 1995 Ontario TESL (Teaching English as a Second Language) Conference, Mrs. Lo told our audience that she saw the acceptance of student multilingualism in group work as a way to foster positive contributions from English as a second or other language (ESOL) students. It was also a way to enhance their social skills and promote mutual respect and self-worth, which in turn could encourage "responsible participation" and "racial harmony" in the classroom.

Mrs. Lo's association of racially and culturally mixed cooperative learning groups with the promotion of racial harmony is one that is frequently made in North American multicultural education texts.[4] The thinking behind this association goes something like this: Tensions that arise among different racial and cultural groups are based on people's stereotyped perceptions of others and a lack of rapport. Involving students in mixed cooperative learning groups is a way of providing students with an opportunity to develop shared goals. Working together toward these goals can promote positive interpersonal interaction. Frequent, meaningful and mutually supportive contact that characterize cooperative learning activities help students to view each other in nonstereotypical ways.

At Northside, experiments with racially, culturally, and linguistically mixed cooperative learning groups led to both positive and negative interpersonal and intergroup interactions. Sometimes, multilingual practices during small group work did not contribute to racial harmony, but worked against it. Although none of the students in Mrs. Lo's classes talked to us about linguistic tensions in their own small groups, students from other classes at Northside did. Here is an example of what they said. Miriam is a White Anglo-Canadian who was enrolled in a French immersion primary school and often spoke French to Lianne, who is a White Franco-Ontarian.

> **Tara:** In your art class, when the [Cantonese-speaking] students sat with each other, they would speak in Cantonese. They would speak Cantonese quite quietly so they wouldn't "disturb" anybody, but they were speaking in Cantonese. How do you feel about that? Is that a problem for you, is that an issue for you in that class?

---

[4]See Coelho (1994, 1998); Kagan (1986); and Slavin (1983, 1990) for further discussion of cooperative learning and the development of positive race relations.

Miriam: No, not at all. I don't find anything wrong with that. Like, I know a lot of people who do, like, think it's rude and stuff. But I don't see that, you know. I mean if that's what they feel comfortable with, then that's fine. But if you're in a situation where you're, like, in a group or something and you're working on a project and they start talking [in Cantonese], well, then we don't understand. That's weird.

Lianne: I remember in math class in Grade 10, [there was] one girl who didn't speak English…and she was sitting in my math class with a little translator. That bothered me because she had three friends and that's all they spoke. They only spoke, I think it was Cantonese. I'm not sure. But you know, that's all they spoke the whole entire class and that was really annoying 'cause I was stuck in their group and I was, like, the only person that spoke English there…We had to do our work for two classes and I was, I was put with them.

Tara: So it was very hard to enter the conversation. Did you try anything as direct as "I'm sorry, I don't understand, could you speak English?"

Lianne: Yes. I'm, like, "Can we, can we do our work?" And they're, like, "Oh, okay, wait, wait." Okay, so I'm waiting. Ten, 15, 20 minutes. I'm like, "Okay, yeah, that's great." They start doing their work and I start doing my work. I should have stayed with them. They did better than I did. But, you know.

Tara: Had you stayed and been successful, perhaps you would have benefited. But it was just very, very hard to break in.

Lianne: Yeah. There were three of them; they were all friends and everything, too. It's kind of hard to try and get into a group, you know, if they are friends. You're there, speaking a different language. It's just hard. Like, it was my first year and I didn't want to like, push anymore, so I sat back and let everything happen.
[*Exchange,* February 26, 1997]

Codeswitching to Work Across Linguistic Differences

While many students spoke of feeling excluded when working in linguistically diverse groups, others had positive experiences. For example, one linguistically mixed group in Mrs. Lo's math class worked together very effectively to solve classroom practice problems. When asked by Veronica to explain how the collegiality in their group had been initiated and nurtured, the students had this to say. Solomon was born in Iran and spoke English in the math class. Susie and May were from Taiwan. They spoke English to Solomon and Mandarin to each other and the three other Taiwanese students in the group. The seventh member of the group was Mario, a White Euro-Canadian who was born in Italy and spoke English in the class.

Veronica: So we wanted to find out how this collaborative effort of helping each other started.

Solomon: Well, they [Susie, Cindy, and May, three Taiwanese girls] are very attractive, right? So … there's no other way around it.
(Susie and May laugh).

Susie: Sure. That was something!

Solomon: Every time I tell a joke [in English], they [Susie and May] translate it to her [Cindy, who isn't as proficient in English as Susie and May] and it's like an echo. Ten minutes later, she [Cindy] gets it.

Veronica: And he [James, one of the two Taiwanese boys] gets it and he starts laughing.
[*Exchange,* July 25, 1994]

The students at this linguistically mixed table codeswitched from English to Mandarin to share jokes and maintain the collegiality necessary for solving math problems together. Here, Mrs. Lo's hope for positive interpersonal and interracial interaction was momentarily realized. Susie and May, who played the role of language brokers were at the center of this successful negotiation of linguistic difference. However, there were times when it was Solomon's (limited) use of Mandarin that was important in building and maintaining collegiality. Several times during our observations, the five Mandarin-speaking students would socialize in Mandarin for extended periods of time. Not being able to join in these social conversations, Solomon would interrupt them by asking Susie or May for the time in Mandarin. This was a question that he had asked Susie to teach him early on in the course. Solomon's request for the time in Mandarin, which was always received with laughter, let the Mandarin speakers know that he wanted to join in the conversation. Each time Solomon interrupted a Mandarin conversation by asking for the time, the conversation would resume in English. Susie, May, and Solomon's practice of codeswitching during classroom practice provided all of the students at their table with an effective way responding to the issue of exclusion raised by Miriam and Lianne. In asking for the time in Mandarin, instead of asking if the members of the group could speak English or get to work, Solomon was able to work across linguistic differences in a way that other students were not.[5]

Commenting on this strategy sociolinguist Angel Lin (personal communication) suggested that Solomon's codeswitching worked because it invoked a different "storyline" than the one imposed by the school's institutional Eng-

---

[5]See Rampton (1995) for a discussion on adolescent codeswitching in a multilingual community in England.

lish dominance. In this storyline, Solomon, as an English speaker, was willing to learn the others' language. His act of asking for the time in Mandarin invoked a storyline that assumed an egalitarian, mutually respectful, reciprocal relationship in which both parties were interested in each other's languages and cultures.[6]

The issue of exclusion in group work was discussed time and time again in our interviews with teachers and students at Northside. The difficulty of dealing with the issue in positive ways was one of the reasons monolingual English-speaking students and teachers expressed a desire for English monolingualism in their classrooms. In the pedagogical discussion that follows, I look at the way one of the Northside teachers dealt with the issue of exclusion in small group work. Additional discussion on group work in multilevel, multilingual classrooms is undertaken in chapter 4.

In addition to tension around student multilingualism in group work, there was also some tension around the teachers' use of languages other than English in their classrooms. To illustrate, Max Yeung, one of the Cantonese-speaking students in Mrs. Lo's math class, talked to us about his concern for the Canadian students (those born in Canada) who may have felt alienated or angered by the use of Cantonese and Mandarin in the classroom. Max suggested that even though Mrs. Lo was good at speaking Mandarin, Cantonese, and English, "maybe the Canadian students don't feel very well, sometimes … Canadians are multicultural and they know that, but they don't prefer that situation." This concern had an influence on Max's own language practices with Mrs. Lo. Whenever there were English-speaking students within hearing distance, he accommodated their linguistic practices by speaking to the teacher in English. Max used English, even though he preferred working in Cantonese, and Mrs. Lo was able and willing to help him in Cantonese.

Max's concern about English-speaking students feeling angry or alienated by the use of languages other than English was substantiated in an interview with a student from Mrs. Lo's class who did not speak Cantonese or Mandarin. Theresa Lubov, a White, Euro-Canadian student who had been born in Russia and had learned English as a second language, told us that she got frustrated when she asked Mrs. Lo a question about a math problem and Mrs. Lo was not able to explain it clearly. When she heard Mrs. Lo helping students in Cantonese or Mandarin, she felt as though they had "more advantage" than she did. Underlying this perception of the Cantonese and Mandarin speakers having more advantage was the assumption that the reason that Mrs. Lo's ex-

---

[6]For a discussion of different possible storylines in crossethnic interactions, see Lin, Wang, Akamatsu, and Riazi (in press).

planations were clearer when she explained a problem to the Cantonese and Mandarin speakers because she was able to use her first and second languages rather than English, which was her third language.

What Theresa had not examined here was the possibility that her difficulty with understanding Mrs. Lo's explanations had to do with issues around her own learning. Earlier in our interview, Theresa had spoken candidly about the difficulty she was having focusing on her academic work and completing it outside of class time. However, the fact that Theresa perceived herself as less advantaged than the Cantonese and Mandarin speakers in the class presented a dilemma for both Max and Mrs. Lo. While Mrs. Lo's use of languages other than English in the private spaces of her classroom was beneficial for ESOL students like Max, it could also result in other students feeling linguistically disadvantaged despite the fact that they could access assistance in English. As mentioned earlier, Max's strategy for managing interethnic/interracial tensions arising from multilingualism in the classroom was to accommodate the English-speaking students at the expense of his own language preference and learning. For teachers like Mrs. Lo, who believed it was important for students like Max to be able to use his primary language of Cantonese if he was stuck, resolving this dilemma in this way was problematic. Further discussion of the ways multilingual teachers might begin to work through this dilemma is taken up in the pedagogical discussion to follow.

This commentary on teaching and learning in languages other than English has looked at the strategy of accepting and legitimizing both student and teacher multilingualism by creating a "shared stage" on the classroom floor. It has also looked at the tensions that can accompany the legitimizing of multilingualism and the way that one group of students worked through the problem of feeling left out. As mentioned in the Introduction, one of the goals of this book is to examine various teaching and learning practices undertaken at Northside in terms of their effectiveness in challenging coercive relations of power and inequities facing ESOL students at the school. A discussion of the way Evelyn Lo's legitimizing of languages other than English can been seen as a challenge to linguistic inequities in multilingual schools is taken up in the Conclusion.

PEDAGOGICAL DISCUSSION:
ON LINGUISTIC ACCOMMODATION

While Max Yeung's linguistic strategy in the multilingual math classroom was to accommodate the English-speaking students' preference of English, Evelyn Lo's strategy was to use English in the public role of teacher and reserve the use of Cantonese and Mandarin for private exchanges when her students were stuck or sought her out for advice on academic and personal issues. Neither of these linguistic strategies, however, prevented Theresa from feeling disadvantaged in the math classroom. Such a situation not only presented a dilemma for Mrs. Lo, who needed to respond to Theresa's concern at the same time as she as she responded to Max's learning needs, it also raised questions for other educators working in multilingual schools. Should teachers who are able to bring multilingual teaching practices into their classrooms be encouraged to do so? Who is accommodated? Who is not? Who benefits? Who doesn't?

In answer to the question of whether teachers should be encouraged to use languages other than English in their classrooms, many educators and parents would say "No." And they, like Theresa, would support their answer with arguments centered on issues of favoritism and fairness in the classroom. However, when we revisit how beneficial and efficient it is for students like Rose and Max to work with Mrs. Lo in Cantonese, an efficiency recognized by the *Learning for Learning* policy, it is a waste of linguistic resources to simply respond with the answer, "No." Furthermore, if English is the only language that is used by a multilingual teacher in a multilingual classroom, it could be argued that those students who use English as their primary language have an unfair advantage over the students who do not.

Perhaps it is not a question of whether or not we should bring multilingual teaching practices into our linguistically diverse classrooms, but a question of how. One way of beginning to deal with issues of linguistic advantage and disadvantage in multilingual classrooms is by talking about them in a direct, forthright manner. Teachers like Mrs. Lo, who have linguistic resources that, when used, can benefit students in their classrooms, might wish to talk to their students at the beginning of the year and initiate a discussion concerning language practices in the classroom. Language practices, like other classroom practices, can be discussed and even negotiated with students. If teachers and students establish some expectations at the beginning about when, how, and why languages other than English will be used in the classroom, students like Max would not feel that they had to use their less developed language in order to maintain positive interethnic/interracial relationships in the classroom.

That being said, I know that it is important to remember that negotiation around classroom language practices occurs in a larger, educational, political, and economic context. In a discussion about this issue, my educational colleague, researcher Judy Hunter, has told me that she has overhead conversations among White, English-speaking students that suggest that there is strong resentment of Cantonese-speaking students. This resentment has to do with the favorable stereotypes teachers seem to have of them,[7] their perceived and actual membership in privileged economic classes, and their perceived social exclusiveness. Teachers who want to initiate a discussion or negotiation of multilingual classroom practices need to take such resentment into account. We need to understand that the acceptance and legitimizing of multilingualism can lead to conflicts in our economically stratified, multilingual, multicultural, and multiracial society. Although I have never undertaken a discussion or negotiation of multilingualism in my own teacher education classroom (which, like other university classrooms in Toronto, imposes English on students), my students and I negotiate classroom rules for talking about issues of discrimination in schooling. Not everyone in the classroom has agreed with all the rules I suggest at the beginning of each term, but my students have always agreed they could "live with them" and would "try them on." When we revisit the rules halfway through the course, there is an opportunity to refine the rules in light of our classroom experiences. Such a process may be helpful to the discussion or negotiation of language practices as well.

Moving from the issue of multilingual teaching to the issue of exclusion when languages other than English were used to learn in small group work, I would like to discuss an approach used by Anglo-Canadian English teacher Greg Dunn, who placed his students in linguistically and racially mixed groups that worked together for the entire 4-month semester. Unlike the student groups in Mrs. Lo's class, which were unassigned, self-selected, and sometimes fluid (i.e., had students moving from one group to another), the groups in Mr. Dunn's class had been put together purposely with a view to provide students with more opportunities to practice English. As will be recalled from the Introduction, students who socialized and worked almost exclusively in Cantonese at school reported that they did not have many opportunities to practice English. To the extent it was possible, Mr. Dunn separated students who spoke languages other than English so that students would be encouraged to communicate with other group members in English, which was a common language they all shared. However, because of the large number of Cantonese-speaking students at the school, there was usually more than one Cantonese speaker in each group. Sometimes two or three students who shared Mandarin or Korean were assigned to the same group. Mr. Dunn began his first group work activity by asking students to write out the things

---

[7]See chapter 4 and Lee (1996), Maclear (1994), and Nakanishi and Nishida (1996) for a discussion of how Asian students are stereotyped as the "model minority."

they liked and didn't like about group work on a piece of flipchart paper. This activity provided an opportunity for team or community building. Each group's likes and dislikes were then presented to the rest of the class. These presentations provided a space for the issue of exclusion to emerge and a space for Mr. Dunn to talk about the issue of working across linguistic difference with the students in his class. It is in such a space that language use practices might be negotiated by students and teachers. In classrooms like Mr. Dunn's, where students are working together in the same groups all semester long, each group can negotiate and develop their own rules and strategies for managing linguistic differences among themselves.

In this chapter, I have discussed how the practice of accepting and legitimizing the use of languages other than English to teach and learn at Northside productively responded to some of the difficulties ESOL students faced at school. I have also discussed how accepting multilingualism created a number of difficulties for teachers and students. I have argued that given how beneficial and efficient it is for ESOL students to work in their primary languages, teachers at schools like Northside do well when they accept and promote multilingualism. However, I understand that accepting and promoting multilingualism sometimes requires educators to deal with feelings of resentment and exclusion. The following activities for further reflection and discussion allow my students and me to talk about resentment and exclusion and other issues associated with negotiating dilemmas of multilingualism at school.

FOR FURTHER REFLECTION AND DISCUSSION

A Collective Reading of **Hong Kong, Canada.**   In *Hong Kong, Canada*, a fictional play I wrote about some of the tensions and dilemmas that arose at Northside, students and teachers begin to work through some of the difficulties that can accompany linguistic diversity at school. The play is included in Appendix A at the end of the book.[8] In a group setting, read or perform the play out loud. A small group of readers/actors can perform the play for the rest of the group or the entire group can be involved in the reading by doubling or tripling up on parts. For example, in one class that worked with the play, half of the group played roles from scenes 1 through 7 while the

---

[8]For a discussion of turning ethnographic data into a fictional play, see my methodological essay in Appendix B. For a discussion on using Readers' Theater for the purpose of qualitative data display, see Donmoyer and Yennie-Donmoyer (1995). For a discussion of the issue of stereotyping in performed ethnography, see Goldstein (2002).

other half played roles from scenes 8 through 16. The advantage of this second approach was that the readers could compare their different interpretations of each character's words, actions, and feelings.

Emotional Responses to Hong Kong, Canada: Personal Reflection. Plays can represent everyday dilemmas and tensions in ways that allow performers and spectators to participate more fully in the emotional process of resolving conflicts. Performers and spectators are not merely observers of the dilemmas in the story, they become participants. It is possible to use the power of our emotional responses to a play to reflect on what we have taken away or learned from it. After the first reading or performance, individually respond to any of the following questions that appeal to you. What provoked a strong emotional response for you? What made you angry? What made you sad? What made you feel bad? What was satisfying? What was not? What confirmed something you believed about students, teachers and/or schools? How did that feel? What challenged something you believed about students, teachers and/or schools? How did that feel?

Issues and Dilemmas Raised in Hong Kong, Canada.   Having reflected upon which scenes provoked strong responses to the play, list the issues and dilemmas facing each of the characters in the emotionally provocative scenes that have just been discussed. In large classes or workshops, participants have done this work in small groups. Compare the lists each person has created. This should provide the entire group with a rich analysis of the issues and dilemmas facing different students and teachers at multilingual schools like Northside. In the chapters that follow, a number of these issues and dilemmas are discussed in detail.

Private and Public Spaces: Personal Reflection.   Within the public space of her classroom, Mrs. Lo created a private space in which students could legitimately use languages other than English to enhance their understanding and learning of math. In his autobiography, *Hunger of Memory: The Education of Richard Rodriguez*, writer Richard Rodriguez tells us that growing up, he had a different understanding of constituted public and private spaces. "Outside the house was public society; inside the house was private." Spanish was "the language of the home," associated with family intimacy and comfort. English was the language of public life.[9] Rodriguez

[9]See Rodriguez (1982, p. 16). I would like to acknowledge the unpublished master's research paper written by Heidi Levine on Richard Rodriguez' memoir, which has informed my own work with his writing.

was not permitted to bring Spanish into the classroom while growing up and he writes that he is glad this was so. Unlike Mrs. Lo, who thinks it was important to create private spaces within the public space of her classroom and school, Rodriguez believes that his private and public identities had to be separated. His ability to recognize himself as an "American," to assimilate, to access opportunities and privileges, would have been jeopardized if the private language and culture of his home had been allowed to permeate the boundaries of school. Thinking about your own schooling experiences, what messages did you receive about the use of languages other than English in school? In what spaces, if any, was the use of languages other than English considered legitimate? Were these public spaces or private spaces that were off center stage of the classroom floor? Thinking about your own classroom, have you created any kinds of space for students to use languages other than English?

The Possibilities of Words Unspoken.   In the play, *Hong Kong, Canada,* Sarah barely passed her first calculus quiz. In scene 3 she tells the audience that lots of the students from Hong Kong are getting 90% or more on their quizzes because they have already taken calculus in Hong Kong. In scene 7, both Sarah and Carol find themselves in the same empty classroom doing calculus homework. Sarah considers asking Carol for help, but in the end decides not to. Working in pairs, have one person reread Sarah's lines in scene 7 until her last line. Instead of saying Sarah's last line, have her approach Carol. With the second person playing Carol, spontaneously play out an exchange between Carol and Sarah. Share your experience of what happened with other pairs in your in group. This activity of interrupting and reinventing a theatrical scene has been developed and written about by educator Augusto Boal. For further reading on this kind of work, see Boal's book, *Theatre of the Oppressed,* listed in the Reference section.

3

Promoting and Legitimizing English

Students who do not have access to the politically popular dialect form in this country are less likely to succeed economically than their peers who do.
[From Lisa Delpit's essay,
"Ebonics and Culturally Responsive Instruction"][1]

In the previous chapter, I discussed the pedagogical approach of promoting student multilingualism. In this chapter, I look at the work of teachers who promote English monolingualism in their classrooms. The chapter begins with an excerpt from an interview with Hong Kong-born English teacher Anne Yee, who implemented an English-only policy in her classroom as a way of providing her English as a second or other language (ESOL) students with more opportunities to practice English. Like African-American educator Lisa Delpit, whose quote on the importance of access to linguistic capital opens this chapter, Mrs. Yee believed that her students' future economic prospects depended on their ability to communicate fluently and effectively in English.

Anne Yee has been working as a teacher for 17 years. She first came to Canada as a high school visa student. She completed her high school, university, and teacher training education in Toronto and went back to Hong Kong to teach. After teaching for 4 years, Mrs. Yee worked in the Education

---

[1]See Delpit (1998).

Department of Hong Kong as an education officer. In this position, which she held for 2 years, she was responsible for supervising the work of government-funded schools in Hong Kong. Mrs. Yee then returned to Toronto where she began teaching again. At the time of the interview, she had been teaching in Toronto for 12 years. Mrs. Yee is currently an English and ESOL teacher, and the head of the ESOL Department and Literacy Committee at Northside. Over the years, she has taught ESOL and "regular English" students from Caribbean, Asian, Middle-Eastern, African, and Eastern-European backgrounds. In describing her experiences of working with students from such diverse backgrounds, Mrs. Yee says they have helped her to become a sensitive, tolerant, and accommodating teacher. They have also made her aware of the need to work toward equity and antiracism. In describing the impact of her own educational experience on her teaching practice, Mrs. Yee had this to say:

> Having acquired English as a second language myself and having attended schools and universities as an ESL student in Ontario, I understand the extreme importance of oral English on the lives of ESL students and newcomers. I feel that it is crucial for my ESL students to acquire maximum fluency in oral English before the end of their adolescence, since my linguistic training has taught me that the articulation flexibility that is required for second language acquisition will start to deteriorate after adolescence. I also understand that it takes a lot of courage for a second language learner to speak in English due to linguistic and cultural barriers. The English-only policy is thus introduced into my class to maximize the opportunity for my ESOL students to practice oral English. These students have minimal opportunity to speak English at home and outside their ESOL and English classroom.
>
> [*Response to Questionnaire*, November 9, 2001]

The following interview excerpt, "A Commitment to English," begins with me asking Anne Yee about her beliefs about bilingual teaching. The rest of the data used in this chapter comes from observations and interviews undertaken in Mrs. Yee's Grade 12 English class. Excerpts from additional student interviews and discussions also appear in this chapter. The ethnographic text, the commentary, and the pedagogical discussion in this chapter have been member checked by Mrs. Yee.

A COMMITMENT TO ENGLISH

Tara: I wanted to ask you about [English/Cantonese] bilingual teaching. Why was it an appropriate strategy in Hong Kong, but not appropriate for a group of students in a Canadian setting?

Anne: There are at least two differences [between school settings in Hong Kong and Canada] that I will talk about. The first difference is in Hong Kong; it is a homogeneous culture. If you are using a bilingual approach, then everyone is able to understand that approach. So, when I am explaining something in their mother tongue, they can understand. There isn't any problem of equity …. The second difference is that back there they expect you to use bilingual approaches to help students understand English because the whole approach of teaching English is different. There [in Hong Kong], there is a lot of emphasis on reading and writing. Spoken English is not emphasized because you don't need to speak it, because it is a Chinese-speaking society. You don't need English for your daily lives … Of course, parents or schools would like to see students being able to speak English fluently, but it is not a survival skill. Here [in Canada, or more specifically Toronto], you need to speak it because it is the language of the mainstream and it is a survival skill …. There is more flexibility or there is more room for using bilingual approaches there.

Tara: Right. So the English-only policy that you have used in your classroom [at Northside], you would not necessarily use that policy in Hong Kong.

Anne: It depends on the level of the students. For grade 12 and the OAC (Ontario Academic Credit/high school leaving credit) equivalent, I didn't use Cantonese at all. It was for the junior grades, to help them a little bit. Usually I used it for explanation, like the meaning of vocabulary, new words.

Tara: So the challenge for someone who does have the bilingual skills you do, here [at Northside], is that you have [students with] a range of [different English language] abilities. You have Barry, who has just arrived and is very much a beginner …. Someone like him could probably benefit from your bilingual approach. Yet, he is in grade 12 and you have other students who are advanced. I know that in your class you have an English-only policy and there are chores for students who speak languages other than English to do [when they are overheard speaking other languages]. When you were thinking about your pedagogy and your strategies, how did you come up with an English-only policy in light of the fact that you knew your class was going to be mixed in terms of [English] proficiency levels?

Anne: Well, personally, I have a strong commitment to make sure that they speak only English in class because I think I understand the family backgrounds. Not just the Chinese kids' [backgrounds], the ESOL kids' [backgrounds]. I mean they don't speak English at home. Their parents don't usually speak English with them and their parents very often expect them to be able to retain their mother tongue.

So, these kids, if we don't force them to speak English at school, they'd have no chance of speaking the target language or the language that they need to acquire. And if we cannot provide such an environment for them, I think we are doing them a disservice. Secondly, time is short. If we don't enforce an English-only environment, I am sure that when they get to universities, no one is going to do that. And since Canada is an English-speaking country, for the sake of the future of the students, I think we have to make them speak English. It is a different country, it is a different environment, and for the benefit of their own future, their own careers, they better equip themselves with good spoken English, because it does make a difference when they are looking for a job.

Tara: Right. If a student like Barry was to come to you for help, and was really struggling, because you have the ability to use Cantonese, can you imagine a situation in which you would use Cantonese? With a student, like, whom you felt it would be more efficient to use Cantonese to—

Anne: No, I won't.

Tara: Not here [in Canada]. Can I ask you why?

Anne: Well, okay. As far as learning is concerned, I think they should get used to being able to communicate with their teachers in English, regardless of what subject it is … I don't want to set any precedent. If I do that, then they'll save their questions and see me after class, hoping I will give them instructions in their mother tongues. It is not fair for other students and it is not a wise use of my professional time or their time. So in order to encourage them to maximize their learning opportunity during class, if they come and see me after class, I usually speak in the same language [I always use with them, English] … I will break the rule in one situation: if they come to me and want counseling. If they are having some personal problems and they can't express themselves that well in English. Only under that kind of circumstance, when the student is desperate, and wants some help, and counseling is needed, I may conduct a counseling session in a student's first language. But as far as teaching and learning is concerned, I think it is rather illegitimate.
            [*Interview*, May 27, 1998]

COMMENTARY: INSISTING UPON ENGLISH

Unlike Evelyn Lo, who accepted her students' use of languages other than English, Anne Yee tried to limit such use by introducing an English-only policy in her classroom. As discussed in the interview above, students who were overheard speaking languages other than English while they were in class were assigned classroom chores to complete. These chores included such tasks as cleaning the chalkboard and handing out books or assignments. The names of those students who had been given chores to complete were written in a corner of the chalkboard and were erased once the students had completed them.

Mrs. Yee's interests in promoting English monolingualism in her classroom had to do with her belief that the more opportunities that ESOL students had to practice English during the school day, the better access they had to the socioeconomic benefits associated with English, the dominant language of mainstream society. This belief was supported by the understandings she had of her ESOL students' linguistic communities both inside and outside of school. Having been a high-school student from Hong Kong herself, Mrs. Yee had a personal understanding of the dilemma for Cantonese speakers articulated in the Introduction. Although socializing and working almost exclusively in Cantonese at school helped students succeed both socially and academically, it did not provide them with many opportunities to practice English. Nor were there many opportunities to practice English at home where family members usually communicated in Cantonese.

Commenting on the argument Mrs. Yee offers for her classroom English-only policy, sociolinguist Angel Lin (personal communication) suggested that the "maximum exposure" argument is one that is frequently constructed, reinforced and invoked in the media and academic discourses in Hong Kong. "Parents, teachers, school principals and government officials in Hong Kong," she says, "frequently draw on the 'maximum exposure' argument to rationalize English only or English dominant policies in the schooling system. This argument has followed from the cognitive 'input-output' model, which was dominant in the Second-Language Acquisition (SLA) and Teaching English as a Second or Other Language research (TESOL)."[2] Lin also suggested that Mrs. Yee's beliefs about the importance of English only in her classroom may have been constructed by her SLA/TESOL education which privileged the input–output model of second language learning over other models. Although Anne Yee did not mention the input–output model of second language learning when asked about important influences on her teaching practice, she did mention another dominant SLA discourse that helped construct her teaching beliefs, the discourse of "articulation flexibility." The English-only policy in Anne's classroom was related to her belief

---

[2]For further discussion of how the "maximum exposure" argument has followed from the input–output model, see Lin (1997a).

that it is crucial for her students to develop their oral English skills in high school because the articulation flexibility required for second-language acquisition deteriorates after adolescence. Importantly, the discourse of articulation, like other psycholinguistic and Universal Grammar approaches in the field of SLA, assumes a generic language user. It disregards any variation between individuals as "noise," that is, a distraction that cannot be avoided, but which cannot in any way contribute to our understanding of the universal facts of SLA (Piller & Pavlenko, 2001). However, as mentioned in the Introduction, a more recent model of second language learning and teaching conceptualizes language learners as complex social beings who learn and use the second language in a variety of social contexts. This sociolinguistic, sociolcultural model of language learning suggests that it is the desire to construct particular identities that underlies a learner's investment (or the lack of investment) in language learning.[3] If second-language learning hinges on community building and identity construction rather than, or perhaps in addition to, exposure to the target language, then the "maximum exposure" and "articulation flexibility" arguments, which have been used to justify many English-only or English-dominant policies and practices in our schools, are problematic. Further discussion of the maximum exposure argument appears later in this chapter in the Pedagogical Discussion.

In addition to her interest in her ESOL students' academic and economic future, Mrs. Yee's promotion of English can also be linked to her interest in avoiding classroom conflicts that can accompany multilingual practices. For Mrs. Yee, the use of languages other than English in her classroom could create a "problem of equity," such as Theresa Lubov's perception, discussed in chapter 2, that Cantonese- and Mandarin-speaking students had "more advantage" than she did in Mrs. Lo's math class.

Student Responses to English-Only in the Classroom

When we asked Mrs. Yee's students about their feelings toward the English-only policy in their classroom, we heard mixed views. On one hand, many Cantonese-speaking students welcomed the policy as a tool for helping them practice English, the language of academic and political power, both inside and outside of school. On the other hand, the enforcement of the policy was sometimes seen as embarrassing, as the following interview excerpt with Cantonese-speaking student Cathy Lee illustrates:

---

[3]See the Introduction, Norton (2000), and Norton Peirce (1995) for further discussion on investment in second-language learning.

Tara: What are your feelings about English-only policies and the different ways that teachers try and enforce that rule?

Cathy: Like, the teacher who makes this policy is, like, good for us. Well, I'm thinking it's good for us because it will motivate ourselves to speak more English, because the teacher is trying to help us improve our English. Like speaking skills, especially. It's good. Like, I think it's good but—It's good to set a policy, but—It's—What I'm thinking is—is that it's not good that you not set a policy—right? Okay? You understand what I'm talking about?

Tara: Tell me a little more.

Cathy: Because, you would naturally speak Chinese when you—when you are not in an English policy rule—like—class. So I don't think—I don't really mind that you speak Chinese in the hall, but I would prefer more [people] to speak English in the class.

Tara: And you think it's the policy that helps you, helps everybody to do that?

Cathy: Yeah. If you have a policy in the class where you have to speak in English—like, this is a policy. You can't change it, right?

Tara: Right. So if you speak Cantonese—ah, usually with your friends—and then you change to English, then they think you're showing off. But in the classroom, if there is an English language policy, everybody knows you are just obeying the policy—

Cathy: Yeah.

Tara: So then no one can accuse you of showing off.

Cathy: Yeah.

Tara: Okay. I got it now. Now, it seems to me there's a difference between having a policy and then also punishing people when they don't have—ah—when they don't speak English. So, let's use Mrs. Yee's class, for example. She has chores.

Cathy: Yeah.

Tara: She doesn't take off marks. She doesn't—um—take money. How do you feel about the chores, a punishment for not speaking English?

Cathy: It's not as big a punishment as money I don't think.

Tara: Right. If you were in a class where the teacher asked you to give them money if you spoke your own language or a class in which they said, "I'm going to deduct some marks," how would you feel?

Cathy: That's too strong (Laughs). But I think the students really don't care about chores.

Tara: No.

Cathy: They don't. Not really. But, like, it's a shame that your name is put on the board. It's like embarrassing, you know?

Tara: Yeah. Would you prefer that she didn't put your name on the board?
Cathy: Yes.
            [*Interview*, April 30, 1998]

In addition to thinking about the issue of student embarrassment, teachers who want to implement a classroom English-only policy also need to think about student resistance. In a discussion of the promotion of English at school, Gertrude Chow, a Cantonese-speaking student who was not in Mrs. Yee's English class pointed out:

> I think that even though teachers tell students not to speak Cantonese, it doesn't work. 'Cause students can talk Cantonese quietly, secretly. Or they even write letters, in Chinese, but not in English.
>
> [*Small group discussion*, November 28, 1996]

Mrs. Yee believed that only the use of English was legitimate in her classroom. In her interview, she said that although she might conduct a counseling session in a student's first language, as far as teaching and learning was concerned the use of languages other than English was "rather illegitimate." Some students, like Cathy Lee, shared Mrs. Yee's belief that it was important to practice English as much as possible and supported her use of a classroom English-only policy even though she felt embarrassed when it was implemented. Others, as Gertrude explained, contested this legitimizing of English by speaking other languages quietly so they were not overhead or by writing notes in languages other than English. In other words, not all students had an "unconditional investment" in speaking English. Some were ambivalent or resistant.

Upon reading both Cathy and Gertrude's comments on Mrs. Yee's English-only policy, my colleague Angel Lin (personal communication) had this to say:

> What stands out from Cathy's story seems to be her argument that the teacher's English-only policy has become a resource for her to draw on to avoid the social interpretation of her "showing off her English ability." She can always say, "Oh, I have to speak English because I dare not offend the teacher by violating her rule." This is interesting because you can see that there are at least two different [groups] of students in the classroom. One [group] wants to practice using English (and has the ability to do so), but dares not do so because of the social sanctions by their peers. For them, the teacher's English-only policy has become a resource to counter those social sanctions...Another [group] of students are those who are diffident about their English accent and limited proficiency. They will not speak English anyway, and so, this policy serves as a resource for them to construct another

identity, that of "brave teacher-contester" who keeps on speaking in Cantonese to one another, albeit in whispers.

Using this analysis to think about what is problematic about an English-only policy in a multilingual classroom, Lin suggested that such a policy not only creates embarrassment for students, but does nothing to increase students' confidence and interest in using English despite accents or limited proficiency. An English-only policy also fails to rally the first-language resources that students might have to support their learning of English:

> It's basically a countereffective strategy in the sense that those who need most help, that is to say, those who are diffident about their English and are actually limited in their English skills, will not be encouraged by this policy to speak English, but will be pushed to speak even more of their first language in defiance of this policy.

To further my thinking about the advantages and disadvantages of implementing a classroom English-only policy as a strategy to provide students with more opportunities to practice English, I turned to work that had been written in response to the American "Ebonics Debate," which raged during the 1996–1997 school year. In the pedagogical discussion that follows, I engage with this work for insights into "best practices" for promoting English in multilingual classrooms.

PEDAGOGICAL DISCUSSION: LEARNING FROM THE AMERICAN "EBONICS DEBATE"

On December 21, 1996, the Oakland School Board in the state of California unanimously passed the Ebonics Resolution, requiring all schools in the district to participate in the Standard English Proficiency program (SEP). The Standard English Proficiency program was a statewide initiative that had begun in 1981 but had not yet been fully implemented in the Oakland district. Acknowledging the systematic, rule-governed nature of Ebonics (also known as Black Language and African American Language), the program took the position that this language should be used to help African-American children read and write in Standard English.[4] This resolution,

---

[4]Standard English has been defined as "…the variety which forms the basis of printed English in newspapers and books, which is used in the mass media and which is taught in school …" (Yule, 1996). Ebonics/Black Language/African American language has been defined as " … Linguistic and paralinguistic features which on concentric continuum represent the communicative competence of the West African, Caribbean, and United States slave descendants of African origin" (Williams, 1975).

similar in intent to the *Language for Learning Policy*, was only one element
of a broad strategy developed by an African-American task force, and was
aimed at improving the school performance of African-American students.
At the time, the African-American students enrolled in Oakland school district in California comprised 53% of the student population, but accounted
for 80% of the school system's suspensions and 71% of students classified
as having special needs. Their average grade was a D+. It was these painful
realities, reflective of the Oakland school system's inability to ensure academic success for African-American children, that motivated the school
board to approve the Black Language/Ebonics resolution.

The school board's approval of the Ebonics Resolution led to a heated national American debate on Ebonics. In her analysis of the debate, African-American educator Theresa Perry noted that, with few exceptions, the
mainstream media in the United States misrepresented the Oakland resolution as a decision by the school board to abandon the teaching of Standard
English and, in its stead, teach Black Language/Ebonics. Not only was this
not the intent of the resolution, this was not what the original resolution
stated. Editorial writers, columnists, talk show hosts, educational leaders
and well-known spokespeople for Blacks in the United States vigorously
opposed the Oakland Resolution. In thinking about the reasons for this op-
position, Perry believed a variety of factors were at play.[5] One of these was
the existence of a dominant White conversation about schooling that discussed "generic solutions to broken schools." [6] This conversation did not examine the specific ways race affected (and continues to affect) the school
lives of African-American children in different communities and educational contexts. Consequently, it did not see the potentially positive impact
the use of Ebonics at Oakland schools might have for students' academic
success. A second factor had to do with the way Black language was
equated with slang on television news reports about the Ebonics Resolution.
Perry explained that there are multiple varieties of Ebonics/Black Language
in the United States: oral and written, formal and informal, standard, non-
standard (slang), and literary. For African Americans who wanted their
children to gain oral and written competence in all the varieties of Black
Language as well as "White" Standard English, an Ebonics Resolution
equated only with slang seemed to narrow their educational options.

As African-American educator Lisa Delpit (quoted at the beginning of
this chapter) has written, the national Ebonics Debate created "much more

---

[5]For a fuller discussion of this analysis see Perry (1998).
[6]See Perry (1998).

heat than light" and did little to clarify the public misunderstandings about Ebonics or the intent of the resolution. The debate also did little to assist educators in developing curriculum and pedagogies that used Ebonics to help African-American children acquire fluency in Standard English.[7] In response, she and Theresa Perry guest edited a special issue of the journal *Rethinking Schools* and published a set of essays that provided a "careful conversation" about the important educational, political, and linguistic issues that were embedded in the Ebonics Resolution.[8] The pedagogical discussion that follows draws on these essays, which have since been republished in the form of a book.[9]

In her own essay on Ebonics and culturally responsive instruction, Lisa Delpit writes that teachers working with African-American students need to respond to two realities. On one hand, they need to recognize that the Black Language linguistic forms their students bring to school are "intimately connected with loved ones, community, and personal identity." When teachers suggest that these forms are "wrong" (or illegitimate) in some way, they are suggesting that something is wrong with the students and their families. But, it is equally important for teachers to understand that the life chances of African-American students who do not learn to use Standard English fluently and effectively will be hampered. Delpit recognizes that having access to the politically mandated language form will not guarantee economic success and cites the growing numbers of unemployed African Americans holding doctorates as an example. However, she maintains that not having access will almost certainly guarantee failure in the economic market.[10]

Although the strategy of implementing an English-only policy responds to the second of Delpit's two classroom realities, the need to provide students with access to English, I am uncertain about how well it responds to the first reality. In its insistence on the sole use of English in the classroom, an English-only policy delegitimizes other languages. It was not Mrs. Yee's intention to suggest that there was something "wrong" with languages other than English or the students in her class who spoke them. On the occasions when she reminded her students of the classroom English-only policy, she included the following words with her reminder: "I do not want to take away your mother tongue. I want to build up your second language." Because Mrs. Yee's own first language was Cantonese, the words sent a strong mes-

---

[7] See Delpit (1998).

[8] This special issue of *Rethinking Schools* is available from: Rethinking Schools, 1001 E. Keefe Ave. Milwaukee, WI 53212. Available at RSBusiness@aol.com

[9] See Perry and Delpit (1998).

[10] See Delpit (1998).

sage. However, even with such a reminder, I am concerned that an English-only policy carries other messages, particularly when it is implemented by educators who use English as a first language. This concern is rooted in my own experience as an acting director of a 6-week residential ESOL program at the University of Manitoba during the summer of 1985.

When I assumed the acting directorship of the program, I inherited its English-only policy, which mandated that the adolescent students enrolled in the program speak English at all times, both inside and outside the classroom. All staff, including the program's secretary, teachers, and "monitors" who organized the co-curricular and recreational events, were expected to report any students who were overheard speaking a language other than English to the director. Students whose names were reported to the director three times were asked to the leave the program, which was funded by the Canadian government. Although I was uncomfortable with having to send students home for speaking their primary languages, I accepted the position of acting director and the responsibility for implementing the English-only policy. Like Mrs. Yee, my own ideas about language learning had been influenced by the "maximum exposure" argument, which was dominant at the time.

Despite my fervent hope that none of the students would be "caught" speaking any languages other than English more than twice, and that I would not have to ask anyone to leave, one of the students continued to resist the program's delegitimization of her language. Despite two "warnings" that her continued use of French would result in her being sent home, the student continued to speak her primary language and was overhead speaking French a third time. Having agreed to implement the program's English-language policy, I felt I had no choice but to ask the student to leave the program. Further resistance to the implementation of the policy followed when the student's entire class protested my decision to send their classmate home. Despite the protest, the student was sent home and I was left with the task of rebuilding student morale and investment in the program. I was also left wondering if there were less coercive ways of promoting the learning of English. I know there are differences between the classroom English-only policies in place at Northside and the program policy I upheld. I also know there are differences between assigning students chores and asking them to leave a program of study as a consequence for speaking languages other than English. Yet, the issue of language and coercion still concerns me. As Angel Lin suggested earlier, the University of Manitoba's English-only policy was counterproductive. It did not encourage the resistant student to speak English. Instead it pushed her to speak even more French. So what are the alternatives to an English-only policy? How might educators provide access to English without delegitimizing their students' primary languages? African-American educator Carrie Secret, who has taught African-American students at Prescott Elementary School since 1966, provides us with a very helpful set of responses to these questions.

Prior to the passing of the 1996 Ebonics Resolution, Prescott had been the only school in the Oakland school system where the majority of teachers had voluntarily agreed to adopt the Standard English Proficiency program. In a 1997 interview about "embracing" Ebonics and teaching Standard English, Ms. Secret was asked if she ever allowed students to use Ebonics in her classroom. This was her answer:

> The word that bothers me is "allow." Students talk. They bring their language to school. That is their right. If you are concerned about children using Ebonics in the classroom, you will spend the whole day saying, "Translate, translate, translate." So you have to pick times when you are particularly attuned to and calling for English translation.
>
> When the children are working in groups together, say three or four of them, I try to keep them in an English-speaking mode, but I don't prevent them from using Ebonics. I want to give them enough time to talk through their project in their comfortable language. It's like a re-write to me. But at some point, they have to present their project to me and these are required to be presented in their best English.[11]

When asked if there were particular times during the school day when her students were required to speak Standard English, Ms. Secret, who was teaching fifth grade at the time of the interview, said this:

> In fifth grade, I encourage the students to practice English most of the instructional time. I say "encourage" because "required" is a word that sends a message that if you don't use English, then you are operating below standard. Let's say that in fifth grade, students are requested and encouraged to speak in English almost all the time.
>
> … When writing, the students are aware that finished pieces are written in English. The use of Ebonic structures appears in many of their first drafts. When this happens I simply say, "You used Ebonics here. I need you to translate this thought into English." This kind of statement does not negate the child's thought or language.
>
> Some days I simply announce: "While you are working, I will be listening to how well you use English. In your groups, you must call for translation if a member of your group uses an Ebonic structure." Some days I say, "Girls, you are at Spelman and boys, you are attending Morehouse College [histori-

---

[11]See Miner (1998).

cally Black colleges]. Today you use the language the professors use and expect you to use in your classes, and that language is English."

I once had some visitors come to my class and they said, "We don't hear Ebonics here." But that is because I had explained to my children that company was coming, and when company comes, we practice speaking English. Company is the best time to practice because most of our visitors are from a cultural language context different from ours.[12]

In line with her beliefs that it is important for teachers not to imply that a student's language is inadequate and that different language forms are appropriate in different contexts, Carrie Secret also had her students become involved with the standard form of English through various kinds of role-play. For example, memorizing parts for drama productions provided her students with an opportunity to practice Standard English while keeping their own linguistic identities and investments intact.

Carrie Secret's strategies for promoting English runs less risk of passing on the message that there is something "wrong" with languages other than English (and the people who speak them) than does the strategy of implementing a classroom English-only policy or program. Secret's strategies are also less coercive in that they do not result in any punitive consequences for speaking one's "comfortable" language while learning another one. As a result, there is less resistance in her classroom to using Standard English.

In concluding her essay on Ebonics and culturally responsive instruction, Lisa Delpit suggests that "all we can do is provide students with access to additional language forms. Inevitably, each speaker will make his or own decision about what to say in any context."[13] Delpit also reminds us not to become so overly concerned with the language form that we ignore "academic and moral content." She argues that while access to Standard English may be necessary, it is not sufficient to produce "intelligent, competent caretakers of the future." Further discussion of the ways teachers might develop curriculum that provides students with relevant academic and moral content takes place in chapter 4 and chapter 5.

The pedagogical discussion in this chapter has looked at various strategies that can be used to promote English in multilingual schools. Further discussion of the way these strategies both challenge and reproduce linguistic and economic inequities in multilingual communities is taken up in the Conclusion. Below, are a set of activities that continue to engage with the work undertaken by Ebonics writers and educators in the United States.

---

[12]See Miner (1998).

[13]See Delpit (1998).

FOR FURTHER REFLECTION AND DISCUSSION

Private and Public Linguistic Identities: Personal and Professional Reflection.   In the reflection activities included in chapter 2, writer Richard Rodriguez was represented as believing that his ability to access opportunities and privileges in the United States depended on his ability to assimilate. Successful assimilation depended upon keeping his private and public linguistic identities separate. In an autobiographical essay about her own Black Language/Standard English bilingual education, literature scholar Joyce Hope Scott writes:

> We were taught specifically that we had a public and a private face, and different languages through which the two distinct personas could be animated. These languages were in a dialogic relationship with each other, and our responsibility was to understand and master this linguistic paradigm rather than to perceive the languages as in conflict with each other."[14]

Like Richard Rodriguez, Joyce Hope Scott was taught to separate her public and private identities through language. However, unlike Rodriguez, whose parents, following the advice of Richard's teachers, only spoke English at home once Richard began school, Scott also learned that there was a place for both languages in her communal experience:

> My mother taught me the beauty of both Standard and Black English by reading to me when I was young, first the classic fairy tales then later Dickens, and English and American poets ... European tales, such as *East of the Sun and North of the Wind* or the legends of Thor or Zeus, were read or told in Standard English. Local folk tales, lore and African-American tales were told in the Black vernacular."[15]

Thinking about your own bilingual education, to what extent, if at all, did you learn that there was a place for different languages in your communal experience? In what ways, if at all, were you taught the languages you spoke could exist along side each other? Thinking about the bilingual education of your own students, in what specific ways can you play a role in teaching them that there is a place for all the languages they speak?

Journal Writing in English.   In scene 3 of *Hong Kong, Canada* (included in Appendix A), English teacher Ms. Diamond tries to encourage a student Carol Shen to practice English through journal writing. Carol resists

---

[14]See Scott (1998).
[15]See Scott (1998).

the activity and tells Ms. Diamond, "What is in my heart, I want to write in Chinese." Ms. Diamond responds by suggesting that Carol write about school things, like the talent show, if writing about personal things in English is difficult. Carol hesitantly, or perhaps reluctantly, takes up this suggestion when she "slowly unfolds her hands, picks up her pen, and begins writing." What do you make of Ms. Diamond's intervention in this scene? Do you see journal writing about school things as an effective way of helping students practice English and learn that there is place for English in their everyday experience? Why or why not?

Imagining Carol's Journal Entry.   Assuming the character of Carol Shen in *Hong Kong, Canada,* write a journal entry in English that describes either how you feel about performing in the upcoming talent show or how you felt after performing in the talent show. Share your entry with the rest of the group and compare the different ways you imagined how Carol felt about performing in the talent show. If you are able to use a language other than English, write a second journal entry in that language. What are the differences between the two entries you have written? How do these differences relate to Carol's desire to write about personal, heartfelt matters in Chinese? Do these differences change your views on journal writing explored in activity 2 above?

Looking at Intersections of Race, Language, and Class.   While I have turned to work from the Ebonics debate in this chapter, it is important to point out that the speakers of Cantonese at Northside were in a different economic, political, and social position than the speakers of Black Language at Prescott. African French psychiatrist, Frantz Fanon, has written that "every dialect, every language, is a way of thinking. To speak means to assume a culture." Applying Fanon's words to the Ebonics debate, African-American sociolinguist Geneva Smitherman has written that speakers of Ebonics have assumed a cultural legacy of slave descendants of African origin. "To speak Ebonics is to assert the power of this tradition in the quest to resolve the unfinished business of being African in America."[16] This cultural legacy, the ongoing struggle to fight poverty, linguism, and racism, is different from the struggle faced by Cantonese speakers at Northside, who experienced discrimination from a more privileged economic position. In the words of antiracist psychologist Beverly Daniel Tatum,

---

[16]See Fanon (1967) and Smitherman (1998).

Not all people of color are equally targeted by racism. We all have multiple identities that shape our experience…When one is targeted by multiple isms—racism, sexism, classism, heterosexism, ableism, anti-Semitism, ageism—in whatever combination, the effect is intensified. The particular combination of racism and classism in many communities of color is life-threatening."[17]

In what ways might the schooling experience of Cantonese speakers at Northside differ from the schooling experience of Black Language speakers at Prescott? In what ways might the benefits of living and attending school in a middle- and upper middle-class community have mediated the Northside students' experience of different forms of discrimination?

Ambivalent and Changing Investments in English. Following Euro-Canadian researcher Bonny Norton, I have argued that ESOL learners can experience ambivalence around their investment in English. Norton has also suggested that, in addition to feeling ambivalent about their investment in English, some ESOL learners experience change in their investment or lack of investment in English. Learners' investments are not fixed in time or space. In the last scene of *Hong Kong, Canada,* Wendy reflects back on her strategy of choosing to only speak English at school so that she would have more opportunities to practice. How is Wendy's investment in English ambivalent and/or how does her investment change throughout the play?

---

[17]See Tatum (1997, p. 13).

4

Responding to Silence

"What do you know about Asians?" a young Chinese American woman asks Mark, a young White man of Italian descent. His response:

I'm going to be honest with you. I completely believed the stereotype. Asian people are hard workers, they're really quiet, they get good grades because they have tons of pressure from their families to get good grades ... are quiet so people can't have a problem with them.
[From the video, *Skin Deep: College Students Confront Racism*][1]

The exchange that opens this chapter captures the essence of the current stereotypes that currently circulate about Chinese North Americans. While the "model minority" characterization may initially seem to be a positive and beneficial one, it has some negative effects. As antiracist researcher and educators Beverly Tatum and Stacey Lee explain, in terms of intergroup relations, the model minority stereotype has served to pit North-American Asians against other groups targeted by racism. The accusing message to other people of color is, "They overcame discrimination—why can't you?" It has also contributed to White resentment, leading to an increase in anti-Asian violence.[2] As well, uncritical acceptance of the stereotype has also concealed the needs and problems of those Asians who have not experienced the success of good grades. Writers Jeff Yang, Dina Gan, and Terry Hong have put it this way:

---

[1] This exchange was reproduced in Tatum (1997, p.160) and can been heard in the video "Skin Deep," produced and directed by Reid (1995).

[2] For information on anti-Asian violence, see Chan and Hune (1995).

Are we or aren't we? Only the Census Bureau can say for sure. What started out as a seemingly harmless observation has grown into a scary sociotheoretical monster, devouring all racial groups in its path. Holding up Asian Americans as paragon and proof that racial discrimination need not be a barrier to social advancement, the "Model Minority" thesis drove a wedge between racial groups trying to forge coalitions after the Civil Rights movements of the 1960s. Thirty years since its inception, the end result of the Model Minority myth has been resentment of Asian Americans by Blacks, Whites, and even those Asians themselves who didn't fit the stereotype of the hard working, lots-of-money, good-grade getting, all-in-the-family-keeping whiz kids.[3]

Although the young man in the opening quote believes that being quiet can protect Asians from people having a problem with them, this was not always the case at Northside. On the contrary, the fact that many of the students from Hong Kong were often quiet in class was considered burdensome and resented by some of their non-Chinese and Canadian-born Chinese classmates. In this chapter, the issue of student silence in multilingual classrooms is explored. The chapter begins with excerpts from two student interviews. The first interview was with a Cantonese-speaking student, Victor Yu, who spoke about the issue of "showing off" in the Introduction. The second interview, conducted by research assistant Gordon Pon and me, was with Mina Henry, a Canadian-born woman of Indo-Caribbean ancestry, who was a student in Anne Yee's grade 12 English classroom discussed in chapter 3. Both Victor and Mina talk about the silence they associated with Asian students in their classes. The Commentary, which was co-written by Gordon and me, analyzes the different ways Victor, Mina, and other students in Mrs. Yee's English class have understood Asian silence at Northside. In the Pedagogical Discussion, Gordon and I look at the ways teachers might assist their students in negotiating the dilemmas and tensions associated with silences in the classroom. Here, we make use of the work undertaken by Northside English teachers Anne Yee, Greg Dunn, and Leonard Robertson, all of whom have member checked the ethnographic interview excerpts, commentary, and pedagogical discussion that appear in this chapter.

"I CAN KEEP IT IN MY HEART"

Tara: Tell me some of the differences between going to school in Hong Kong and going to high school here in Toronto.

Victor: Oh, there's a big difference. In Hong Kong, right? The teachers are really dominating, like, they, they, want everything under their con-

---

[3]See Yang, Gan, and Hong (1997).

trol because there are 40 people at least in one class, even in grade 7. So, there are many people, right? If one student gets, like, out of control, right? Everyone will be out of control. So that teacher wants absolute control. And in this case, the good students will have no questions. They will always follow the teacher instruction. So, in here, right? Maybe the teacher, teacher will say that, "This guy is doing really good in, in his task, in his, his, work. How come he doesn't answer any questions?" Or "How come he doesn't answer any of my, how he come didn't answer my questions?" Because this is a different culture.

Tara: Right. Tell me more about that. You were telling me before I turned on the tape [recorder] about that. You were telling me this is something I should tell my [pre-service teacher education] students.

Victor: Yeah. If, if you see a student, right? Like especially from Hong Kong or from Asia. Like, they, they do their work really good. But they're quiet, right? Don't blame them because this is like what they used to be in the school in Hong Kong, or in, in their country. Because they, they think that, "If I don't have any problems for the teacher, the teacher will think I am good." So they keep quiet. They don't know that if they don't, like, answer questions, then they are not really participating in the class. Right? It's, it's, they will, like, the teachers will see them as not really good students. So this is, this would be a difference from the school in Hong Kong and here.

Tara: Let me ask you [this]. Was it very hard for you when you first came to Toronto to get used to the presentations and the group work and the speaking out in class?

Victor: Yeah. It was really, really hard. 'Cause, okay, 'cause I, when I want to answer some questions I was thinking about, "If I answer," right? "What will other Cantonese students or students from Hong Kong think about me?" If I, like, they may be thinking about how I am showing off my knowledge. I mean, yeah, I know the [answers to the] questions, right? I know it. That's, that's good. I can keep it in my heart. But then, if I put my hand up and then say, "Sir, I understand" and then answer the question, right? They will, they may think, think I am showing off. So it is really hard.
[*Interview,* October 9, 1999]

"EVERYONE HAS TO CONTRIBUTE"

Gordon: Can I ask you a little about the group work in Mrs. Yee's class?

Mina: Well, first of all, like, I thought it was unfair because it was only me and Gregory (a Hong Kongese student) in the group doing the ISP

[Independent Special Project] and there were five other people [in other groups] ... Other groups had five people, we had two people ... And then with Gregory, he didn't do anything ... I did the whole, I planned out every single thing. If you looked at our presentation, it was all on what I had and what I put into it. She [Mrs. Yee] does a lot of stuff with group work. But then, the people that can't speak English or not [well], you know what I mean? They don't contribute anything and I'm, like, left to do the work for them and they get the same mark as me, which I don't find fair.

Tara: Group work is a very important topic for our work. In what ways is it good and in what ways is it bad?

Mina: I think group work is good, but you have to have people at the same level, you know what I mean? Everyone has to contribute. Of course, there is always going to be someone to take the lead ... but you need other people to contribute, right? And they don't. Especially in this class, they don 't. There's a lot of Chinese people, like, no offense, right? And they can't speak English properly, you know what I mean? And, like, she [Mrs. Yee] makes us, like, teach them. Well, like, I'm in a grade 12 Advanced English. My English is not that great myself, like, you know what I mean? I can speak proper English, but I am here to learn how to write properly for my OAC level [Ontario Academic Credit/high school leaving credit level]. I don't want to have to teach people, like, basic work. I need to learn how to write an essay properly. I need to learn the basic skills. In math class, the Chinese people are all good. They don't teach me math, you know what I mean? They sit there and do their own work. They go to private school and learn math. None of them help me, you know what I mean? But here I have to teach them basic primary skills. And my English is not that good.

Tara: I want to ask you a question on that. There is no question that you take on a leadership role in the class ... Do you think that in some unexpected way, being in a class like Mrs. Yee's—and I hear everything you're saying about how difficult it is for you and that's very important—

Mina: I don't mind multiculturalism, right? My friends, they're of all races. They speak Greek, they speak whatever. But, you know what I mean, when it comes to my work, I have to achieve. I have to achieve the marks.

Tara: Absolutely. But do you think the fact that you take on more leadership in these groups in Mrs. Yee's class than you do in other classes, is a good thing? I know there is that whole problem about the essay, but is the fact that you do take on so much leadership, is that a good thing for you in some ways?

Mina:	I like taking on the leadership role, I've always been like that. In any class I will be, like, a leader. I like speaking my mind and I like having discussions, but I like—
Tara:	But you're concerned about the essay.
Mina:	Not even the essay writing. Okay, I say my part, but like there's no like other stimuli from any other person in the class. They just sit there, you know what I mean? There's nothing there to, like you know, conflict with. In my other classes, I have other people [who] will say things, will disagree with me, will give me—in this class I have nothing. Everyone in that class just sits there like this. They're really quiet, they don't do nothing, like, you know what I mean? In other classes, I have other people that are on the same level in the same way as I am, so I have something to conflict with me. Seriously, I don't think half of those people in that class should be in a grade 12 advanced class. That's honestly what I'm saying. They shouldn't, they can't speak proper English ...
Tara:	You talk a little bit about the silence and I want to know why do you think there is so much silence? 'Cause we've noticed the same thing in Mrs. Yee's class. You mentioned it. It could be [English] language proficiency. That is probably a big reason. Is there any other reason you think that people are quiet?
Mina:	I have no clue. In most of my other classes people are just loud, and most of my classes are more [linguistically and racially] mixed. In this class, there are more Orientals and Orientals I find to be quieter people, like, you know, maybe that's why. I have no clue why, but like everyone in that class is like really quiet.
	[*Interview,* May 6, 1998]

COMMENTARY: SILENCES
IN THE MULTILINGUAL CLASSROOM
CO-WRITTEN WITH GORDON PON[4]

In their interviews, Victor and Mina present two very different views on the importance of speech in the classroom. Mina, who had always attended school in Toronto, desired conflict and debate in whole group classroom discussions and believed that everyone should contribute to smaller group discussions. Victor, who had completed most of his schooling in Hong Kong, worried about being perceived as "showing off" if he contributed to classroom discussions in the way Mina desired. Knowing that her grade 12 ad-

---

[4]The ideas in this Commentary and in the Pedagogical Discussion are also discussed in Pon, Goldstein, and Schecter (in press).

vanced English class consisted of primarily Chinese-Canadian students—many did not speak English as their primary language, and several had been in Canada for less than 2 years—Mrs. Yee expected that many students would be quiet and not verbally participate in class. Likewise, she anticipated that many of these students would want to use languages other than English in the classroom. Accordingly, she established a classroom English-only policy (discussed in chap. 3) and often asked students to work in racially and linguistically mixed small groups so that low English proficiency students would have opportunities to practice speaking with more proficient students. Despite these pedagogical strategies, silence, particularly among Hong Kong-born students, characterized many of the classes Gordon and I observed. We noted that many of the Chinese-Canadian students spoke very little and some not at all, both during whole-class discussions and in small group work. Moreover, many of the Chinese-Canadian students never raised their hands to volunteer responses, offer commentary, or to pose questions.

Burdensome Silence

The reluctance to speak English on the part of the Chinese-Canadian students in a classroom where students were asked to work extensively in linguistically mixed groups gave rise to particular racial tensions between Hong Kong-born Chinese, Canadian-born Chinese, and non-Chinese students. As Mina asserted in her interview, in many sessions of small-group work that we observed, the Hong Kong-born Chinese students spoke little, whereas the Canadian-born Chinese and non-Chinese students assumed a leadership role in an attempt to elicit verbal participation from the quieter members. For Mina, this reticence was burdensome ("I am left to do the work for them") and threatened the quality of her education ("In my other classes, I have other people [who] will say things, will disagree with me … in this class I have nothing"). These feelings were echoed by Marilyn, a White, Canadian-born young woman in Mrs. Yee's class, who had this to say about assuming the responsibility for doing most, if not all, of the talking in her small, linguistically, and racially mixed group:

> I feel like I'm just there to teach them and then—And I'm not really learning anything, I'm not getting anything out of it. Whereas if I was working with someone at the same level, then we could put in our ideas and it's not going to be just my ideas. And then the outcome will be like—we'd probably get better marks, I think because when we're doing presentations and stuff its not just one person or two people's ideas out of a group of five.
>
> [*Interview*, April 30, 1998]

Mina and Marilyn's interview comments equate silence with a lack of understanding and passivity. They also link silence with students' inability to work at a grade 12 level. Such comments reflect the findings of other North American educational researchers, such as Sandra McKay and Cynthia Wong, who have argued that in multiethnic and multilingual schools such as Northside, colonialist and racialized views find daily expression. [5] One such common expression is the belief that English-speaking ability is not only associated with academic success, but is also an indication of cognitive maturity and sophistication, and degree of "Americanization" (or, in this case, "Canadianization"). Likewise, Mackay and Wong note the common belief that immigrant status and limited English proficiency are considered states of deficiency and backwardness. Mina's comments about the inability of her Chinese-Canadian classmates to speak "proper English" invoke such colonialist and racialist discourses. Mina's understanding of her classmates' silence as being part of their Asian nature and her use of the word "Orientals" ("Orientals I find to be quieter people") also demonstrates the legacy of colonialist worldviews that North-American teachers and students have inherited (see "A Word About Language" at the beginning of the book for further discussion on the use of the term *Oriental*).

In analyzing what is at stake in the linguistic and racial tensions in Mrs. Yee's classroom, we see a conflation of at least two things: First, the invocation of colonialist and racialized discourses that pathologized the quiet "Oriental" students in Mrs. Yee's class; second, the very real or material pressure for high grades and academic success (cultural capital) that weighed heavy on the minds of Marilyn and Mina. Thus, the silence of some Chinese-Canadian students functioned to affirm, in the minds of some non-Chinese students, dominant negative stereotypes of Asians. These negative reactions became more strident when Asian reticence pulled down the collective marks of a group.

The comments offered by Mina and Marilyn show us that Mrs. Yee's purposeful pedagogical maneuver of establishing linguistically mixed groups was interrupted by silence and the forces of stereotyping and the pressure for high marks and academic success. Thus, student silences can be disenabling for positive race relations in multilingual classrooms. Yet, what Mina, Marilyn, and other students did not understand was the complex social and political forces that shaped the speech and silence dynamics of their Chinese-Canadian classmates. As discussed in the Introduction, these dynamics were often the result of linguistic dilemmas or double binds that

---

[5]See McKay and Wong (1996).

trapped students into silences. Moreover, these dilemmas had little to do with being Asian, as suggested by Mina. As explained in the Introduction, they were peculiar to the immigration process that had created Cantonese-speaking communities in schools like Northside.

Inhibitive and Attentive Silences

After reading through a variety of different literatures on student silences, we found that Asian-American scholar King-Kok Cheung offered us new ways of understanding the silences that troubled students like Mina and Marilyn. In her book, *Articulate Silences,* Cheung proposes at least five differing, and often overlapping, modes or tonalities of silences.[6] They are stoic, protective, attentive, inhibitive, and oppressive.

Attentive silence is a form of silence in which there is acute listening, empathy for others, and awareness of even the subtlest signs from a speaker. In essence, attentive silence is a quiet understanding. Such a mode of silence, argues Cheung, is empowering and thus the antithesis of passivity. *Oppressive modes of silence* include forms of racism that arise at the confluence of social policy and hatred. The infamous Chinese Exclusion Act of 1923, which barred Chinese immigration to Canada until its repeal in 1947, is one example of oppressive silence.[7] The Chinese Exclusion Act of 1882 in the United States is another example. Stoic modalities of silence include the quiet forms of suffering exhibited by Chinese immigrants, such as the *Issei,* in Joy Kogawa's novel titled, *Obasan.*[8] Cheung asserts that this stoic silence is characterized not by weakness but rather by endurance and tremendous fortitude.

Cheung argues, however, that all modes of silence can fluctuate between being enabling and debilitating. For this reason, she warns against romanticizing or eroticizing silences. For instance, she notes that the desire among some Asian, North-American parents to shield their children from harsh histories of racism exercise a mode of silence that she calls *protective.* Cheung believes that although this variety of silence can certainly enable children when they are young, it can infantilize them through an enforced innocence as they get older. A fifth silence, *inhibitive silence*, can also be debilitating and is of particular relevance to this commentary.

The general silence of some of the Cantonese-speaking students in Mrs. Yee's class may have been attributable to their fears that their English pronunciation and Cantonese accent would be laughed at. This self-imposed or

---

[6]See Cheung (1993).

[7]See Chan (1983) for further discussion of Chinese immigration to Canada.

[8]See Kogawa (1981).

inhibitive silence is articulated by the words of Cathy Lee, a Hong Kong-born student in Mrs. Yee's English class, who was interviewed in chapter 3. In the interview excerpt now presented, Cathy described why she believed many of the Cantonese-speaking students were silent:

> They're embarrassing of the English. They can't speak. They scared that people will laugh at them, because I try that—I'm in that stage before—right? So I know how they think and how they feel.
>
> [*Interview*, April 30, 1998][19]

Alternatively, as Victor explained both in his aforementioned interview and in the Introduction, Cantonese-speaking students might be silent in class because speaking English and answering questions could be perceived by their peers as showing off. This form of silence resonates with Cheung's term, *attentive silence*, which is also inhibitive. Also of interest is the suggestion made by Barbara Ishii, the current principal at Northside, that some Asian students feel that there is no need to reiterate an opinion that has already been aired by another student. Here, the silence of Asian students would also be an attentive silence. Through their silence students would be demonstrating to their teacher that they had been listening to their classmates' opinions and had nothing new to add. Such attentive silence, however, traps students into a linguistic dilemma or double bind. They are caught in a "lose–lose" situation. On one hand, they stand to lose grades and also risk the resentment of their non-Chinese and some Canadian-born Chinese classmates if they do not speak English, answer questions, and express their opinions in class. On the other hand, if they do use English with their Cantonese-speaking classmates in group work, answer the teacher's questions in front of other students, or reiterate an opinion that has already been offered, they stand to draw the negative reactions from their Hong Kong-born friends.

> The negative reactions on the part of Hong Kong-born Chinese toward their English-speaking Chinese peers may in part relate to friendship formations that are staked in racial identity politics. For example, when we asked Charles, who is a Hong Kong-born Chinese student at Northside, about how his Cantonese-speaking friends would react if he spoke to them in English, he replied: "They'd think I'm Whitewashed."
>
> [*Interview*, April 30, 1998]

---

[9]Related to our own discussion on inhibitive silence is Cristina Igoa's book, *The Inner World of the Immigrant Child*, where she outlines the psychological stages many immigrant children seem to go through as they integrate into North-American classrooms.

Charles' association of English with being "Whitewashed" is similar to the association of English with being "too Canadianized," discussed in the Introduction. In our research at Northside, we found that Hong Kong-born, Chinese-Canadian youth sometimes referred to Chinese peers who did not speak Cantonese as "*juk-sing*." This was a pejorative term used by these youth to describe the Canadian-born Chinese. It literally means the empty spaces in bamboo that obstruct the flow of water. The term alludes to the manner in which Canadian-born, Chinese youth are considered to be stuck in a void; neither fully Chinese nor fully Canadian. This term is conceptually analogous to the label *banana* which is also used by Chinese people to refer to someone who is considered to be "yellow on the outside but White on the inside."[10] It is possible that the attentive and inhibitive silences experienced by Victor were linked to identity politics and his desire to not be considered *juk sing*. Such a desire can also be linked to the ambivalence some Canadian students from Hong Kong feel about investing in English.

Desires for Whispered Cantonese

Another linguistic dilemma or double bind facing students like Victor Yu can be found in the Canadian-born Chinese and non-Chinese students' desires for Chinese speech to be whispered when it was spoken and thus relegated to the private realm of intimate conversation. In the following interview excerpt, Tony, a Chinese-Canadian student who was born in China and came to Canada at a young age, expressed his feelings toward students who speak loudly in Cantonese:

> Cantonese [speakers] tend to shout out—that annoys me. We [English speakers] don't shout ... Many Chinese shout and the Cantonese accent—it always has the long tail, a stretched-out sound—it annoys me.
>
> [*Interview*, April 30, 1998]

Tony's annoyance with the loudness of Cantonese resonates with writer Anne Jew's characterization of the way people talked in Chinatown. In the short story excerpt that opens Part I of this book, Jew writes, "Everyone talked loudly and waved their arms. I couldn't understand why they had to be so loud. It seemed so uncivilized."[11]

At the same time, as many Hong Kong-born, Chinese students opened themselves up to possible disparagement for being "loud" speakers in Can-

---

[10]See Yang, Gan, and Hong (1997) and Yee (1993) for further discussion of the terms *juk-sing* and *banana*.

[11]See Jew (1992).

tonese; when they spoke in English they were often considered to be inaudible. Like the narrator of Maxine Hong Kingston's book, *The Woman Warrior*, which also opens Part I of this book, they were regularly exhorted by students and teachers to speak "louder."[12] In other words, Cantonese speakers were caught in a bind where they were considered to be too loud in Cantonese and too quiet in English.

Tony's feelings about the loudness of Cantonese may reflect an internalization of racism and its disparagement of the peoples, cultures, and languages of "others." The literatures of Asian North America have long critiqued how North-American society and schools have served other Asian people.[13] The "othering" of Asian people has acted to produce in many Chinese youth, particularly among those born in North America, an ambivalence, even a loathing of "Chineseness," including the Chinese language.[14] This ambivalence suggests that the double binds facing Cantonese-speaking students at Northside can be linked to dominant Western perspectives on speech and silence. On one hand, students at Northside admonished Cantonese-speaking students for being too quiet and passive. On the other hand, students devalued them when they spoke loudly and assertively in Cantonese. In this way, dominant perspectives on speech and silence function to valorize not all speech, but specifically, English speech. Speech in any language other than English was devalued and not regarded as powerful, worthy, or reflective of agency on the part of the speaker. Its utterance in the public realm had to be whispered so it could not be heard and disturb or embarrass others. Tony's own linguistic development over the course of his life also reflects the devaluation of languages other than English. He informed us that over the years since immigrating to Canada, he had become "not that good in Mandarin anymore" (*Interview*, April 30, 1998).

Tony's irritation on hearing loud Cantonese heightens the disenabling aspects of the linguistic dilemmas or double-binds discussed at the beginning of the Commentary. Not only did Hong Kong-born, Chinese students who chose to speak English and answer questions stand to lose friendships among their peers from Hong Kong, if they chose to speak Cantonese, they were "annoying" and often much too loud, according to some local-born Chinese. These tensions placed them in a trying bind, caught between an immigrant Cantonese youth culture that valued not showing off English and a dominant Eurocentric culture that only valued the use of English.

---

[12]See Kingston (1989).

[13]See, for example, Hogue (1996); Kim (1982); Kingston (1989); and Wong (1993).

[14]See Hwang (1990); Jew (1992); and Ma (1998).

In this Commentary, we have suggested that the Cantonese-speaking students at Northside were continually engaged in a negotiation of linguistic double binds. These double-binds contributed to a reluctance to use English on the part of many students. The consequent silence of many Cantonese-speaking students caused some students to resent their classmates. In the pedagogical discussion that follows, we will explore what kinds of pedagogical interventions might better enable students to negotiate the linguistic dilemmas of inhibitive and attentive silences and alleviate the racial tensions that develop from the various double-binds, stereotypes, and academic pressures that frame the education of Hong Kong-born, Chinese Canadians.

PEDAGOGICAL DISCUSSION: SILENCES IN THE MULTILINGUAL CLASSROOM
CO-WRITTEN WITH GORDON PON

In thinking about what pedagogical maneuvers might alleviate the racial tensions just described, it is helpful for pedagogy to, first of all, acknowledge that various silences are at play in the multiracial, multiethnic, and multilingual classroom. Accordingly, each silence probably benefits from differing pedagogical engagements. In thinking about the ways teachers and students might work with different kinds of silences, we turn to the interviews we had with English teachers Anne Yee, Greg Dunn, and Leonard Robertson. To contextualize the pedagogical approaches suggested by Mrs. Yee, Mr. Dunn, and Mr. Robertson within their own life experiences as teachers and learners, we offer a brief biographical account of each teacher's career.

Anne Yee, Greg Dunn, and Leonard Robertson

As recalled from chapter 3, Anne Yee has been working as a teacher for 17 years. She first came to Canada from Hong Kong as a high-school visa student. She completed her high school, university, and teacher training education in Toronto and went back to Hong Kong to teach. After several years as a teacher and administrator in Hong Kong, Mrs. Yee returned to Toronto where she began teaching again. She is currently an English and ESOL teacher, and the head of the ESOL Department and Literacy Committee at Northside (see chap. 3 for a fuller biographical account of Mrs. Yee's life and work as a teacher).

Greg Dunn has worked as a teacher for 21 years. Jobs were very scarce when he graduated from the Faculty of Education of the University of To-

ronto in 1980, so he taught summer school, night school, and did a little sup-
ply work. Mr. Dunn got his first full time teaching job in January of 1981 at a
private school for Visa students called Eastern College. The school had
been set up for Asian students who wanted to attend Canadian universities.
Most of the students were from Hong Kong who had been sent to study in
Canada because of the uncertainty about the future of Hong Kong after
1997. All of the students at the school were learning in a second language. In
talking about his work at Eastern College, Mr. Dunn had this to say:

> I think my work with the students at Eastern College has had a great impact
> on me. These students were alone in Toronto coping with culture shock,
> homesickness, and language difficulties. You could not be anything but
> sympathetic to them and their situations. I learned from working with them
> how crucial it is to the learning process to create a positive and comfortable
> learning environment where everyone can feel safe and secure. As a class-
> room teacher, I work very hard to create a positive environment so all stu-
> dents feel comfortable enough to risk being wrong when they answer a
> questions, or can say, "I don't want to read aloud today."
>
> [*Answers to Questionnaire*, November 19, 2001]

Mr. Dunn was first hired at Northside in October, 1987. The following year,
he was declared surplus and assigned to another school where he taught
ESL classes. However, 1 year later, a new position opened up at Northside
and Mr. Dunn was able to return to the school. He has taught there ever since
and over the years has almost always worked with students who do not use
English as their first language. This work has taught Mr. Dunn that "one always needs to be understanding of our students' situations and keep what
we are doing in perspective":

> When we are dealing with students who may be living on their own—cook-
> ing, cleaning, carrying a full timetable, and studying in a second language so
> that the half hour of homework we gave may indeed take well over an hour.
> We have to be willing to accommodate and facilitate their learning and not
> penalize them with late mark deductions and lectures about working harder
> to achieve success. Maybe it comes down to respect. We need to respect our
> students as individuals, and accord them respect in the way that we like to
> receive respect from our co-workers and administration.
>
> [*Answers to Questionnaire*, November 19, 2001]

During the research we conducted at Northside, Leonard Robertson was
in his 32nd and 33rd years of teaching. Prior to beginning high school teaching, he had spent 1 year as a tutor at the University of Toronto, while pursuing his masters degree in English. Mr. Robertson began his teaching career

in Burlington, Ontario, a small town south of metropolitan Toronto. He describes the White Anglo-Canadian high school he worked at as racially and
culturally homogeneous. In those first 3 years of teaching (1967 to 1970),
he taught junior classes, and was most successful with classes of students he
would now identify as coming from a working class background. "As I look
back," he says, "I attribute that success to my patience, my humor, my story
telling abilities, and my refusal to view my students as unable to succeed."
Mr. Robertson taught at Northside from 1970 until 1998, with a break of 5
years. In 1971, he became the assistant head of English and in 1972 the head
of English. He remained the head of English, teaching all of the grades from
1972 until 1990. During that time, the demographics of the student body
changed from a population that was predominantly White and Jewish in the
1970s to one that was predominantly Asian (from Taiwan, Hong Kong, Ko-
rea, then eventually Vietnam, and mainland China) in the 1980s. In the
1990s the school became even more diverse when it enrolled students from
the Indian subcontinent and the Middle East.

From 1990 to 1995, Mr. Robertson was a consultant in staff development
with the school board and worked with elementary and high school teachers
on instructional strategies. He also worked on "outcomes" education and
strategic planning with school principals and on team building and conflict
resolution with business and support staff. In 1995, a year before the study
began, Mr. Robertson returned to Northside, and resumed his teaching responsibilities.

When he returned to the school, the high enrollment of students who spoke
English as a second or other language (ESOL) led Leonard to seek out new
ways to ensure that his students were successful in English classes. He says
that there were three very significant professional development activities that
shaped the last years of his teaching practice at Northside. During the 1980s,
Mr. Robertson was involved in school board committee work that focused on
antiracist education. At the same time, he completed a masters degree in Education. Leonard's masters research into language development, pedagogy,
reading, and writing reinforced his commitment to antiracist education, stu-
dent-centered learning, and the belief that all students must have clear models
of the work that they are expected to produce. Finally, Mr. Robertson's work
as a consultant with instructional strategies such as cooperative learning and
multiple intelligences helped him refine the skills he needed to work with student groups. "I no longer saw students who worked together as copying from
each other, but as aiding each other in learning." Working with this principle
of adult learning, Mr. Robertson says, enhanced his work with ESOL students
at Northside. Having provided a brief account of Anne Yee, Greg Dunn, and

Leonard Robertson's life experiences as teachers and learners, we turn now to what they had to say about working with silences in the classroom.

Working With Inhibitive and Attentive Silences

In an interview about the silences in her classroom, Anne Yee told us that she believes that:

> ... silence is a signal for lack of trust. It also means insecurity: I don't feel good about my English. I want to hide it, I don't want to hear it, I don't want to be picked on. It requires a lot of courage for me to say something in a language in which I know I have an accent, in which I know that I may not be able to use the right word. I may use it wrong and people may laugh at me. I am not going to show you something that I am not good at.
>
> [*Interview*, May 27, 1998]

Working with Mrs. Yee's understanding of inhibitive silences as being related to feelings about accents and language use, pedagogy that works toward helping students negotiate silences is pedagogy that asks teachers and students to deconstruct the myths and stereotypes they hold about accents and different varieties of English. Some excellent work in this area has been undertaken by American linguist Rosina Lippi-Green. In her book, *English With an Accent: Language, Ideology and Discrimination in the United States*, Lippi-Green discusses the way linguistic discrimination manifests itself in the classroom, the court, the media, and corporate culture.[15] Of particular interest to teachers in multilingual schools is Lippi-Green's examination of how the notions of "nonaccent" and "standard language" are really myths used to justify social order and how language ideology affects students. Of additional interest are Lippi-Green's discussions of how the media and the entertainment industry promote linguistic stereotyping and how employers discriminate on the basis of accent. The work that has been undertaken by Lippi-Green could be used to develop a classroom unit on language awareness that aims to engage students in critical analytic skills around issues of language, power, and racism.

Greg Dunn, whose work with mixed linguistic and racial groups was discussed in chapter 2, suggested direct teacher intervention as a way of responding to inhibitive silences that emerge in group work:

> I think the teacher has to be watching for the dynamics in the various groups and intervene when they see [silence] happening. And go and

---

[15]See Lippi-Green (1997).

sort of find out and see what's going on and sometimes maybe talk to the students individually about what's happening. Suggest ways for the group leaders to encourage the students who feel they maybe don't have something to contribute. Have them prepare something, maybe even show it to me ahead of time. Show me what you are going to give your group today so that they have something to contribute and they know that it's okay.

[*Interview*, May 13, 1998]

The strategy of encouraging students to bring something they have previously prepared for their next group meeting gives the rest of the group members something with which to work. Showing the work to teachers or sympathetic classmates before the group meets for approval or suggestions for improvement challenges the likelihood that students are not going to show group members something "that they are not good at."

Mrs. Yee told us that one of her strategies for a response of "dead silence" to a question she has asked the class is to ask students to talk about the question with a partner for a couple of minutes. When she asks the same question again, the students are able to answer the question with greater ease and she is able to elicit participation from students who were silent the first time. Another one of Mrs. Yee's strategies is calling on students who don't volunteer answers. When Tara suggested that calling on students in this manner may put them in "a bad position," both Mr. Dunn and Mrs. Yee told her that they have used the strategy with success.

Tara: ... I've learnt to call on people who don't speak out because you recognize sometimes they need that space created for them. But when there is no answer, it's just, you feel like you've put somebody in a bad position.

Greg: Yes. And what do you do? 'Cause if you just sort of come off and call on someone else, then they look bad. So how do you handle it? I used to say, "It's okay to say if you don't know right now. You can think about it and we'll come back and look at your response later." To give them that option rather than just saying, "You don't know, we'll go to someone else."

[*Interview*, May 13, 1998]

Tara: ... some teachers feel that they may embarrass the kids. If the kids don't volunteer, they are afraid to call on the kids' 'cause it will be embarrassing.

Anne: I think the first time they may feel embarrassed, and the second, third, fourth, and the fifth, they'll get used to it.

[*Interview*, May 27 1998]

Earlier in this chapter, Victor's understanding of the use of English among Cantonese-speaking peers as "showing off" was associated with Cheung's attentive as well as inhibitive silence. As theorized by Cheung, attentive silence is characterized by acute listening and empathy for others. In that such silence supports important social relationships between Cantonese speakers that can be linked to both academic and social success at school, the practice of choosing silence over English in the classroom can be seen as empowering and enabling as well as inhibitive. Imagining pedagogy that can assist students in negotiating attentive silence is difficult. As has been discussed in previous chapters, the practice of attentive silence is rooted in issues of identity, the pursuit of friendship and academic success, and resistance to the linguistic colonialism of English in both Hong Kong and the North American diaspora. Perhaps the most helpful way forward is working toward alleviating the racial tensions that emerge from the practice of attentive silence.

Alleviating Tensions in Small-Group Work

One place to begin is to attempt to address the concerns of students like Mina and Marilyn who feel burdened by having to assume the responsibility for doing most, if not all, of the talking in group work. In the interview excerpted, Marilyn suggested that group work would be more productive for her if the teacher could ensure that each member of a group had similar proficiency in English. This strategy, however, would result in placing ESOL students and students who use English as their primary language in separate groups. This kind of separation is problematic for teachers who purposefully establish linguistically mixed groups to provide opportunities for the ESOL students in their classes to practice English. Yet, to effectively manage the tensions that can emerge in such mixed groups, it may be helpful to be flexible in grouping arrangements and alternating the kinds of groups in which we ask students to work. Alternating grouping arrangements provides teachers with a space to encourage rather than restrict the use of languages other than English during particular activities. Although students working in their primary language lose an opportunity to practice English during these activities, they gain the opportunity to speak about academic material in ways that are enabling and might better prepare them for the kind of interaction, debate, even conflict, that Mina desires and that is valued in North-American classrooms. Thus, students can be given the opportunity to first work on a particular assignment in their primary language and then be asked to share their work in English with the teacher or others in a linguistically mixed group. After reading an earlier draft of this chapter, Leonard Robertson shared the following experience with me:

> Although I generally formed mixed language groups for the ISP in grade 11 and OAC (Ontario Academic Credit [courses]), I always chose who worked with whom, and there was one occasion when I allowed students from the same language background to work together. This interestingly enough involved four girls who spoke only English to work together on a project about Iceland, and four girls who spoke only Cantonese to work on a project about Greece. Having read your research, I am beginning to think I was intuitively reacting to a type of racist tension that emerged when the ISP was assigned. I'm not sure I taught these students anything about racist attitudes, but I did relieve what I perceived to be racist tension. By the way, both groups did equally well on the ISP project.
>
> [*Member Checking Response*, June 12, 2001]

A second way to work toward alleviating tensions in small group work is to give recognition to students who take on leadership roles and try to work effectively across linguistic differences. This is another strategy Leonard Robertson had used successfully. In Mr. Robertson's class, recognition meant extra marks as they were the most valued form of recognition at Northside. Other forms of recognition recommended by multicultural education consultant Elizabeth Coehlo are a letter of commendation from the teacher or a school administrator (in a language that the students' parents can understand) or acknowledgment in a school assembly.[16]

A third strategy for alleviating group work tensions involves the careful monitoring of the progress students are making on group work assignments. Mr. Robertson managed this monitoring work by asking students to document their individual responsibilities to the group in writing:

> Whenever there is group work going on in my class, particularly with the ISP, there is always a form to fill out … They [the students] fill out only one form, but everyone gets a copy of it. So everybody has something in writing which says that student A will be writing two articles on this, student B will be writing two articles on that, and student C will be writing something else on something else, and when the next meeting is. There is a written record that everybody has in writing. There is a common understanding that they can look at.
>
> [*Interview*, May 20, 1998]

By asking his students to document their responsibilities and progress on major group work assignments, Mr. Robertson knew when a particular stu-

---

[16]See Coehlo (1998).

dent was not contributing to the group work. He could take action to alleviate the anxiety of the other group members who were worried that they
would all be penalized for that student's lack of participation.

> … Now, there was one student who never produced any work … She had al-
> ways been absent during any type of group work … I thought this was
> avoidance, and I confronted her on the avoidance, and on the necessity of be-
> ing in class, and then gave her some deadlines for producing work … [I told
> her,] "If you do not have this work by Friday, you are no longer a member of
> the group, and your credit is in jeopardy."
>
> [*Interview*, May 20, 1998]

Concluding this discussion on alleviating tensions on small group
work, we'd like to touch on Mina's comment about being asked to work in
groups in her English class, but having to solve math problems on her own
without the support of students who might assist her when she runs into
difficulty. If Mina had felt that she had access to assistance from classmates in her math class, perhaps she would have felt less resentment in
providing assistance to classmates in her English class. Engaging with
such a possibility means thinking about school-wide pedagogical interventions that encourage students to assist each other in a variety of classes.
It means asking teachers and administrators to work across subject areas
and departments to collectively plan ways of encouraging students to use
their different academic strengths to assist others. Such planning can be
complex and difficult, but may be a positive way to alleviate the resentment described earlier in the chapter.

Lowering the Stakes of Small-Group Work

Yet, given the tensions that can surface in cooperative small group activities that are connected to high-stake projects, like the ISP, which are worth
a lot of marks, it is possible to ask whether reserving group work for lower
stake activities might be helpful. This can be done in at least two ways.
First, group work can be reserved for activities that are not evaluated and
make up part of the students' final grade, but are designed to help students
prepare for individually graded assignments. Such a strategy would be
similar to Mrs. Lo's "classroom practice activities" described in chapter 2,
which helped students prepare for quizzes and tests. To illustrate what
such a strategy might look like in an English classroom, I turn to a group
work activity Mr. Robertson designed to help his grade 11 students prepare individual essays on William Shakespeare's, *Macbeth*. The students'
task was to develop arguments to support one of eight different statements

about the play. An example of such a statement was "Lady Macbeth has sometimes been called the 'fourth witch.' Construct a thesis that argues that she should be regarded as the fourth witch, and support it in an organized essay." A contrasting statement asked students to argue that Lady Macbeth should not be regarded as the fourth witch. Students were placed in eight different linguistically mixed groups and each group was asked to create a flipchart (poster), which provided a thesis statement and supporting evidence for one of the eight statements. After each group had finished their flipchart, they were hung up on the walls of the classroom. Each student then worked individually on a plan for the essay they had chosen to write. Just before the students were scheduled to write their in-class essay, Mr. Robertson gave them a class period to talk to any one of their classmates about their plan and consult the flipcharts on the wall one more time to improve their plans. Tara observed this class period and noted that a number of students worked together in Cantonese as well as English. A lot of students used the period to talk to Mr. Robertson about their plan as well as other students, and many students consulted the flipcharts on the wall. Here group work was planned as a way to assist students to produce strong, individually assessed work. As Mr. Robertson explained, "I was trying to structure the learning for all students in order to ensure that students had good examples of a solid argument of which the teacher approved, and which they could use with full confidence that they would be rewarded" (*Member Checking Response*, June 12, 2001).

A second way of lowering the stakes of group work activity is to evaluate group processes rather than group products. Teachers can use specific performance criteria to provide students with feedback on how well they approach mixed group tasks; for example, seeking assistance from peers, providing assistance to peers, codeswitching to facilitate group communication, and participating in problem solving.

Alternatives to Small-Group Work

In addition to lowering the stakes of the group work, teachers can also alleviate linguistic and racial tensions by alternating small-group work with whole-group work. Examples of whole group work that provides students with opportunities to practice English include reciting self-enhancing poetry or prose in chorus, and asking students to answer questions in unison. Tara noted that when students in Mr. Robertson's class answered questions in unison, several Cantonese-speaking students who were usually silent responded to the question.

In conclusion, the pedagogical engagements presented in this chapter for responding to silences and linguistic and racial tensions in multilingual, multiracial schools ask teachers to work with students' feelings of embarrassment, frustration, anger, and dynamics of identity. They also bring teachers face to face with everyday racism and the legacy of colonialism. The following activities for further reflection and discussion have been created by Tara to help her and her students work with issues arising from inhibitive and attentive silences in multilingual classrooms. The activities can be adapted for use in high-school classrooms and are offered as examples of ways we might develop rich academic and moral content for multilingual classrooms.

FOR FURTHER REFLECTION AND DISCUSSION

Unearthing and Deconstructing Stereotypes Around Varieties of English.   Anne Yee believes that silence can be a sign of insecurity and that students who do not speak English as their primary language sometimes worry about others laughing about their accents. In chapter 5 of her book, *English With an Accent: Language, Ideology and Discrimination in the United States*, Rosina Lippi-Green unearths and deconstructs the way Disney animated films such as *Three Little Pigs*, *Aladdin*, and *The Lion King* teach children to discriminate against other people on the basis of the way they speak. Listening to one of these animated films with critical ears helps us understand what we have learned about people who speak different varieties of English or English with different accents. After renting or borrowing a copy of *The Lion King* from a video store or library, analyze the different varieties of English each animal character speaks. Which characters speak standard American English? Which characters speak with a British accent? Which speak a variety of Black Language/Ebonics? Link the different ways the characters speak to the different characteristics they portray in the film. For example, which varieties of English are associated with intelligence, strength, bravery, and self-reliance? Which are associated with weakness, foolishness, and dependence? Thinking about the different varieties of English the students in your own classes speak, what kinds of messages about the ways your students speak have you and your students absorbed? How are you and your students perpetuating and reinforcing these negative messages? How can you both begin to challenge them?

The Myth of the Non-Accent: Personal Reflection.   As far as linguists are concerned, it is not possible for adults to substitute one accent for another *consistently and in a permanent way.*[17] Yet, as Rosina Lippi-Green explains in chapter 2 of her book, *English With an Accent,* many people believe that if we only try hard enough, we can acquire a perfect language, one that is clean, pure, and free of variation. They also believe that language that is not perfect does not have to be accepted. Such beliefs are problematic as they can lead to people using accents to discriminate. For example, Lippi-Green tells us about the court case of James Kahakua, a Hawaiian meteorologist with 20 years of experience and considerable educational background, who applied for a promotion, which required that he read prepared weather reports on the radio. Mr. Kahakua was not given this promotion, because as a bilingual speaker of English-Hawaiian Creole English (HCE) (often referred to, mistakenly, as Hawaiian Pidgin), he had a Hawaiian accent. Mr. Kahakua sued his employer under Title VII of the American Civil Rights Act, on the basis of language traits linked to national origin. He lost his case because the judge, who was not a native of Hawaii, believed that it was reasonable to require that radio announcers speak "Standard English." The speech pathologist who testified on behalf of the employer gave the judge ammunition when she testified that "Pidgin can be controlled" and suggested that Mr. Kahakua seek professional help to lessen his "handicap."[18] Thinking back on your own personal experiences and those of family members and friends, in what ways did particular ways of speaking impact on opportunities that were available to you? Have you or others you know ever been discriminated against on the basis of accent and dialect?

Developing Communicative Competence and Confidence: Professional Reflection.   Rosina Lippi-Green reminds us that accents have little to do with what is generally called "communicative competence" or the ability to effectively use and interpret language in a wide variety of contexts. She provides us with a list of ESL speakers who never lost their accents, but have demonstrated that they can use English in effective ways. This group includes such public and political figures as Corazon Aquino, Benazir Bhutto, Cesar Chavez, Joseph Conrad, Boutros Boutros-Ghali, and Henry Kissinger. As teachers working in multilingual classrooms, many of our students will speak English with a variety of accents. How can we assist our

---

[17]See chapter 2 in Lippi-Green (1997) for further discussion of the myth of nonaccent.
[18]See Lippi-Green (1997, pp. 44–45) for a fuller discussion of this case.

students to develop the communicative competence and confidence they need to thrive in a world that sometimes discriminates against the ways people speak?

Performing and Engaging With Silence.   During an Australian reading of the play *Hong Kong, Canada* (included in Appendix A), the student who played the character of Carol left the classroom in the middle of the reading because she knew that she did not have to speak for the rest of the play. She returned before the reading ended, and in the discussion that followed, revealed that she had felt excluded from the story of the play because she only spoke in one of the 16 scenes. She also said this feeling of exclusion was followed by a feeling of alienation from the others in the group who were actively engaged in performing the story of *Hong Kong, Canada.* Educated in an Australian school, the student playing Carol associated *speech* with agency and being part of the story and *silence* with absence from the story. However, as Asian-American scholar King-Kok Cheung writes, some modes of silence, such as attentive silence, can be empowering. *Attentive silence*, which demonstrates a quiet understanding is the antithesis of passivity and absence. At the same time, Cheung argues that all modes of silence can fluctuate between being enabling or debilitating. Looking back at the scenes in which Carol appears, but does not speak, discuss the mode or tonality of silence (stoic, protective, attentive, inhibitive and/or oppressive) with which Carol is performing or engaging. Is her performance or engagement with silence in the scene enabling or debilitating?

Speaking English and Acting White.   In the commentary, Charles associated English with being "Whitewashed." In the play *Hong Kong, Canada* Sam accuses Wendy of "acting White" when he finds out that she has made a personal decision to only use English at school. In linking speaking English to acting White, Sam points to the way the dominance of Whiteness and English intersect to produce a culture of dominance that some high school students and their parents feel is in their best interest to comply with. Wendy's compliance makes Sam very angry. Why? How might we understand Sam's anger?

II

Dilemmas
of Discrimination

CHINESE CANADIANS

Our environment is changing due to 1997.
New immigrants are coming from Hong Kong.
New immigrants have come here to start a new life, new history and a new journey.
Toronto is becoming a new Hong Kong.

We no longer want to be silent.
We want to scream and shout.
We have black hair and yellow skin.
We were born in Canada.
We are Chinese Canadians.

We are disguised as Hong Kong people. But we are not accepted by them.
We try to blend into White people. But we are not accepted by them either.
We don't want to be discriminated against.
We are Chinese Canadians.

We are not all mathematicians or scientists. Many of us don't even like English.
We may not be able to speak, listen or write in Chinese.
We cannot communicate.
We are Chinese Canadians.

We feel little or no attachment to Hong Kong.
Our parents instill old traditional values of the East on us, but we live in the West.
We are Chinese Canadians.
There are internal struggles within us.
We don't know where we belong.
We are Chinese Canadians.

We want to be treated as individuals.
We are not "pure Chinese" stereotypes.
We are not "pure English" stereotypes either.
We have feelings, we have thoughts, we are unique.
We are Chinese Canadians.

—By Evelyn Yeung, a Chinese-Canadian Student at Northside

5

Resisting Anti-Immigrant
Discourses and Linguicism

Until I can take pride in my language, I cannot take pride in myself. Until I
can accept as legitimate Chicano Texas Spanish, Tex–Mex, and all the other
languages I speak, I cannot accept the legitimacy of myself. Until I am free to
write bilingually and to switch codes without having to translate, while I
still have to speak English or Spanish when I would rather speak Spanglish,
and as long as I have to accommodate the English speakers rather than having them accommodate me, my tongue will be illegitimate.
        [From Gloria Anzaldúa's *Borderlines/La Frontera: The New Mestiza*][1]

In this well-known quote, Latina writer and poet Gloria Anzaldúa talks about
her desire to communicate in multiple voices, to feel pride in the many languages she speaks, and to have her multilingual tongue legitimized. The journey toward pride can be a difficult one in multilingual communities where the
use of particular languages or language varieties is devalued, trivialized, or
vilified. This chapter recounts a journey undertaken by a young Chinese–Canadian born artist named Evelyn Yeung, who needed to reconstitute who she
was in a city and a school that had recently seen the arrival of a large number
of immigrants from Hong Kong. The data in this chapter was collected in
Evelyn's enriched art class, which was beginning a painting assignment when
we began our observations. Evelyn's art teacher, Leslie Edgars, had asked her
students to write reflection pieces in their art journals during the painting pro-

---

[1]See Anzaldúa' (1987, p. 59).

ject. The chapter begins with excerpts from Evelyn's first two art journal entries, which were tape recorded when she read them aloud to me. At the end of that school year, I asked Evelyn to join the research team and paid her to write a final reflection piece about creating her art piece, *Journey to Acceptance*. Excerpts from this final reflection piece also open this chapter. In the Commentary, I analyze Evelyn's artwork as a pedagogical project that not only encouraged linguistic pride, but that also challenged anti-immigrant ideas that structured students' relationships at school. Drawing, in part, on the work undertaken by Leslie Edgars, the Pedagogical Discussion looks at how teachers might prepare themselves for work in multilingual, multiracial schools where issues of language, identity, and discrimination need to be negotiated on a daily basis. The ethnographic excerpts, the Commentary, and Pedagogical Discussion that appear in this chapter have been member checked by Evelyn Yeung and Leslie Edgars.

JOURNEY TO ACCEPTANCE

Beginnings

> ... Yesterday I was reading in the *Toronto Star* and there was an article on how people, not, not only Chinese, are learning Mandarin because of China and Hong Kong. The doors in Mainland China are slowly opening. I am disgraced that other people of other backgrounds learn Mandarin and Cantonese when I, of Chinese background, cannot read or write my own dialect of Chinese ... It's frustrating going into Chinese malls when, where everywhere it's Chinese, and I'm practically illiterate.

> Last month when I was shopping at the Bay with my friend, out of the P.A. system came someone speaking Chinese. My friend and I felt embarrassed. What made me feel more embarrassed was that there was a customer that was complaining to a cashier about it and looking directly at me. Sometimes I wish there was a distinct way of separating us Canadian-born ones with the ones from Hong Kong ... Earlier this year I read in the newspaper about how the people in Richmond Hill (a suburb located north of Toronto) were complaining about the signs on the stores. They said that the English is too small and the Chinese is too big on the stores, store signs. There were more complaints but I do not remember them right now ... The Chinese immigrants of the past few years, I heard a lot of them say that they will return to Hong Kong after university, or if, or if Hong Kong is okay [politically and economically stable after the return of Hong Kong to China in July, 1997]. I get mad sometimes when they say that because they are competing for the same spots in university as, as us. And they are changing the whole Toronto, yet they are going back to Hong Kong ...

> [*Journal entry 1*, read aloud in an interview, November 20, 1996]

After reading Evelyn's first journal entry, Ms. Edgars suggested that Evelyn consider doing a painting that expressed how she felt about the Chinese language. The two talked about Evelyn undertaking an abstract painting and then discussed the idea of Evelyn creating her own alphabet or her own language. A third option was Ms. Edgars' suggestion that Evelyn learn how to write in Chinese from one of her classmates from Hong Kong. She thought that the experience of learning to write in Chinese might provide Evelyn with something that she could use for her painting. Taking up Ms. Edgars' third suggestion, Evelyn began learning how to write Chinese characters from several of her classmates who were born and educated in Hong Kong. The characters that Evelyn asked her classmates to teach her were those that had some meaning or relevance for her. Many came from the journal entries she was keeping. The first word that Evelyn asked her classmate Peter to teach her was "Hong Kong."

> The black ink brought back all memory, all the memories of Chinese school on Saturday, where the Chinese, where the teacher walked around criticizing the way you held the brush … For the first couple of characters, I followed Peter's brush stroke. But I sort of knew that he was sort of uneasy 'cause I didn't follow it completely, properly. As well, there was my audience of grade 11 and grade 12s [Evelyn was a grade 13 student] who kept saying that it wasn't right … I really didn't want to disappoint them by writing it wrong … I felt sort of uncomfortable that everyone was looking at my characters … [S]ome people in the class were sort of poking fun at my characters … Sometimes when I am talking to people from Hong Kong, they poke fun at my Chinese if I don't pronounce it clearly. Same thing when I'm speaking English. People poke fun at my pronunciation. I wish I never belonged to either [group], I wish I either belonged to either [one group] or [the other]. I never knew that learning how to write Chinese could in, involve interaction with so many people. Two other grade 11s [who were not critical] came over to see what I was doing. What a surprise! I felt that everyone wanted to be part of my process. And at that, that moment, [came] my peace. It felt great to write Chinese again. Writing Chinese helped me interact more with the grade 11s and 12s, something I wasn't expecting. Even though my Chinese, my Chinese characters are not going to earn me an award, they did help me communicate and learn from other people in the class …
>
> [*Journal entry 2*, read aloud in an interview, November 20, 1996]

Final Reflections

> My final art piece has evolved from my surroundings, my experiences and myself … I am a Chinese Canadian born and being raised in Western society with Eastern values and beliefs. Going to a school like Northside with a pre-

dominantly Oriental population has given me predominantly Oriental friends ... Not until recently, when flocks of Chinese people have immigrated to Toronto from Hong Kong, have I started to feel lost and uncomfortable with my surroundings ... I felt terrible when people (of Western background) thought I was from Hong Kong because I wasn't. I couldn't read or write Chinese. I couldn't read Chinese signs or menus. I didn't understand all the jokes at the movies or even on TV. I felt terrible when Hong Kong people called me a Banana.[2] They poked fun of my pronunciation. I started to feel awkward around Hong Kong people, because I thought I couldn't talk to them. I questioned my spoken Chinese ... It was almost vice versa for Western society. I did know how to speak the language and I did know how to write the language, but I didn't know who each and every [Canadian] entertainer was. I am also a very shy and cautious person, which doesn't make conversation easy ...

... It took me a long time to have my first [writing] lesson. I was scared. I was scared of Peter. I was scared of the brush. I was scared of what the other students would think. I was scared of everything. It wasn't until a couple of characters later that I was more relaxed. I really started to have fun. I talked to many of the grade 12s and they were eager to help me. It wasn't like I thought. People were willing to help you ...

... My feelings have not changed about where I am at right now. I am still in the middle. I am learning to enjoy the advantages and learning to accept the disadvantages. I still can't read or write Chinese, but I will be taking a course in Chinese at [the University of] Waterloo (Mandarin not Cantonese). (I am sort of disappointed, but with Hong Kong switching hands, I understand). I have lost the bitterness I felt toward Hong Kong people, because I had the opportunity to know some of them better. I know that they are losing a home back to China. They don't know what is going to happen in China. Some of them don't even know what they are now. They don't have China citizenship, but they don't have a Canadian passport yet. They don't have a place of birth. They are in the middle, too, like me. I sympathize with them, but when Hong Kong was given back to China on July 1, I felt nothing. I was just an observer of a historical moment in history, but many of my friends were scared of what might happen to their family and friends. I am beginning to see their side of the story. I have become closer to many classmates from this experience. I have learned that there are Chinese people from Hong Kong who want to be your friend and that not all people are mean and cruel.

[*Final Reflection*, "Tackling the Fine Art of Chinese Brush Writing,"
July 31, 1997]

---

[2]The term *Banana* is a derogatory term meaning "Yellow on the outside and White on the inside." The term is used by Asian Americans to refer to other Asian Americans whom they perceive as denying their Asian heritage or identity (from Yang, Gan, and Hon, 1997).

COMMENTARY: NEGOTIATING IDENTITIES
IN "HONG KONG, CANADA"

It's not just another wave of immigrants. Over 20 years, 142,000 from Hong Kong have moved here. With ambition, money and a strong identity, they're changing the city's face.
[Headline of a report on Hong Kong immigration to Toronto by Vanessa Lu, staff reporter, *The Toronto Star*, November 10, 1996, B1]

The following commentary discusses Evelyn Yeung's artwork, *Journey to Acceptance*, as a symbol of Evelyn and Leslie Edgars' efforts to negotiate new identities in a school and a city that had recently seen increased immigration from Hong Kong. The importance of teachers undertaking such work and providing opportunities for students to engage in such work has been discussed by educational theorist Jim Cummins, who believes that the negotiation of identities at school is central to student learning.[3] Cummins writes that identities are formed and negotiated through everyday interactions between teachers, students, and the communities to which the students belong. Importantly, these interactions are never neutral. In varying degrees, they either reinforce "coercive relations of power," the exercise of power *over* people, or promote "collaborative relations of power," the creation of power *with* people. By reinforcing coercive relations of power, teachers (and, I would add, students) contribute to the subordination of (other) students and communities targeted by discrimination. By promoting collaborative relations of power, teachers (and, I would add, students) are able to participate in "a process of empowerment" that encourages (other) students and communities to challenge the operation of coercive power structures and processes.[4] Analyzing Evelyn's artwork as a project that challenges coercive relations of racial and linguistic discrimination at school, I try to illustrate how Leslie Edgars was able to provide an opportunity for her students to resist what writer Charles Taylor has called society's "confining or demeaning or contemptible picture of themselves."[5]

In my examination of the journey Ms. Edgars and Evelyn undertook together, I draw upon Rosina Lippi-Green's ideas on the language subordination process. It is this process that underlies linguistic discrimination or *linguicism*, discrimination based on language use. But first, to introduce readers to the discourses that Evelyn and Ms. Edgars needed

---

[3]See Cummins (1996).
[4]See Cummins (1996, p. 19).
[5]From Taylor (1994, p. 25).

to negotiate, I begin with an analysis of what it means to teach and learn in a city and school that has recently seen increased immigration from Hong Kong.

Teaching and Learning in "Hong Kong, Canada"

As can be seen in the quotation that opens this commentary, there is some anxiety about the number of Hong Kong immigrants who have come to live in Toronto. The headline printed over Vanessa Lu's report in *The Toronto Star* characterized Hong Kong immigrants as people who were "changing the city's face" from one that had historically been mostly European and White to one that was increasingly Chinese.[6] The title of the report, "Hong Kong, Canada," was typed in enormous bold-faced letters that dominated the page on which the story appeared. The headline shaped what Canadians were to make of this latest "wave" of immigration. Canada was being invaded by large number of immigrants from Hong Kong. We were no longer living in Canada; we were living in "Hong Kong, Canada."

The discourse of invasion that emerged from the "Hong Kong, Canada" feature can be related to a perceived threat of shifting economic power bases in Canada. In her contribution to the feature, demographics reporter Elaine Carey began her article with the following lead:

> They're younger, more educated and they hold better jobs than the average person in the greater Toronto area. They're the 142,300 Hong Kong immigrants who have flocked to the GTA, largely in the past 20 years. They now make up 15 per cent of all new immigrants to Canada each year—an average of about 40,000—making them the largest group from any one country, as well as the wealthiest.[7]

There was much reporting about the wealth that some Hong Kong immigrants bring into Canada throughout the "Hong Kong, Canada" feature. For example, there was a picture of the owner of Toronto's Metropolitan Hotel,

---

[6]See *The Toronto Star*, November 10, 1996, p. B1. The perception that Toronto's "face" has been mostly European and White ignores the historical and contemporary presence of Canada's Aboriginal/First Nations people who have always been part of the city's face. It also ignores the historical presence of non-European and non-White immigrants who have not only been part of the city's face since the beginning of what Aboriginal scholars call "the contact period," but who have contributed to the building of the city and the country.

[7]See "Skilled, Young, Wealthy and Loyal to Canada," *The Toronto Star*, November 10, 1996, p. B4.

sandwiched between two headlines: "To Canada, With Cash" and "Hong Kong Money Likes GTA." There was also a description of how Hong Kong immigrants had "changed the look of much of the city" by financing the building of 50 "Chinese malls" in the Greater Toronto Area.[8] However, what was missing from the "Hong Kong, Canada" feature was any detailed reporting on the immigration polices that brought Hong Kong capital into Canada (see chap. 2) or the fact that, overall, Hong Kong immigrants are poorer than Canadian-born people and other immigrants. At the very end of her article, Carey reported that 25% of all immigrants from Hong Kong live below the low-income cut-offs compared with 15% of those who were born in Canada and 19% of all immigrants. Highlighted in a different way, with pictures of Hong Kong immigrant families struggling to make ends meet in a new country, such statistics could have done much to challenge the idea that all Hong Kong immigrants were wealthy. Buried at the very end of the article, however, the statistics on the poverty of 25% of Hong Kong immigrants did not make much of an impact on the reader. *The Star's* discourse of invasion went unchallenged, and made its way into a Northside art classroom through Evelyn's art journal entries.

Opening Small Doors

> My role for these kids is to open doors ... And whether they go through them is always their choice. But that's the teaching technique ... They're small doors that we open—to allow them to open the bigger doors ... As teachers [that's] what we have to do, whether we're educators, parents, we open small doors.
>
> [Leslie Edgars, *Interview*, February 1997]

Leslie Edgars has worked as an educator for 28 years. She began her career in inner city Philadelphia in the United States at a bilingual (English/Spanish) school. Ms. Edgars' teacher training from Temple University included only 3 months of practice teaching, but she says she was fortunate to have as a practice teaching supervisor a woman who had worked in the infancy schools in England. Leslie's supervisor and her husband had worked in several schools, both in England and North America, which promoted open classrooms, team teaching, and learning activity centers. She and Leslie visited "free schools" in New York City, which were also based on these pedagogies and encouraged students to work on individual tasks tailored to their individual needs.

---

[8]See *The Toronto Star*, November 10, 1996, pp.B1 and B4. "Chinese malls" are shopping malls in which the names of stores are written in Chinese. Sometimes store signs are bilingual, written in both Chinese and English.

Upon moving to Toronto, Ms. Edgars says that she was fortunate to find work in a school like Northside, which allowed her to continue working collaboratively with students as a facilitator and mentor.

As can be seen in the aforementioned quote, Leslie Edgars is a teacher who wants to open small doors for her students so that they can open the bigger doors for themselves. Doors can be understood as metaphors for insights into life and identity issues. When Ms. Edgars' students start opening doors, they are able to shed light on the social, political, and identity issues that impact on their everyday lives. As explained by educational theorists, Carmen Luke and Allan Luke, diasporic identity is not stable, or fixed, or predictable. It is always in a state of change and flux. At the heart of this state of change is the way people find themselves needing to work with "place-bound discourses," such as the anti-immigrant discourse of "Hong Kong, Canada," that mark their difference in particular ways.[9] After reading Evelyn's journal entries, Ms. Edgars recognized that Evelyn needed to work through the uneasiness and discomfort she felt about being marked as an immigrant from Hong Kong even though she had been born in Canada and could not read or write in Cantonese, her own dialect of Chinese. As mentioned earlier, Leslie suggested that Evelyn learn to write in Chinese so she could work on a painting that expressed her strong feelings about using the language. Such a suggestion was typical of Ms. Edgars' belief that it is helpful to learners be able to communicate ideas and feelings in both images and words.

As Evelyn began working with her classmate, Peter, she began to remember childhood experiences of learning to write in Chinese. These memories and critical comments from some of her classmates made her feel uneasy and uncomfortable. The feelings were so strong that she wished that she had only learned English or Cantonese as a child. Growing up monolingual would have meant that she would have been able to speak in a way that would have prevented people from "poking fun" at her pronunciation (in either English or Cantonese). It would also have meant that she would have been able to write Chinese "properly." In thinking about how and why people learn to value some varieties of language (like mainstream/standard English or Chinese) and not others (like Cantonese English or English Cantonese), Rosina Lippi-Green's model of the language subordination process is very helpful.[10] The model Lippi-Green presents grew out of her analysis of public commen-

---

[9]See C. Luke and A. Luke (1999).
[10]See Lippi-Green (1997).

tary on English language use and language communities. She found that people learn to value a particular variety of language over another through the following processes and practices:

*language is mystified;
You can never hope to comprehend the difficulties and complexities of your mother tongue without expert guidance.

*authority is claimed;
Talk like me/us. We know what we are doing because we have studied language, because we write well.

*misinformation is generated;
That usage you are so attached to is inaccurate. The variant I prefer is superior on historical, aesthetic, or logical grounds.

*non-mainstream language is trivialized;
Look how cute, how homey, how funny.

*conformers are held up as positive examples;
See what you can accomplish if you only try, how far you can get if you see the light.

*explicit promises are made;
Employers will take you seriously; doors will open.

*threats are made;
No one important will take you seriously; doors will close.

*nonconformers are vilified or marginalized;
See how willfully stupid, arrogant, unknowing, uninformed, and/or deviant and unrepresentative these speakers are.[11]

Of the eight practices Lippi-Green has identified, two seem particularly relevant to thinking about Evelyn's feelings of uneasiness around learning to write Chinese characters: claiming/giving mainstream language authority and trivializing non-mainstream language. At the very beginning, when she attempted to follow Peter's brush stroke, Evelyn felt that he was uneasy because she wasn't following his strokes "properly." As well, a number of stu-

---

[11]See Lippi-Green (1997, pp. 67–69).

dents watching her initial attempts to follow Peter's brush strokes told Evelyn that she wasn't "doing it right." Here Evelyn and her audience gave Peter's brush strokes authority. Evelyn absorbed Peter's (perceived) uneasiness because she was not writing like him—a person who learned to write characters in Hong Kong, a person who wrote well. When some of her classmates poked fun at her first attempts to draw Chinese characters, Evelyn was reminded of the times other people from Hong Kong had poked fun at the variety of Chinese she spoke and of the times that English-speakers had poked fun at the variety of English she spoke. Here Evelyn's use of non-mainstream language—both Chinese and English—was being trivialized.

Although Evelyn experienced feelings of discomfort as she began to learn how to write Chinese characters, she also experienced some excitement, as her classmates become interested in her art project. Their interest helped her connect to positive feelings associated with writing Chinese. As she says in a final reflection piece that I asked her to write at the end of school year,

> I was delighted and relieved that they were excited to help and teach. Although some of them criticized my character strokes, it didn't matter. I was the center of attention. And I really, really enjoyed it.
> [Final Reflection, Tackling the Fine Art of Chinese Brush Writing, July 31, 1997]

Evelyn's delight with the recognition she received from her classmates mitigated the discomfort she felt when people criticized her brush strokes. Even though her first attempts at drawing characters were trivialized, Evelyn herself was not "vilified" or "marginalized" as a nonconformer. This was something she had been anticipating.

> The first word was shaky. In fact, the first column was shaky. I braced myself for all the nasty comments that would burst out of the mouth of the students. But there wasn't any. I was surprised. The second column was less intimidating. As the columns progressed, I became more confident ... The strokes were more powerful and expressive.
> [Final Reflection, Tackling the Fine Art of Chinese Brush Writing, July 31, 1997]

Evelyn's use of the words "less intimidating," and "more powerful" in this reflection asks us to think about her work in terms of power. Jim Cummins tells us that the process by which students and teachers negotiate identities in classroom and school interactions can play a major role in determining how students feel about themselves and how they feel about others. In her interactions with Evelyn around her journal entries, Leslie Edgars opened a small door and provided Evelyn with a space to do some identity work by learning to write Chinese characters from a classmate from Hong Kong. As Cindy Lam and I have argued, in a school and a city that was struggling with the use of Cantonese in public spaces, this work can be seen as a pedagogical project that challenges both coercive relations of power underlying standard English ideology and traditional roles of authority in the classroom.[12] Outside Ms. Edgars' art classroom, there was debate in the student newspaper around the publication of bilingual Chinese–English advertisements, the use of Cantonese at the students' annual talent night, and the use of Cantonese at a karaoke event scheduled during Spirit Week. Inside Ms. Edgar's art classroom, Evelyn Yeung learned to write in Chinese characters, using both Cantonese and English, so she could express her feelings about being a Canadian-born, Chinese woman living in "Hong Kong, Canada." Importantly, the students' use of Cantonese to complete the project required Ms. Edgars to negotiate a new identity for herself as a teacher in her classroom. Not able to understand the Cantonese the students are using while they assisted Evelyn in learning to write Chinese characters, Ms. Edgars had to ask the students to translate what they were saying into English so that she could enter their dialogue. Having to ask students to translate their words shifted traditional relations of authority in Ms. Edgars' classroom: She had to request and be given permission to enter her students' conversations.

> I've always dialogued with the kids but you can't do that around here if, if they are speaking Cantonese ... So you have to engage more with the students ... [Y]ou almost have to bring up a chair and kind of just sit there and say, "Okay I'm here now and you, I, I don't understand what you're talking about. So either you have to teach me your language or let's talk, let's find a place where we can talk because this is my job and I need to know what you're doing. So can I come in?"
>
> [*Interview*, February 13,1997]

Returning the ethnographic gaze back on Evelyn, there are a number of questions we can raise: What was Evelyn able to do with the collaborative space she was provided with in Ms. Edgars' classroom? What kind of impact did her artwork have on how she felt about others and how she felt about herself? In answering these questions, I return to the excerpts from Evelyn's last written reflection.

Journey to Acceptance: Challenging Assumptions and Rejecting Linguicism

Learning to write Chinese characters in her art class provided Evelyn with an opportunity to interact with people who she had resented. The interpersonal

---

[12]See Goldstein and Lam (1998).

space that she and her Cantonese-speaking classmates created through their work together challenged some of the assumptions that she had been holding. Evelyn found out that "It wasn't like I thought. People were willing to help you." And she valued her classmates' interest in her project: "Even though my Chinese, my Chinese characters are not going to earn me an award, they did help me communicate and learn from other people in the class."

While Evelyn's identity work had just begun ("My feelings have not changed about where I am at right now. I am still in the middle"), she did feel that she had moved forward in her journey to self-acceptance. She was "learning to enjoy the advantages" and "accept the disadvantages" of her current subject position, a position that was powerfully described in her poem "Chinese Canadians," that opens Part II of this book. Evelyn also was planning to take a course in Chinese at university, which will make new discourse repertoires available to her. From these new repertoires, Evelyn will continue to make sense of her relationships to others and continue to construct her identity and identifications with others.

Working on her art piece, *Journey to Acceptance*, also provided Evelyn with an opportunity to reject some of the linguicism she had internalized. This work is essential for developing the multilingual pride Gloria Anzaldúa writes about and an important part of learning how to enjoy the advantages and accept the disadvantages of being "in the middle."

Although Evelyn uses the metaphor "in the middle" to describe her Canadian-born, Chinese subject positioning, Carmen Luke and Allan Luke have argued that "between two cultures" theorizations do not adequately account for the "hybridity" and "multiply situated character" of diasporic identities.[13] Instead, they suggest that the metaphor of "third space" used by cultural theorist Homi Bhabha allows teachers and researchers to better understand the situations in which students like Evelyn find themselves.[14] Quoting Homi Bhabha, Luke and Luke describe the notions of hybridity and third space in the following way:

> ... hybridity is not to be able to trace two original moments from which the third emerges, rather hybridity is the "third space" which enables other positions to emerge ... the importance of hybridity is that it bears the traces of those feelings and practices which inform it, just like a translation, so that hybridity puts together the traces of certain other meanings or discourses. It does not give them the authority of being prior in the sense of being original: they are prior only in the sense of being anterior. The process of cultural

---

[13]See C. Luke and A. Luke (1999).

[14]For a discussion of the concept of *third space*, see Chow (1990, 1993) and Bhabba (1994).

[15]See C. Luke and A. Luke (1999, p. 234).

hybridity gives rise to something different, something new and unrecognizable, a new area of negotiation of meaning and representation.[15]

Homi Bhabha's metaphor of "third space" is very helpful in thinking about Evelyn's situation. Evelyn does not speak English like an Anglo-Canadian, nor does she speak or write Chinese like her Hong Kong-born, Chinese classmates. Instead, her linguistic and cultural identities are developing within a "third space," one that bears traces of both Anglo-Canadian and Chinese legacies. Importantly, as Luke and Luke explain, Evelyn's hybrid identity and identifications change through contact with different people and places. The contact Evelyn had with classmates from Hong Kong in her art classroom was particularly important as it challenged some of the negative assumptions she had held about classmates from Hong Kong and allowed her to reject the linguicism she had internalized regarding the Chinese language.

Researchers working in other multilingual communities in North America have also noted the need for young people to engage with their negative feelings about language use. For example, in a study of language and ethnic identity among Puerto Ricans in the United States, researcher Maria Zavala showed how destructive ideas about Spanish speakers in schools could lead to students feeling ashamed about being bilingual.[16] To illustrate, this is what Margarita, one of the young women participating in Zavala's study, told her about bilingual life in her own school:

> In school, there were stereotypes about the bilingual students, big time. [Since] they don't speak "the" language, they don't belong here. That's number one. Number two, they were dumb, no matter what ... Everyone said "that bilingual person," but they didn't realize that bilingual means they speak *two* languages. To them bilingual was not a good thing. There was a horrible stigma attached to them and I think I fell in the trap sometimes of saying "those bilingual people" just because that was what I was hearing all around me.[17]

The bilingual students in Margarita's school were vilified as dumb. In the face of this blatant linguicism, a common coping strategy was to avoid the use of Spanish in public. Christina, another student interviewed by Zavala, told her,

> I remember pretending I didn't know how to speak Spanish. You know, if you pretended that you were that American, then maybe you would get accepted by the White kids. I remember trying not to speak Spanish or speaking it with an [English] accent.[18]

[16]See Zavala (2000). Zavala's work was part of study undertaken by C. Suárez-Orozco and M. Suárez-Orozco (1995).

[17]See Zavala (2000).

[18]See Zavala (2000).

Interestingly, when Christina, the high-school student in Maria Zavala's study who had avoided speaking Spanish, enrolled in college, she began to "reclaim" the language.

> I've been reading a lot of literature written by Latinos lately, some Puerto Rican history. Before [college] I didn't even know it existed. Now I'm reading and writing more and more in Spanish and I'm using it more in conversations with other Puerto Ricans ... My kids are going to speak Spanish and they're going to speak it loud. They're not going to go with the whispering stuff. As a matter of fact, if a White person comes by, we're going to speak it even louder. I am going to ingrain that in them, that you need to be proud of that.[19]

The rejection of linguicism and the reclaiming of Spanish in college—where she began to engage with new discourses represented in Latino literature and Puerto Rican history—resulted in Christina being able to envision a new set of language practices to pass on to her children. She had moved from feeling shame about speaking Spanish to pride.

Given the importance that rejecting linguicism has for students like Evelyn and Christina, educators need to think about how they and their students might challenge negative messages associated with languages other than English. In the pedagogical discussion that follows, I reflect on what we can learn from Christina's work in college and the antiracist work that Ms. Edgars and Evelyn undertook together.

PEDAGOGICAL DISCUSSION: ON REJECTING LINGUICISM

Thinking about what Evelyn was able to do in Leslie Edgars' classroom provides us with an idea of what teachers working in other multilingual, multiracial communities might do to prepare themselves for work in schools where issues of language, identity, and discrimination need to be worked through every day.

First, it is clear that teachers need to develop their own critical literacy skills and learn to recognize the discriminatory discourses with which their

---

[19]See Zavala (2000).

[20]The concept of *critical literacy* emerged from radical educational theory in the 1970s. Brazilian educator Paul Freire (1970) used the term to refer to the ability to use language as a means for articulating a transformative (e.g., antidiscriminatory) political analysis and agenda. For Freire, "reading the word" meant "reading the world," and developing a critical analysis of an economic, social, and political order. This could be achieved through a "dialogic," pedagogical approach that encourages learners to become teachers of marginalized experience. The dialogue between Leslie Edgars and Evelyn Yeung, which began as a result of Evelyn's writing in her art journal, is an application of this approach. Rather than using language as a means for beginning a transformative journey, however, Evelyn uses painting. For further discussion of critical literacy, see the review by Allan Luke (1997).

students might be struggling.[20] These struggles can provoke strong emotions—disgrace, embarrassment, and resentment—that might be worked on in a class project. Such projects are not difficult to imagine in art, language, and social science classes in which activities such as journal writing, painting, drawing, clay work, poetry, playwriting, multicultural literature, and ethnic studies, such as Puerto Rican history can easily become part of the core curriculum. They are more difficult to imagine in math and science classrooms. Yet, innovation is possible in all classrooms.

One of Leslie Edgars' colleagues, who was teaching biology in a school like Northside, asked his students to write a children's book on one of the topics that they had been studying together. He felt that if the students could explain the digestive system or the respiratory system to younger children, they would understand the concepts themselves. Students who paired up with someone who could translate the book into a second language to create a bilingual book received bonus marks. With this one project, the biology teacher accomplished several things. By assigning bonus marks to the use of languages other than English in the project, he increased their status and the status of those speakers who used the other languages as a first language. The project also provided an opportunity for students from a variety of backgrounds to work together across linguistic differences in pursuit of a common project and common goal. For students struggling with the kind of anti-immigrant discourses Evelyn was working through, such an opportunity might produce moments where discriminatory assumptions can be challenged and linguicism resisted.[21]

On Language, Authority, and a Schoolwide English-Only Policy

Engaging students in issues of language, identity, and discrimination, however, is difficult work that can rub against our individual understandings of authority and roles in the classroom. Key to Ms. Edgars' success in facilitating Evelyn's journey was her willingness to work with languages other than English in her classroom. This meant living with the discomfort of not being able to listen in on or understand everything her students said. Because understanding everything students say is central to retaining power and authority in the classroom, Ms. Edgar's work with Evelyn depended on her being able to share power and authority with her students. For Ms. Edgars, sharing linguis-

---

[21]For a good resource on how educators can raise the status of languages other than English in their classroom and provide their students with opportunities to work across linguistic differences, see Coehlo (1998).

tic power and authority did not rub against her understanding of her role as an art teacher. Working with languages other than English did not prevent her from "opening doors" for her students. In fact, it facilitated this work.

However, as discussed in chapter 3, not all teachers believed that working in languages other than English was in their students' best interests. Several mathematics teachers, one who was Japanese-Canadian and two who were White, Anglo-Canadians, explained that listening in on their students' conversations while they were solving assigned math problems was key to confirming that their students had understood the material that had been presented. Unlike Mrs. Lo, whose work is described in chapter 2, they did not speak any of the languages their students spoke. In order for them to understand their students' conversations, the conversations had to be in English. Because being able to confirm students' understanding of math concepts was central to their understanding of their role as math teachers, these teachers, like Mrs. Yee and others, experimented with English-only policies in their classrooms. They also lobbied the principal for a schoolwide language policy that would give their individual classroom policies even more authority. Unlike Mrs. Yee's English-only classroom policy (described in chap. 3), which was based on a pedagogical desire to provide students with more practice and could be negotiated with multilingual students for use in particular learning contexts, the schoolwide policy the mathematics teachers called for was not intended to be flexible. It was intended to ensure that only English was spoken in Northside classrooms. Such a policy would prevent teachers from creating "private" spaces, off center stage of the classroom floor, in which student multilingualism could be promoted. A schoolwide English-only policy was never created because the principal of the school felt that it could not be implemented without engaging in a power struggle between students and teachers that would not serve either group well. As well, the principal was responsible for implementing the school board's, *Language for Learning Policy*, which supported student multilingualism despite the desire of some parents, teachers, and students for classroom English monolingualism.

As was mentioned in the Introduction, one of the core assumptions underlying the policy was the assumption that all students needed opportunities to think critically about the social values and status assigned to different languages by various groups in our society and to explore issues of bias and stereotyping related to language and culture. This was exactly the kind of work that Ms. Edgars and Evelyn Yeung had undertaken together. Such work wouldn't have been possible if there had been a schoolwide policy in place that insisted that English be the only language spoken in all Northside classrooms.

The fact that a group of well-respected and successful teachers at Northside (their students were renowned for their success in national and international math competitions) were actively resisting the school board's *Language for Learning Policy* by calling for a schoolwide English-only policy shows that language policies that work toward collaborative relations of power and authority are not easily implemented. Successful implementation of the school board language policy at a school like Northside would have meant that those teachers who didn't speak the same languages as their students had all agreed to share power and authority in their classrooms in ways they had never done before. It would have also meant that teachers had all agreed to think about their roles in new ways and engage with such questions as "Are there other ways for teachers to check for student understanding without insisting that all students speak English while completing their math problems?"

As a teacher educator whose role is to assist my own students in educating across linguistic differences, what I have learned from my research in Leslie Edgars' classroom is that working effectively in multilingual schools means rethinking traditional learnings and desires around authority in the classroom. It means asking new questions around "classroom management." It means struggling with the vulnerability that comes with sharing power. It means working with students in new ways—ways that are unfamiliar and untested. As mentioned earlier, it also means learning to recognize the discriminatory discourses with which high school students might be struggling. The following activities for further reflection and discussion allow my students and me to begin to do this work together.

FOR FURTHER REFLECTION AND DISCUSSION

The Complexity of "Who Am I?"   In her book, *Why Are All the Black Kids Sitting Together in the Cafeteria? and Other Conversations About Race,* Beverly Daniel Tatum writes that the concept of *identity* is a complex one, shaped by individual characteristics, family dynamics, historical factors, and social and political contexts.

Who am I? The answer depends in large part on who the world around me says I am. Who do my parents say I am? Who do my peers say I am? What message is reflected back to me in the faces and voices of my teachers, my neighbors, store clerks? What do I learn from the media about myself? How am I represented in the cultural images around me? Or am I missing from the picture altogether?[22]

How are your own bilingual students of color represented in the cultural images surrounding them? Choosing one group of students you work with, look at the ways these students and their families are represented on radio talk shows, newspaper articles, television programs, cartoons, comic strips, or the movies. What kinds of images and messages about your students are you and your students taking in? How are you and your students perpetuating and reinforcing the negative messages that are so pervasive in our culture? How can you both begin to challenge them?

Working With Controversial Language Issues. In scenes 2 and 3 of *Hong Kong, Canada* (included in Appendix A), radio talk show host James Wolfe runs a show on the topic of "To Canada, With Cash: Hong Kong Money Likes Toronto." Joshua is impressed with the show because he believes that such controversial topics bring in a large audience. In scene 6, Sam warns Joshua that while creating a language controversy in the school newspaper may bring in more readers, it will also increase racial and linguistic tensions in the school. If the role of a teacher advisor to the school newspaper team had been included in *Hong Kong, Canada*, what could he or she have said to Joshua, Wendy, and Sam about the situation? Write a scene in which a teacher advisor talks to Joshua, Wendy, and Sam about publishing the controversial issue. Read aloud or perform several of these scenes one after another and discuss the similarities and differences between them.

Not Understanding What Is Being Said: Personal Reflection. In the last scene of *Hong Kong, Canada*, in response to the various comments she has heard at the school hearing, Ms. Diamond says, "I was moved by the argument that many non-Cantonese speaking students in this school feel left out when they hear Cantonese being spoken in the hallways and classrooms of our school. I must admit, I often feel left out myself." Thinking about your own teaching practice, how important is it that you understand what your students say? Why is it so important? How is understanding what your students say linked to how you see your role as a teacher? Considering the advantages associated with students speaking their primary languages at school, how might teachers check for student understanding and engagement without insisting that all students speak English?"

---

[22]See Tatum (1997, p. 18).

Responding to a Call for a Schoolwide English-Only Policy.   The play, *Hong Kong, Canada,* concludes in an open-ended way. No solution is provided for the audience. It is up to them to think about the ways principals and teachers might provide leadership around the difficult task of negotiating across linguistic differences. In pairs or small groups, write an ending to the play in which the principal of Pierre Elliot Trudeau, addresses the students who came to the hearing in the last scene. Decide if you want Trudeau to belong to a school board or school district that has a language policy that is similar to the *Language for Learning Policy* described in the Introduction. The existence of such a policy could have an impact on how the principal responds to what the students have said in the hearing. Once again, read aloud or perform several of these endings one after another and discuss the similarities and differences between them.

6

Oral Presentations, Accent Discrimination, and Linguistic Privilege

The school's programs emphasize the acquisition of learning skills as well as academic content. Technology is successfully integrated into the curriculum of the school, through the use of networked computer systems. As a result, students demonstrate sophisticated research and presentation skills.

[Northside *School Profile*, 1996–1997]

And the presentation, right? Because we don't have such a thing in Hong Kong ... I cannot adapt to it. I'm really embarrassed. I mean I am really shy. I'm really, I don't have the confidence to speak in front of such a big class.

[Victor Yu, *Interview*, October 9, 1996]

The two quotes that open this chapter point to the importance that was placed on the display of strong English oral presentation skills at Northside and the difficulty some students had in developing these skills. While many of the students who used English as a primary language were creating imaginative and sophisticated classroom presentations, using television game and talk show formats as well as computer technology, others were struggling with strong feelings of embarrassment at having to speak English in front of a large group of people. Chapter 6 begins with a short play written by Northside student Timothy Chiu (not a pseudonym), entitled *No Pain, No Gain*. The play dramatizes the difficulty of preparing an oral presentation in a second language and the disappointment of a giving a performance that does not live up to the presenter and his family's expectations of excellence. *No Pain, No Gain* was written and performed as a final activity during a 12-session student playwriting workshop held in July, 1998. As mentioned in the Preface, the goal of the playwriting project was to provide 15 students from Anne Yee's English class with an opportunity to develop their English language skills by writing and performing their own ethnographies through the genre of playwriting. The workshop was created as a way of responding to the student dilemma of not having enough opportunities to practice English. It also provided a small group of Northside students with a chance to represent their own experience as paid student researchers on the project.

The commentary uses Timothy Chiu's play to look at some of the issues that arise when students speak in different accents and teachers must evaluate students working in a second or other language. The Pedagogical Discussion explores ways teachers might respond to these issues. The data from the summer playwriting workshop included in this chapter is supplemented by data from an interview with Timothy Chiu and field notes from the playwriting workshop. The play, *No Pain, No Gain*, the Commentary, and Pedagogical Discussion that appear in this chapter has been member checked by Timothy Chiu.

NO PAIN, NO GAIN
by Timothy Chiu

Characters (in order of appearance)

Timothy: A Canadian student born in Hong Kong
Mike: Timothy's Canadian-born friend
Mom: Timothy's mother
TV: the television
Millie: Timothy's sister
Mr. Kendall: Timothy's English teacher

Setting

At school, Timothy's bedroom at home, the family living room at home, at the dinner table, English class. Timothy, Mom, and Millie speak English with a Cantonese accent.

SCENE 1

(At school)

TIMOTHY   Oh, no! The presentation is tomorrow and I HAVE to get at least 80%. But I am so nervous! Oh, my God, my hands are shaking.

MIKE   You are kidding me, Tim. You got your speech ready and all you have to do is say it in class tomorrow. I am not even half done.

TIMOTHY   So what? Even though I am finished my speech, I am nervous about delivering it! I don't know why, but I always have problems speaking in public and especially in class.

MIKE   Stop saying you are nervous. It's no big deal! Besides, you are doing much better than me in English class.

TIMOTHY   I got my marks from studying and all that, but when it comes to participating in class, well ...

MIKE Don't worry. Just speak as you would normally and things will work as planned. You know what? I think your speech is really good!

TIMOTHY Really?

MIKE Yeah, of course. But meanwhile, help me do my speech 'cause I am really dead.

TIMOTHY Sure, man.

MIKE You're the best!

SCENE 2

(At home, Timothy's bedroom)

TIMOTHY Okay. No pain, no gain! If I have to get a decent mark, I gotta practice and practice until I feel comfortable and confident. *(Coughs)* Good afternoon, fellow students. No! That's not good enough. It should be (Brightly, with much enthusiasm) Good afternoon, fellow students! 1997 marks an important date to the people in Hong Kong. It's a transition of 156 years of British administration to Chinese sovereignty, a transition from a Crown Colony of the United Kingdom to a Special Administrative Region of the People's Republic of China.

(Timothy goes on and on and on in a lowered voice, walks around and looks at himself in the mirror. He then walks around again and again.)

Ha! I got it all in my head! Right now, it's just a matter of time before it is finally finished. Done. Finito. Woo, hoo! *(He jumps up and down.)*

(Mom enters the living room and calls out to Tim.)

MOM Tim? Are you all right in there? You locked yourself in the room for nearly 4 hours now. It's time for supper!

TIMOTHY   Okay, Mom. I'm just rehearsing my speech for tomorrow's class. You can eat first, Mom. I still have to fix something in the speech.

MOM   That's weird, he's usually hungry at this time of day. I'll watch the news then.

(She sits down and turns on the TV.)

TV   A new study suggests that teenagers should not study more than 2½ hours each day. A new found mental disease called "Nerdkazophobia" is proven to be fatal and parents should be aware if their children stay in their room for over 2½ hours. Symptoms include murmuring, loss of appetite, and extreme hyperness. If your children have the above symptoms, please contact your local health and mental authorities immediately.

MOM   Could this be my son? Oh, I really have to pray to the Buddha![1]

SCENE 3

(At the dinner table)

TIMOTHY   Okay, let's eat.

MILLIE   Hey, Tim, what's got into you? You were locked in your room for nearly 4 hours.

TIMOTHY   Just rehearsing a speech for a presentation.

MILLIE   Four hours to rehearse? Come on, it's a piece of cake.

---

[1] In a post-workshop interview, after he had seen a videotape of his play being performed, Timothy Chiu explained that Mom's line "Oh, I really have to pray to the Buddha!" means, "Son, don't become crazy!" Chiu also told us, "When I was performing the dinner scene in the play, I wanted to accentuate what traditional Chinese families are like … [Praying to the Buddha] is a very traditional, Chinese characteristic, something that a family would do. I wanted to show this in the play. I feel that the effect is pretty good; I like it."

MOM   What cake? I didn't buy a cake!

TIMOTHY Ha, ha, ha. Mom, it's just a figure of speech.

MOM   What? What?

MILLIE   Anyway, I think you shouldn't worry too much. You'll be fine. Have a good night's sleep!

TIMOTHY *(Eating)* Okay.

MOM   By the way, what is your speech about?

TIMOTHY Mom, it's about my research on the handover of Hong Kong.

MOM   Ha! That's my boy. You gotta tell all your students that we Chinese people are no longer enslaved by Whites!

TIMOTHY Well, I didn't plan to be cocky, but I am telling the class about the significance of this major event as well as my well-planned analysis.

MOM   You better get a good mark on English or you will never get a raise in allowance. You got me?

TIMOTHY Yes, Mom. Let's eat.

SCENE 4

(The next morning at school)

TIMOTHY *(To himself)* Okay, everything is set for the presentation. All I got to do is say it.

(Mike approaches)

MIKE   Hi, Tim. Ready for the presentation?

TIMOTHY   Uh, huh. How 'bout you?

MIKE   Same here. I notice that you were answering most of the questions in Biology class today.

TIMOTHY   Yeah, it is the stuff that I know most of all and feel comfortable in answering.

MIKE   I thought you had problems in class, but all of a sudden you are so articulate.

TIMOTHY   Am I? Maybe, you are right. Our Bio teacher is a funny guy and he makes the class environment much mellower for me so I can speak up in class. But in English class, our teacher doesn't talk much and he doesn't say funny stuff to us. Even though I know something, I just can't say it. And the people in the class made gestures to me the last time I spoke, as if they didn't understand what I am trying to tell them.

MIKE   I see. It's the environment of the class that's bugging you, right?

TIMOTHY   Sort of. And sometimes I just don't feel comfortable speaking when there's lots of people staring at me.

MIKE   It's time to go. I'll see you at lunch.

TIMOTHY   See ya.

SCENE 5

(English class, before the presentation)

TIMOTHY   *(To himself)* I am going to do it and everything is gonna be fine. Come on, you can do it, man! Just do it!

MR. KENDALL *(In a low voice)* Okay class, today we begin the ISP presentations. Next up is Timothy. Timothy, anytime when you are ready.

TIMOTHY *(To himself)* Okay, right now it's show time! Come on, it's only 5 minutes. *(Reading from a script)* Good afternoon, fellow students. 1997 marks an important date to the people in Hong Kong. It is a transition of 156 years of British administration to Chinese sovereignty, a transition from a Crown Colony of the United Kingdom to a Special Administrative Region of the People's Republic of China.

(Students are staring at Tim and as he goes on and on, he gradually gets more and more nervous. His hands and body begin shaking. He speaks more softly, covers his face with the presentation script and begins to mumble.)

TIMOTHY *(Talking to himself and the audience)* How can this be? It went well yesterday at home and now it's totally different.

(Timothy finishes his speech.)

MR. KENDALL Good analysis. Your reading was good, but you were a bit nervous and sometimes your words didn't come through. But it's good for an 85%.

TIMOTHY *(Sadly)* Thank you, Sir!

SCENE 6

(English class, after the class has ended)

MR. KENDALL You did well today, Timothy. Why are you still disappointed?

TIMOTHY I don't know, Sir. But I have problems speaking in public.

MR. KENDALL I think you only have this problem while speaking in class, right?

TIMOTHY   That's right, Sir. But in other classes, I do fine.

MR. KENDALL   It's okay, Timothy. Just speak more in public when you have opportunities and you will improve, trust me.

TIMOTHY   Thanks for the advice, Sir.

MR. KENDALL   Not at all, Timothy. I appreciate your effort.

SCENE 7

(Center stage)

TIMOTHY   After this incident, Timothy began to practice English wherever he could, and in the process, he met a lot of new friends and his ability to speak in public improved.

(The End)

COMMENTARY: SPEAKING WITH DIFFERENT ACCENTS

On Classroom Presentations

Student presentations, performed both individually and in small groups, were a popular assignment among English and social studies teachers at Northside because they provided students with an opportunity to practice their public-speaking skills in English. For most English as a Second or Other Language (ESOL) students, giving an effective classroom presentation was an extremely demanding activity. Students were evaluated on their use of Standard English grammar and Standard English phonology (pronunciation). They were also evaluated on their strategies for repairing and enhancing communication (for example, their ability to paraphrase and effectively use gestures and eye contact) and their understanding of the sociolinguistic and cultural norms associated with giving a classroom presentation.

The presentations given by the ESOL students at Northside were assessed in comparison to the performances of students who used English as a primary language and/or had attended elementary school in Toronto. For many of these students, giving classroom presentations was not perceived as an unfamiliar or particularly difficult activity. To illustrate, when the character of Timothy tells his Canadian-born friend, Mike, that he is nervous about his upcoming presentation in scene 1 of *No Pain, No Gain*, Mike thinks he must be kidding. Timothy's speech is already completed, and all Timothy has to do is "say it in class." Mike, on the other hand, hasn't finished his speech. For Mike, preparing the speech is the difficult task, not presenting it. Elementary school students in Ontario begin making classroom presentations as early as in grade 1. This means that students like Mike have already accessed what sociologist Pierre Bourdieu has called the linguistic and cultural "capital" needed to produce effective classroom presentations. However, for students like playwright Timothy Chiu, who did not (completely) do their elementary education in Toronto (Timothy arrived in Toronto at the age of 10), performing a presentation in front of other students required learning new and uncomfortable ways of talking and acting.

In Chiu's play, the character of Timothy demonstrates that he has mastered quite a few of the linguistic and cultural norms associated with doing a classroom presentation at Northside. For example, in scene 2, we hear that he knows it is common and appropriate to begin a presentation with a greeting such as "Good afternoon, fellow students." He also knows that such a greeting needs to be delivered in a bright and enthusiastic manner. As well, the sample of his presentation speech we hear in scene 2 has been edited so it follows the rules of Standard English grammar. Finally, Timothy understands that his presentation must contain a well-planned analysis and appeal to a wide range of political opinions on the colonial history of Hong Kong. In scene 3, when Mom tells Timothy that he has to tell his classmates that Chinese people are no longer enslaved by Whites, Timothy replies that he doesn't plan to "be cocky."

Yet, despite the sociolinguistic, grammatical, cultural, and political expertise Timothy displays in scene 2 and scene 3 of the play, and despite the 4 hours of practice (which is later critiqued by the playwright as being overzealous when it is described as a symptom of a fictional disease named "Nerdkazophobia"), the presentation does not go as well as Timothy had anticipated. After a strong beginning, Timothy's hands and body begin to shake. He lowers his voice, and then hides his face behind his presentation script so it is no longer possible for other students to hear or understand what he is saying. Mr. Kendall, who appreciates Timothy's effort, gives him a mark of 85% for his presentation, but comments on his nervousness. Timothy, who had practiced for 4 hours and had been anticipating a higher mark, is disappointed.

The audience knows why Timothy became nervous even after 4 hours of practice. Earlier, in a conversation that he had with his friend Mike, Timothy told us that he didn't feel comfortable speaking when lots of people were staring at him. As Victor Yu tells us in the quotation that opens this chapter, in Hong Kong, Timothy was not required to make a classroom presentation and it is hard for him to get used to speaking on center stage. The audience also found out that the last time Timothy spoke out in front of his classmates in English class, they made gestures, which Timothy interpreted as a sign that his classmates did not understand what he was saying. The anticipation of not being understood and having to, once again, continue speaking despite distracting and disturbing gestures from classmates contributed to Timothy's nervousness, which, in turn, contributed to his disappointing performance.

At the end of play, Timothy and Mr. Kendall talk about Timothy's nervousness. Mr. Kendall suggests that Timothy practice speaking English in public whenever he has the opportunity to do so. In the last scene of the play, Timothy, speaking in the third person about himself, tells the audience that he followed Mr. Kendall's advice and began to practice English wherever he could. In the process of practicing, Timothy met a lot of new friends and his ability to speak in public improved. The play has a happy ending.

On Sharing the Responsibility of Communication

Both Mr. Kendall and Timothy place the responsibility of achieving this happy ending in the hands of ESOL students. It is up to them to seek out opportunities to practice English with English speakers so that they can improve their skills and increase their confidence. Such a belief, however, does not take into account what playwright Timothy Chiu understands to be at the heart of ESOL students' nervousness in public speaking activities: distracting and disturbing nonverbal signs that members of the audience are not understanding what they are saying.

Critical linguist Rosina Lippi-Green, whose work was discussed in chapter 5, believes that successful communication is based on "mutual responsibility" in which participants in a conversation (or, in this case, classroom presentation) collaborate in the establishment of understanding.[2] One of the things that can get in the way of such collaboration is the way people respond to an accent that is different from their own.[3] Lippi-Green writes that when people are confronted with an accent that is unfamiliar to them, the way that Timothy's classmates are confronted with his Cantonese accent, the first decision they make is whether or not they are going to accept their responsibility in the act of communication. What sometimes happens is that members of the dominant language group reject their role. In Timothy Chiu's play, this rejection is communicated nonverbally. Chiu talked about this in an interview that was undertaken about 8 months after the playwriting workshop had been completed. The Cantonese interview was undertaken, transcribed, and translated into English by research assistant Wing-Yee Chow. The words in **boldface** are words that were originally said in English.

> ... My **play**, it brings out a message to others that when we walk up for a **presentation**, it seems very easy, it's done in 15 minutes. But actually, we do a lot of preparation. I wrote this piece [on the handover of Hong Kong] many times, and also **rehearsed** many times ... Some people don't know about this and just think, "You don't know how to speak English." Once they see that you are Chinese, they think that you're gonna do badly. I feel that this isn't good ...
>
> [*Interview*, April 7, 1999]

For Lippi-Green, breakdown in communication and lack of understanding is due not so much to an accent itself as it is to people's negative social evaluation of the accent in question, and a rejection of the "communicative burden." Using linguistic research to support this argument, Lippi-Green reports that work in accommodation theory suggests that complex interplay of linguistic and psychological factors will establish people's predisposition to understand. Listeners and speakers will work harder to find a communicative middle ground and work toward mutual understanding when they are socially and psychologically motivated to do so. Based on our own personal histories, backgrounds, and social selves, which make up a set of

---

[2]See Lippi-Green (1997, p. 70).

[3]Following Lippi-Green (1997), I believe that it is not only ESOL students who speak with an accent, but that we all speak with an accent. I also don't believe it is possible for ESOL students to replace a non-Standard English accent with the Standard English accent (that is most valued at school) in a consistent and enduring way. See chapter 2 in Lippi-Green (1997) for further discussion of the "myth of non-accent."

"filters" through which we hear other people talk, we all take a communicative stance. Most of the time we agree to carry our share of the burden. Sometimes, if we are particularly positive about the set of social characteristics we see in another person, or if the purposes of communication are especially important to us, we will accept more of the burden. Conversely, if we feel negatively about particular accents and other social characteristics, we feel justified in rejecting the communicative burden, as in the case of the students who made gestures during Timothy's presentation in the play.[4]

Related to Lippi-Green's ideas here is Pierre Bourdieu's (1993) idea that a speaker must possess the authority to speak and that part of this authority is given to the speaker by the listener. Education researcher Jenny Miller writes that people who are considered to have the "wrong accent," nonstandard pronunciation, or faulty syntax, in Bourdieu's terms, lack credibility and an affirming audience of believing listeners.[5]

Returning to Mr. Kendall's advice to Timothy about how to reduce his nervousness during classroom presentations, it seems that working toward happy endings in our own multilingual classrooms requires more than suggesting that our ESOL students look for opportunities to practice speaking English in public. It also requires working with all our students to challenge what Lippi-Green calls "accent discrimination," so that all students in our classrooms have credibility as speakers. Further exploration of such work takes place in the Pedagogical Discussion.

Accessing the Target Language Community

Mr. Kendall and Timothy's belief that seeking out opportunities to practice with English speakers will help English speakers improve their skills is supported by many theories of what makes a good language learner. As explained by critical applied linguist Bonny Norton, these theories have been developed on the premise that language learners can choose what conditions in which they will interact with members of the target language and the learner's access to the target language community is a primarily function of the learner's motivation.[6] Norton critiques this set of assumptions, suggesting that speakers of the target language have the power to influence when ESOL speakers can speak, how much they can speak, and what they can

---

[4]See Lippi-Green (1997, pp. 70–72).
[5]See Jenny Miller (1999, p. 61).
[6]See Norton Peirce (1995, p. 12).
[7]See Norton (2000, p. 2).

speak about.[7] Support for this critique comes from one of our own play-writing workshop sessions.

During a discussion on the some of the difficulties associated with learning English, Marilyn, a White, Canadian-born student who used English as a primary language, suggested that a person's attitude was important to the process of language learning. Marilyn's family had hosted in their home several visiting students from Japan. She talked about the impressive progress one of these students had made after deciding that she would pursue new friendships with English-speaking people and use English as much as possible while in Canada. Marilyn then contrasted this first student's language-learning experience with that of another student who chose to socialize with other Japanese students and frequently used Japanese during her stay. This second student did not make nearly as much progress learning English as the first student did. Speaking up in response to these comments, Cathy, a Hong Kong-born Chinese student, told Marilyn that it was often difficult to pursue new friendships with English-speaking people. English-speaking people must want to be friends with you, she told Marilyn and the rest of the group, before you can become friends with them.[8] Given that the pursuit of interactions with English-speakers can be difficult, providing ESOL students with access to sites where such interactions are possible is important. One of the playwriting workshop's most valued outcomes for many of the students was the opportunity to "make new friends" with people who had been classmates, but not friends. Such a finding supports one of the recommendations made by parents who were interviewed for the 1995–1996 *Quality Assurance School Review*, discussed in the Introduction. These parents felt that Northside's extracurricular program was one of the better sites to foster social interaction among students from different linguistic, cultural, and racial groups and that more noncompetitive or "just-for-fun" activities should be provided at the school.

On Linguistic Privilege

As mentioned earlier, and demonstrated in Timothy Chiu's play, giving an effective classroom presentation is an extremely demanding activity that involves being able to effectively engage with a complex set of linguistic and cultural norms. As was also mentioned earlier, classroom presentations given by the ESOL students at Northside were assessed in comparison to the performances of students who used English as a primary language and had attended

---

[8]For similar findings in an Australian high school context, see Miller (1999).

elementary school as well as high school in Toronto. These students were linguistically advantaged or privileged in that they had already accumulated the
linguistic and cultural capital needed to give a school presentation in English.
They were also privileged in that their Standard Canadian-English accent
provided them with credibility as English speakers and an audience of affirming listeners. Furthermore, the "filters" that Lippi-Green discusses not only
influence students' evaluation of their peers' oral performances; they can also
influence teachers' assessment of their students' oral performances. How
might teachers respond to the inequities associated with linguistic privilege
and accent discrimination in multilingual schools? Several answers to this
question are discussed in the Pedagogical Discussion below.

PEDAGOGICAL DISCUSSION:
ANTI-DISCRIMINATORY EDUCATION
IN MULTILINGUAL SCHOOLS

Responding to Accent Discrimination and Linguistic Privilege

As discussed in the Commentary, there are several ways accent discrimination can disadvantage ESOL students making classroom presentations in
multilingual schools. First, ESOL students who speak with accents that are
different from the Standard English accent most valued at school lack credibility and an affirming audience of believing listeners. As revealed in Timothy Chiu's play, this lack of credibility is sometimes communicated to
ESOL presenters through gestures. Such gestures increase the presenters'
nervousness, which in turn, diminishes their performance and the mark they
get for their performance. Second, teachers who assess ESOL students' presentations make their own subjective evaluations about the way their students speak. These evaluations may be positive, neutral, or negative. A
negative social evaluation of a particular accent can lead to a rejection of the
communicative burden on the part of the teacher, which in turn will lead to
the teacher not understanding what the student is trying to say and a lower
presentation mark.

   There are a number of ways that teachers can challenge the impact of accent discrimination in their classrooms. English teacher Greg Dunn has
given his ESOL students the opportunity to give their presentations in front
of a smaller, self-selected group of students, rather than the whole class.
This smaller audience provided the ESOL presenters with a group of believing listeners and avoided the possibility of them having to speak in the face

of distracting and disturbing gestures. English teacher Leonard Robertson has given his students the opportunity to submit a videotape of their oral presentation in addition to giving their presentation in front of the class. In the event that a student becomes extremely nervous and gives a disappointing performance in front of other students, the videotape of a more polished performance raises the student's presentation mark.

As discussed in chapter 2, in my own teacher education classroom, my students and I negotiate classroom rules for talking about issues of discrimination in schooling. One of the rules is

> Disagreement is a part of life. We understand that there are times when we will disagree, but we will not intentionally humiliate, intimidate, or embarrass each other. If we unintentionally do so, we will apologize. Nonverbal gestures also communicate messages that can humiliate, intimidate, or embarrass people.

This commitment to monitoring the way we respond (both verbally and nonverbally) to what others are saying helps my students and me to productively dialogue across differences of political and educational opinion. Perhaps the inclusion of a similar rule, with reference to audience participation during student presentations, might help teachers and students challenge accent discrimination in their own classrooms. Such a rule is probably most effective when students are also asked to think about the kinds of subjective evaluations they make about different accents. The first activity to follow entitled "Thinking about accent and race," is intended to promote such thinking. This activity may also be useful to teachers who want to think about their own subjective evaluations regarding the way their students speak. As was discussed in Activity 1, "Unearthing and Deconstructing Stereotypes Around Varieties of English," in chapter 4, we have all learned to discriminate against other people on the basis of the way they speak. Educating ourselves to be able to discern between real communicative difficulties and those stemming not from language, but from stereotype and bias, is essential for teachers who want to challenge linguistic inequities in their classrooms.

As mentioned earlier, many of the students at Northside who were linguistically privileged because they spoke with a Standard Canadian-English accent were also advantaged because they had already accumulated the cultural capital needed to give an effective school presentation in English. Providing ESOL students with some explicit instruction around the norms associated with giving a classroom presentation is another way of responding to the issue of linguistic privilege in multilingual schools. To illustrate with an example from our own work at Northside, in the first year of the project, assistant Judith Ngan gave a "demonstration speech" in one of the ESOL Drama classes at Northside. The purposes or learning outcomes of the activity were to (1) help students become aware of the components of a good speech; (2) help students become more knowledgeable about how to give an oral presentation; and (3) reinforce the need for organization. Judith's demonstration speech was about how to use one sheet of paper to make an eight-page booklet. As Judith spoke, she followed her own directions and turned a sheet of paper into an eight-page booklet. After the demonstration speech, Judith gave students a brief lecture on how to prepare and give an oral presentation. Modeling some of what she was suggesting to the students, she prepared an outline of her lecture and put it on a transparency so that students could easily follow her presentation. Judith's demonstration speech, the outline, and the lecture notes themselves are all included in Appendix C. As can be seen from Judith's work, the cultural, linguistic, and paralinguistic knowledge needed to give an effective presentation is quite complex. Providing ESOL students with access to this capital takes time. One ESOL teacher who Judith spoke to told her that it took her an entire semester to have the students complete the process of practicing how to make a presentation, that is to say, from choosing a topic, to handing in the speech, to composing an outline, to presenting the speech. Clearly, Judith's demonstration and lecture was only the first of many other activities that needed to take place to provide students with the kind of instruction and practice they needed to access the linguistic and cultural capital associated with giving an oral presentation.

Of all the advice contained in Judith's lecture, perhaps the most valuable pieces were "Watch how other people do it," and "Practice as much as you can" (see Appendix C). Sociolinguist James Gee writes that students develop school discourses, such as the discourse of making classroom presentations, through "apprenticeship."[9] He believes that discourses are acquired in natural settings rather than learned through overt teaching. Knowing "about" the language (of classroom presentations) does not mean knowing how to "do" the language. If mastery of a discourse comes through acquisition, not learning, as Gee believes, teachers wanting to assist their students

---

[9]In talking about developing school "discourse" rather than school "language," or discourse acquisition rather than language acquisition, Gee (1996) is putting forth the idea that our knowledge of how to use language at school is more than a knowledge of words and how to combine them to form grammatical sentences. It is knowledge of ways of being in the world of school. This knowledge includes "words, acts, values, beliefs, attitudes, and social identities, as well as gestures, glances, body positions and clothes" (p. 127).

in accessing the capital associated with giving classroom presentations need to create the conditions for such acquisition as well as provide explicit instruction. Returning to Judith Ngan's lecture and Timothy Chiu's play, *No Pain, No Gain*, for an illustration, we can see it is possible to teach students to begin a presentation with "Good morning," or "Good afternoon," as Judith did in her lecture (see Appendix C). However, Timothy's knowledge that the greeting should be said brightly and with much enthusiasm ("*Good* afternoon, fellow students!"), comes from having heard other students greet their audiences in such a way. In fact, when the play was presented to participants in the playwriting workshop, the phrase, "*Good* afternoon," received a big laugh because it sounded just like the "*Good* morning" greeting Northside's student council president uttered every day before making her announcements over the intercom.

Given the complexity of the discourse of classroom presentations that needs to be acquired by students, teachers who want to respond to the inequities of linguistic privilege in their classrooms might want to reconsider the role classroom presentations play in their curriculum or the way they assess their students' performances. Teachers can replace or supplement classroom presentations with other kinds of oral activities that are more familiar to their ESOL students. They can also lower the stakes associated with the performance of any one presentation by assessing the entire process of making a presentation: the choice of a topic, the preparation of a speech, the composition of an outline, the creation of visual aids, and the rehearsal of the speech as well as the final presentation of the speech.

Acquiring Discourse Competence

James Gee's idea that discourses are acquired in natural settings and that discourse competence is realized socially through interaction also emerges in the last scene of Timothy Chiu's play, *No Pain, No Gain*. After his disappointing presentation performance in Mr. Kendall's class, Timothy began to practice English wherever he could. In the process, he tells the audience, he met a lot of new friends, with whom he could interact socially, and his ability improved to speak English in public.

Moving from the ethnographic fictional world of *No Pain, No Gain* to playwright Timothy Chiu's own world of schooling, one way that Chiu, himself, tried to "practice English wherever he could" was to join the 12-session summer playwriting workshop that was facilitated and videotaped by our research team. Through the discussion, reading, and reading activities undertaken in the workshop, Chiu was able to develop his English language, or, in Gee's terms, discourse skills through inter-action with others.

What follows is another excerpt from the post-workshop interview Wing-Yee Chow undertook with Chiu. At the time of the post-workshop interview, Timothy was in his last year of high school and taking the last set of Ontario Academic Credit (OAC) courses he needed to complete in order to gain admission to university.

Wing-Yee: Did you find that the **workshop** has had any impact on you since it ended, 7, 8 months ago?

Timothy: The whole, the whole **workshop** aimed to help us to **improve public speaking skills.** I feel that after I attended the workshop I regained some confidence ... Actually, today, I have brought something for you to see. This is my **speech,** English **OAC.** I am happy because I got 100%.

Wing-Yee: **Wow!**

Timothy: I used what I have learned from the play: Not to be afraid. That is, you know what you are talking about. You [need to] walk up, no matter how many people there are, even if there is a group of people, even if there are several hundred people. I think that the workshop has helped me in achieving the result this time.

Wing-Yee: How did the **workshop** help you? In providing opportunities to practice?

Timothy: Yes, [I] got the opportunities and I could **explore,** that is, I could talk about why we faced obstacles. [We] could **discuss** and realize that the classroom **environment,** the **conversations** between the teacher and student can also change the **classroom performance.** And [it was] very relaxed. **Tara** made us feel very **comfortable.** "It's okay, just say whatever you want to say." I find this pretty good. [*Interview*, April 7, 1999]

Using this interview excerpt to think about the ways the playwriting work-shop helped Timothy Chiu to develop the discourse competence that he needed to make more effective presentations, two things seem important. First, that fact that Timothy was actually given an opportunity to spend the month of July using English to write, read, and listen to others' ethnographic reflections, dialogues, and dramatic scenes was important ("Yes, [I] got the opportunities."). As well, because the workshop took place during the summer break, the participants had the opportunity to practice English outside a traditional school or classroom setting. Workshop designer and lead facilitator Victoria Shen responded to the students' work, but did not evaluate it by assigning it a mark or grade. The stakes associated with performing in English were lower than they were during the school year ("And [it was] very relaxed."). Because there were only 15 students enrolled in the workshop (six spoke English as a primary language whereas nine were ESOL speakers), we sat on chairs in a circle where everyone could see each other's face. This arrangement helped us create an affirming audience of believing listeners for the ESOL speakers in the group.

The second thing that helped Timothy Chiu develop the discourse competence he needed was the opportunity to explore and talk about the obstacles ESOL presenters faced in multilingual classrooms. As can be discerned from Timothy's interview, some of the discussions we had in the workshop centered on issues of linguistic discrimination. Such discussions were deliberately pursued in the design and facilitation of the workshop curriculum. To illustrate, in a session on the theme of language and identity, Victoria handed out a chapter from Momoye Sugimon's book, *Jin Guo: Voices of Chinese Canadian Women,* entitled "How Come You Don't Have an Accent?"[10] In this chapter, 18 Chinese Canadian women talk about their personal experiences with issues of language and identity. Victoria randomly divided the workshop participants into small groups and gave each group a different question to answer about a particular excerpt from the chapter. When the participants finished their work, they returned to the circle they usually sat in and reported on their small group work to the others. Some of the issues that arose in this discussion included, "Are Chinese people who are born in Canada less Chinese than those who are not?" (this was an issue Evelyn Yeung struggled with in chap. 5); choosing to live in Toronto's Chinatown and Little India rather than choosing to live in a mixed or English-speaking community; and the difficulty of speaking Spanish with an English accent and English with a Cantonese accent. The issue of accent discrimination discussed in this chapter was raised and discussed in a direct way, and it was this kind of talk about "why we face obstacles" that gave Timothy the story line for his play, *No Pain, No Gain.*

Performing the play, with the assistance of his playwriting colleagues, gave Timothy Chiu an opportunity to dramatize the obstacles he faced and imagine a way of moving forward. As well, his own performance in the role of Timothy allowed him to begin moving forward by providing him with an opportunity to practice speaking English in front of an affirming audience. Both of these opportunities helped Timothy acquire the discourse competence and confidence he needed to make more effective classroom presentations.

---

[10]See Sugiman (1992).

Re-creating the opportunities that were made available for Timothy Chiu in the playwriting workshop is difficult for teachers who work with groups of 30 to 40 students rather than 15 and who also have the responsibility of grading their students' work. However, knowing what kinds of opportunities are helpful to students struggling to acquire the discourse competence associated with public speaking at school may help teachers think of ways that they might be able to create such opportunities for students in their own schools.

FOR FURTHER REFLECTION AND DISCUSSION

Thinking About Accent and Race: Personal and Professional Reflection. In her book, *English With an Accent: Language, Ideology and Discrimination in the United States*, Rosina Lippi-Green reports on a research study undertaken to see how American university students' expectations of instructors born outside the United States played into their attitudes and learning experience.[11] Sixty-two undergraduate students who spoke English as their primary language participated in the study. Each student listened to a 4-minute lecture on an introductory topic that was prerecorded on tape. While listening, the students saw a projected slide photograph, which was meant to represent the instructor speaking. *Both of the recordings* heard were made *by the same speaker,* who was a primary speaker of English from central Ohio. However, there were *two possible projected photographs*: half of the students saw a slide of a White woman lecturer, and the other half saw a woman similarly dressed and of the same size and hair style, but who was Asian. Immediately after listening to the 4-minute lecture, each student completed a test of listening comprehension. Students were also asked to fill out a questionnaire that asked them to rate the accent (*speaks with an American accent* or *speaks with an Asian accent*) and the quality of teaching of each speaker.

The results of the study showed that the perceived race of the instructor, on the basis of the photograph, influenced the ways students evaluated the instructors' language use. Some of the students looking at an Asian face were convinced that they were hearing an Asian accent despite the fact that the prerecorded language they had listened to was that of a primary English speaker from Ohio. Other results of the study showed that overall, students scored lower in the comprehension test when they believed that the lecturer was Asian. In commenting on these results, Lippi-Green suggests that the students' preconceptions were strong enough motivators to

---

[11]See Lippi-Green (1997, pp. 126–130) and Rubin (1992).

cause them to construct imaginary accents and fictional communicative breakdowns. Applying the findings to our everyday world of teaching and learning, Lippi-Green also suggests that although primary speakers of English are usually given the benefit of the doubt to whether or not they are good teachers and communicate effectively, ESOL speakers are often not give a chance at all.

Thinking about the study that has just been described, what kinds of accents do you perceive difficult to understand? Knowing that your own negative expectations of being able to easily understand these accents might lead to a breakdown in communication, what steps can you take to ensure that you assume a reasonable amount of responsibility for working toward mutual understanding?

Thinking About Positive Evaluations of Different Accents: Personal and Professional Reflection. As discussed earlier in this chapter, Rosina Lippi-Green tells us that if we are particularly positive about the set of social characteristics we see in another person, or if the purposes of communication are especially important to us, we will accept more of the burden. Under what circumstances, if any, have you worked to accept more of the communicative burden than you typically do? Why do you think you worked so hard to understand what was being said? How might your answers to these questions impact on your teaching practice?

Thinking About Linguistic Privilege. In the play, *Hong Kong, Canada* (included in Appendix A), Joshua and Sarah have the privilege of not having to worry about being understood or performing effectively in a second or other language. They also don't have to worry about being able to understand the teacher or other students at school. Wendy and Sam do. Wendy and Sam also have to make difficult decisions about which language(s) to speak at school. Thinking about the linguistic privileges Joshua and Sarah have as Standard English-speakers at their school, keep a week-long list of the ways Standard English speakers are privileged in your own school and community settings. To illustrate, "Standard English speakers don't have to worry that people in the audience will wrinkle their noses, shrug their shoulders, or shake their heads during their oral presentation." How might the findings from your list inform the pedagogical choices you make in your own classroom?

7

Conclusion: Challenging Linguistic Inequities in Multilingual School Communities

> My mother does not know the discomfort of trying to speak English all day, everyday. She is in Hong Kong where she can speak Cantonese. Some days my mouth, my cheeks, my lips, my throat hurt. When my mother tells me, "I want you to speak English" she thinks only of the doors that might open. Not the doors that close. An English-only policy will close doors for those of us who speak other languages. Unable to say what we would like to say in English, some of us will remain silent. An English-only policy also closes doors for those of us who want to practice speaking other languages with students who already know them well.
>
> [From *Hong Kong, Canada*]

In the last scene of my play, *Hong Kong, Canada* (Appendix A), English teacher, Ms. Diamond, holds a school hearing so that she can better understand the variety of student views on multilingualism at her school. A petition for an English-only policy has been signed by a small group of students at the school and Ms. Diamond is trying to find out what is behind their desire to eliminate the use of languages other than English. At the same time, Ms. Diamond wants to find out why other students feel that multilingual practices serve their best interests. In the quotation that opens this conclu-

124

sion, the character of Wendy uses the metaphor of opening and closing doors to articulate her thinking on the issue. In her mind, an English-only policy closes doors for students who speak languages other than English.

Like the characters in *Hong Kong, Canada*, the students and teachers at Northside grappled with the politics of language use at their school. As mentioned in the Introduction, the staff at Northside were expected to follow the guidelines set forth in the school board's 1995 *Language for Learning Policy*, which accepted student multilingualism at school. Although all the teachers we spoke to supported and shared the *Language for Learning Policy's* goal of setting ESOL students up for academic success, not all of them shared the policy's assumption that the best way to do this was by accepting institutional student multilingualism. In this short conclusion, I summarize the different ways the *Learning for Policy* was received at Northside by examining the ways particular assumptions underlying the policy were both embraced and contested by teachers and students. I also return to an important purpose of this critical teacher education text, and discuss the question of whether or not a language policy that promotes student multilingualism is able to effectively challenge educational linguistic inequities facing ESOL students in schools like Northside.

CONTESTING AND CHALLENGING STUDENT MULTILINGUALISM AT NORTHSIDE

Every teacher we interviewed and observed at Northside cared deeply about their students' academic success and every one believed that their pedagogical approaches "recognized," "respected," and "valued" their students' linguistic backgrounds as outlined in the *Language for Learning Policy*. The differences between the teachers' individual approaches to working with linguistic diversity had to do with whether or not they supported the *institutional* use of languages other than English at school. Although some teachers demonstrated personal respect for their students' linguistic backgrounds, they believed that their students' language, academic, and economic needs were best met through English monolingualism in the classroom. They contested the school board's assumption that students' first language played an important role in their classrooms with pedagogical strategies that promoted and insisted on the use of English only.

In contrast to those who desired English monolingualism in the classroom, other teachers at Northside supported the assumption that the use of languages other than English could help their students meet academic goals.

They accepted and encouraged the use of languages in a number of ways. For example, in Mrs. Lo, Ms. Edwards, and Mr. Robertson's classrooms, students taught and advised each other in languages other than English as they worked on their different math problems, art, and English projects.

Although it was possible to contest the policy's legitimizing of student multilingualism in a classroom context at Northside, it was not possible to contest multilingualism on a schoolwide basis. As discussed in chapter 5, during the study, several of the math teachers at Northside asked the principal to implement a schoolwide English-only policy so that their individual classroom English-only policies would have more authority. This was something that the principal would not do because she was expected to support all the assumptions underlying the *Language for Learning Policy* and find ways of negotiating the contradictory desires of English monolingualism and student multilingualism at the school. Barbara Ishii, who was one of the vice principals at Northside during the study and is now the current principal at the school, believes that it is important that teachers learn to deliver curriculum in different ways to accommodate students from different backgrounds. She also believes that an English-only policy can not be implemented without taking away what teachers do individually to accommodate differences among students. "Students benefit from many teaching styles and approaches," she says. "It gives the students enriched experiences. An English-only policy compromises the benefits students gain from diversity of pedagogical approaches." As well, she adds, "In the real world, there is no building in the city that has rules about only speaking English." Learning to negotiate across linguistic differences, then, is a life skill that all students living in multilingual communities need to develop. In keeping with this analysis of the importance of linguistic negotiation, I have advocated for a multifaceted strategy of promoting both multilingual and English learning activities that are dependent on the cognitive, skill, and discourse development that needs to take place in a particular learning context.

CHALLENGING LINGUISTIC INEQUITIES IN MULTILINGUAL SCHOOL COMMUNITIES

Moving to an analysis of whether or not the school board policy that accepted student multilingualism at Northside was able to challenge any of the linguistic inequities facing the ESOL students studying there, I discuss some of the pedagogical approaches that supported student multilingualism at the school. Following sociolinguists Monica Heller, Marilyn Martin-Jones, and Makul Saxena, I look at these approaches in terms of whether or not they encouraged the use of languages other than English on or off the "center stage" of the classroom floor.[1]

Students who were learning math from an introductory lecture by Mrs. Lo (before practicing problems on their own or in small groups on a shared stage) did not perform on center stage unless they were asked to explain a problem to other students during the lecture. This center stage performance was always undertaken in English. The association of English with center stage teaching performances can be traced back to the *Language for Learning Policy*, which clearly stated that English was the language of instruction in the school board's schools. Although the policy encouraged institutional *student* multilingualism (for the purposes of assisting each other), the use of languages other than English to *teach* while occupying (as opposed to sharing) center stage was not legitimate. This may explain why Mrs. Lo talked about her work at Northside as encompassing three different roles: teacher, helper, and counselor. It was only in the roles of helper and counselor, off center stage, that she used Cantonese and Mandarin because it was only in those roles that the use of languages other than English was legitimate.

The exclusive use of English for teaching on center stage of the classroom floor sent a strong message to students about the value of different languages used in school. English was the legitimate language at the school and was valued more highly despite the recognition that "all languages and varieties of languages are equally valid forms of thought and communication" (*Language for Learning Policy*, p. 8). However, Mrs. Lo limited the amount of time she spent teaching on center stage and the amount of time English maintained its legitimacy in her classroom. After her introductory lesson on center stage, Mrs. Lo involved her students in "classroom practice activities," which transformed her classroom space into a shared stage. On this shared stage, the use of languages other than English was accepted and challenged the dominance of English. Similarly, during the painting unit in Ms. Edwards' class, students worked on a shared multilingual stage and were able to advise each other in whatever language they desired as they worked on their different projects. As was argued in chapter 5, this establishment of a shared stage not only momentarily challenged the dominance of English, but also challenged coercive

---

[1]See Heller and Martin-Jones (2001) and Martin-Jones and Saxena (2001).

relations of power underlying standard English ideology and traditional roles of authority in the classroom.

Mrs. Lo and Ms. Edgars' creation of a shared multilingual stage in their classrooms, made possible by the acceptance of student multilingualism in the *Language for Learning Policy Language,* allowed them to challenge the linguistic disadvantage of having to always perform academically in a second or other language. Another challenge of linguistic disadvantage occurred—on center stage—in Mr. Robertson's class, when a student chose to make an oral presentation that involved the use of another language. Here the student presenter, who did an analysis of a Chinese poem that he had performed twice, once in Chinese and once in English, was using Chinese on center stage to complete an oral assignment that was being evaluated for academic credit.

To summarize, a school board language policy that accepts student multilingualism at the same time as it names English as the official, legitimate language of instruction in its schools provides teachers with a space to challenge linguistic inequities facing ESOL students in small, momentary ways. At Northside, such work was undertaken by creating a shared, multilingual stage in the classroom. Such a strategy, however, was not unproblematic. Given the powerful discourses of linguistic privilege and discrimination operating in our society, teachers who created a shared multilingual stage in their classrooms found themselves needing to negotiate a variety of dilemmas of speech, silence, and exclusion. Learning how to negotiate these dilemmas effectively is extremely important for teachers who work to create a shared stage in their own multilingual classrooms.

FROM "WHAT IS" TO "WHAT COULD BE"

Moving from a policy discussion of "what is" to a policy discussion of "what could be," a more powerful way of challenging linguistic inequities in schooling would be to create a language policy that supported both teacher and student multilingualism at school. Such a policy would enable teachers to legitimately use languages other than English to assist students in accessing school knowledge. A policy of full institutional multilingualism could also encourage the recruitment of more multilingual teachers and the development of multilingual assessment practices. These hiring and assessment practices would expand the current space available for challenging linguistic privilege and linguistic inequities in multilingual schools. A full discussion of such a policy is beyond the scope of this concluding chapter. However, thinking about the dilemmas and tensions that arose from the implementation of the 1995 *Language for Learning Policy*, it is clear that such an antidiscriminatory language policy would likely involve conflict. Implementation of such a language policy, then, would need to be accompanied by teacher education programming that assisted teachers in learning to respond productively to different kinds of linguistic conflict.

Although I have argued for a future that supports teacher as well as student multilingualism at schools where English is the primary medium of instruction, current policy development in Toronto has not increased the spaces teachers need for challenging linguistic inequities. As mentioned in the Introduction, when several different school boards in the metropolitan Toronto area merged to form the new Toronto District School Board in January, 1998, the policies that had been implemented in each school board were replaced with new policies. A new language policy for the new Toronto District School Board was adopted on May 27, 1998, after our classroom observation work at Northside had been completed. The 1998 *Literacy Foundation Policy* is similar to the 1995 *Language for Learning Policy* in that it articulates the belief that "all languages and varieties of languages are equally valid forms of thought and communication" (p. 2). The 1998 policy also states that "First language literacy is important for second-language learning and for achieving academic success in the second language" (p. 2). However, the new policy does not include the statement that "Students' first languages play an important role in the classroom, in the school program as a whole, and in communication with the home" that was contained in the 1995 policy. As discussed in the Introduction, it was this statement that legitimized institutionalized student multilingualism at Northside. Replacing the statement that students' first languages play an important role in the classroom and the school program is a more general statement about valuing and respecting diversity.

> Valuing and respecting diversity requires an inclusive curriculum which recognizes and affirms the life experiences of all learners, regardless of gender, place of origin, religion, ethnicity and race, cultural and linguistic background, social and economic status, sexual orientation, age and ability/disability. (p. 7)

Although such a statement keeps a space open for the acceptance of student multilingualism at school (accepting student multilingualism is a way of recognizing the linguistic life experiences of learners at school), it is not as powerful a statement as the 1995 statement, which explicitly discussed students' first languages as playing an important role in the classroom and school program. It also does not expand the space for challenging linguistic privilege and inequities in the ways that have been already discussed.

PEDAGOGICAL DISCUSSION: PROMOTING MULTILINGUAL AND ENGLISH LEARNING ACTIVITIES

As mentioned earlier in this chapter and is evident throughout the book, my own pedagogical response to the linguistic inequities experienced by ESOL students at schools like Northside is to promote both multilingual and English learning activities in the classroom. My decisions around when to encourage students to use their primary languages and when to promote (but not require) the use of English would depend on the knowledge, skill, and discourse development I felt needed to take place in the learning activities in which we were engaging. The teachers and students at Northside had much to teach me about such decision making.

Evelyn Lo, who was teaching finite math during the pilot study at Northside, reminded me how much students can learn from their peers through discussions and conversations about a task at hand, especially in large classrooms where one teacher has to respond to the questions of 30 or 40 students. In promoting peer teaching and learning, it is important that students have the opportunity to share knowledge as clearly as possible. For many ESOL students, this entails using a language other than English.

Mina's desire for debate in Anne Yee's classroom reminded me about the kinds of interactions that are valued in North American classrooms and the difficulty many ESOL students have in engaging in such interactions. Similarly, Timothy Chiu's play, *No Pain, No Gain,* taught me about the importance North American schools place on the display of English oral presentation skills and how difficult it is to acquire the discourse of making classroom presentations. For ESOL with limited proficiency in English, preparation for debating complex issues and making classroom presentations are often best taken up in students' primary languages and then rehearsed and shared with others in English.

In concluding this last chapter on challenging linguistic inequities, I return again to the 1998 *Literacy Foundation Policy.* The policy's statement on diversity encourages both educators and learners to see the world in multiple ways and to use the knowledge that comes from multiple ways of seeing to create a more just and equitable society (p. 7). It is my hope that readers of this book will use the ethnographic data, the commentaries, the pedagogical discussions, and the plays, *Hong Kong, Canada,* and *No Pain, No Gain* to engage in new discussions on antidiscriminatory education. I wish you all the best.

Appendix A

HONG KONG, CANADA
A One-Act Play
by
Tara Goldstein
© 2001

Characters *(in order of appearance)*

Rita:	18-year old president of the student council; Toronto-born, South Asian or African descent.
Ms. Diamond:	Creative writing teacher at Trudeau; Toronto-born, Anglo-Saxon Protestant, European descent; early 40s.
Joshua:	18-year-old student in his last year of high school; editor of student newspaper named *P.E.T. Tales*; Toronto-born Jew, European descent; Wendy's love-interest.
Wendy:	17-year old student in her second-to last year of high school; assistant editor of *P.E.T. Tales*; Hong Kong-born Chinese.
Sarah:	18-year old student in a creative-writing English class; Toronto-born Jew, European descent.
Carol:	18-year-old student in a creative-writing English class; Hong Kong-born Chinese.

Sam: 17-year old student in his second-to-last year of high
                  school; advertising manager of *P.E.T. Tales*; Hong Kong-
                  born Chinese.

James Wolfe: CRAB AM's talk show host.

Caller: Caller to James Wolfe's talk show.

Nana: Naomi, Joshua's grandmother, sculptor, recently wid-
                  owed; Montreal-born Jew, European descent; mid-60s.

Setting

Pierre Elliot Trudeau Secondary School
Toronto, Canada
Fall, 1996

Set description

A high school in Toronto, Canada. The front door to the school is upstage
center. On the wall above the front door there is a hand-painted banner
on brown mailing paper that says, "Welcome to Pierre Elliot Trudeau, the
home of *P.E.T. Tales.*"

The rest of the settings—the principal's office, classrooms, the school
newspaper office, the cafeteria, and Wendy's living room appear and dis-
appear as needed.

SCENE 1

*(The house lights come down, a school bell rings, and the audience
hears RITA make the following announcement.)*

RITA   Good morning, Pierre Elliot Trudeau Secondary School.
           This is Rita, your student council president and that was
           your 5-minute warning bell.

(The lights come up on entire stage.

*Rita is standing in front of the old wooden desk in the principal's of-
fice, stage right. On top of the desk is an intercom system. She is reading a school textbook while she waits for the second bell to ring.*

The English classroom downstage left is empty except for MS. DIA-MOND who is correcting papers at her desk. The classroom has six metal desks with wooden tops arranged in two rows. These desks and their orange plastic chairs represent many more. There is a small teacher's desk and chair placed in front of the students' desks.

JOSHUA and WENDY are sitting on the sofa in the newspaper office, center stage, looking at some photographs and laughing together. Joshua has his arm around Wendy's shoulder.

The newspaper office also has an old wooden table and three wooden chairs. There is a small computer and printer on the wooden table and a large radio on a small coffee table beside the sofa.

SARAH walks through the front door and makes her way to the newspaper office. Hearing the laughter, she stops just outside the office, listens for a few seconds, then walks in).

SARAH   *(Brightly)* Hi Josh! *(Coolly)* Hello, Wendy. What's so funny?

JOSHUA   Hey, Sarah. We're just looking at the pictures Wendy took on our camping trip Labor Day weekend. They're great!

(Handing the photographs to Wendy)

What's up?

SARAH   *(Perching on the sofa arm nearest Joshua)*

I just came by to give you a message from your Nana Naomi. I saw her the day before yesterday.

JOSHUA   You were in Montreal?

SARAH   Yeah, I was there for the High Holidays. My grandmother goes to the same synagogue as yours so I saw her at the service Wednesday morning. In fact, I sat right in front of her.

(Wendy gets off the couch, walks over to the table and puts the photos away in her knapsack.)

JOSHUA   Cool. How did she look?

SARAH   Fabulous. She said to give you a big hug for her the next time I saw you so stand up and let me give it you.

(Joshua laughs, stands up and lets Sarah give him a hug. She also gives him a quick kiss on the cheek, which he doesn't expect.)

The kiss is from me. See you later.

(Sarah walks out of the office and across to the English classroom. Wendy glares at her as she leaves.)

JOSHUA   Later.

(A second school bell rings. Ms. Diamond leaves the English classroom and walks to the front door. Rita turns on the microphone and makes a second announcement.)

RITA   Please stand for our national anthem and our thought for the day.

(A tape recording of, "Oh Canada," comes on and everyone on stage stands at attention. Joshua walks over to where Wendy is standing and motions that he wants to see the photos again. Wendy reaches for her knapsack, rummages through, finds the photos, and gives them to Josh. She gives him a big smile and they look at the photos together. SAM and CAROL hurry into school through the front door. When they see Ms. Diamond standing by the door, they stop dead in their tracks. Ms. Diamond motions to Sam to take off his baseball cap. He does. In the English classroom Sarah pulls out a huge calculus textbook out of knapsack, opens it up, and begins reading. The national anthem comes to an end.)

RITA   And here's your thought for the day: "All we own, at least for the short time we have it, is our life. With it we write what we come to know of the world." By writer Alice Walker. That's all for now Trudeau. Have a great day!

SCENE 2

(Wendy sits down on one of the chairs. Joshua goes to sit down on the sofa. Ms. Diamond walks back to the classroom and sits down at her

desk. Carol and Rita walk over to the English classroom and take their seats. Carol sits in the back row alone. Sam walks over to the newspaper office and greets Joshua. After greeting Sam, Joshua turns on the radio and the tape-recorded voice of James Wolfe on CRAB is heard.)

WOLFE Good morning, Toronto. It's time for Talk Radio on CRAB AM. Today's topic: "To Canada, with cash: Hong Kong money likes Toronto." Over 20 years, almost 150,000 people from Hong Kong have moved here. They are changing the face of our city. What do you think Toronto? Are they changing the city for the better? Or is our country turning into "Hong Kong, Canada." Give us a call at CRAB. 737-1111.

SAM *(Reaches over and turns off the radio)*

Hey, Joshua. Can we turn it off? That guy is really bugging me. And it's going to get worse when the phone calls start coming in.

JOSHUA I love this show. I love the phone calls. I love the controversy. Controversy sells ads Sam. Controversy …

WENDY *(Interrupting)* Sorry, Josh, but could we start the meeting? I can't stay too long. Ms. Diamond wants me to be in class in 15 minutes. I don't have a spare like you guys.

(In the English classroom, Ms. Diamond takes a magazine out of her briefcase and motions to the three girls to come up to the desk and look at an article in the magazine. Sarah and Rita go up to the desk and gather around the magazine. Carol stays at her desk.)

JOSHUA Sure, Wen, no problem.

(Walking over to the table and taking a seat next to Wendy)

Now that you're here, we can start the meeting.

(Sam joins the others at the table.)

Okay you guys, here's the problem.

(Lights fade on the newspaper office but remain on the English classroom. Ms. Diamond closes the magazine and walks out from behind her desk to stand in front of the class. Rita and Sarah sit down in their seats.)

DIAMOND   Okay ... This morning I'm going to give you time to work on some journal writing.

(Sarah, Carol, and Rita take their journal books out of their bags.)

I hope that everyone is trying to write for at least 10 minutes every day. Thirty minutes is ideal.

SARAH   It's impossible to find the time to write 30 minutes every day. Especially if you're taking calculus.

(Rita laughs. Carol is silent looking straight ahead at Ms. Diamond.)

DIAMOND   I know it's hard to find time to write everyday, but if you want to become writers, you've got to try.

(Lights fade on the English classroom and come up on the newspaper office.)

JOSHUA   *P.E.T. Tales* is in big trouble. The editorial team last year left us with a deficit and Ms. Diamond says that the school has very little money to fund student activities because of the provincial budget cuts. So, the principal is willing to give us the money to produce the first issue of the paper, but after that we're on our own. So...

(Lights fade on the newspaper office and come up on the English classroom.)

DIAMOND   Let's go over our rules for journal writing one more time.

SARAH   Again?

DIAMOND   Yes. Again. I want you to remember the rules because they are the beginning of all writing.

(Lights fade on the English classroom and come up on the newspaper office.)

SAM   So if we are going to run any more papers after the first one, we've got to find a way to raise enough money to pay for the paper AND pay off the deficit from last year. Because the printer won't publish our paper if we don't pay up by the end of October so...

JOSHUA *(Interrupting)* So we have a month to come up with the money and enough money to run a first paper.

SAM How much do we owe?

WENDY $1,000.

SAM $1,000. That's not too bad. We can try to increase the advertising we get from the business community. We just have to show advertisers that lots of people at our school read the paper.

WENDY There's no way we can prove that lots of people at school read our paper because they don't. Hardly anyone reads the paper–wait a minute, what time is it? *(Looking at her watch)* I gotta go. See you later.

(Wendy rushes out of the newspaper office and runs toward the English classroom. Lights fade on the newspaper office and come up on the English classroom. Wendy walks in and takes a seat beside Rita.)

SCENE 3

DIAMOND Okay, here are your instructions. Begin with the phrase, "I don't know." "I don't know." Got it? Begin with "I don't know" and keep going. Don't stop. If you get stuck and think you have nothing else to say, write, "I don't know," again and again until something comes. Just keep your hands moving.

(Ms. Diamond sits down at her desk. A spotlight shines on Sarah. Her voice, reading her journal entry as she writes it, has been tape-recorded.)

SARAH I don't know … I don't know … I don't know if I should drop calculus or not. I had to miss the second quiz this week because it was on Yom Kippur and I was in synagogue in Montreal. Mr. Majors said he would excuse me but he wouldn't let me write a make-up. I barely passed the first calculus quiz. Not like those kids from Hong

Kong. Lots of them got nineties because they have already taken calculus back home. I wish I were as good in math as they are. There's so many of them in my class. Mr. Majors couldn't give a quiz on Chinese New Year. The class would freak out.

(Lights fade on the English classroom and come up on the newspaper office.)

SAM Maybe we should ask Ms. Diamond to ask the principal to lend us the money to run the paper until December. That will give us some time to increase our readership.

JOSHUA I don't want to wait until December to increase readership. I want to demonstrate increased readership with the very first issue.

SAM Why the big rush?

JOSHUA Applications for journalism school are due in November. I want to be able to talk about the way we saved the paper in that essay they make you write. You know the essay about why they should offer you a place in their programs?

SAM Yeah, I know. But Josh, building up readership takes a long time—

JOSHUA *(Interrupting)* That's why our first issue has to be controversial.

(Lights fade on the newspaper office and come up on the English classroom. Carol puts her pencil down, folds her hands together, and places them on the desk.)

DIAMOND *(Looking up)* Carol you've stopped writing. Why?

CAROL *(Eyes down on her notebook)* I don't know how to write well in English.

DIAMOND I know it's hard, but you have to keep trying. The only way your English will improve is if you practice. Journal writing is a perfect way to practice English. In Hong Kong, don't people keep a personal journal?

CAROL *(Looking at Diamond)* Yes. Many people write in journals in Hong Kong. But we don't write in English. We write in Chinese. So I don't know how to write well in English journals (eyes down on her notebook). What is in my heart, I want to write in Chinese.

DIAMOND And I want you to write in English. It's good practice for you. In university, you'll have to show your professors that you know how to communicate in English. If it's hard to write about personal things in English, then write about school things. Write about the talent show tonight. You're performing in it, aren't you?

CAROL *(Eyes down on her notebook)* Yes.

DIAMOND All right then. Write about Talent Night and how you feel about performing in the show.

CAROL *(Eyes down on her notebook)* Okay.

(Carol slowly unfolds her hands, picks up her pen and begins writing. Lights fade on the English classroom and come up on the newspaper office.)

JOSHUA Carleton, University of Western Ontario, and Concordia in Montreal.

SAM Montreal?

JOSHUA My grandmother lives in Montreal. We're pretty close. My grandfather died about a year ago. If I go to school in Montreal, I can help her out by paying room and board. We'll keep each other company.

SAM What about Wendy? If you're living in Montreal, you won't see her very often.

JOSHUA *(Sounding uncomfortable)* Yeah, I know. But maybe she'll follow me next year after she graduates. If she does a good job this year, she can run for editor of the paper next year and try to get into Concordia too. *(Changing the subject)* A controversial issue. I still think that's what will get people reading the paper. Do you know how many people listen to James Wolfe on CRAB AM? Lots. Do you know why? Because he deals with controversial issues like—

SAM *(Interrupting, sarcastically)* Like "To Canada with Cash?" "Are we living in "Hong Kong, Canada?" C'mon Josh. What kind of question is that? If that's what it takes to attract readers, I don't want to be part of it.

JOSHUA You're too sensitive. The guy is only asking a question— can't we even ask questions any more?

SAM Josh, questions like—

JOSHUA *(Interrupting)* Questions on national policies? Like immigration? Have we become so politically correct that we can't even ask questions?

SAM You want to hear what kind of answers you get to those kinds of questions? Turn on the radio!

(Joshua turns on the radio and the tape-recorded voice of James Wolfe is heard.)

WOLFE Thank you very much. Do you have a comment to make about our topic?

CALLER I sure do Jim. I have lived in Toronto all my life Jim. My father was born here; my grandfather was born here. My grandfather fought in the First World War and my father fought in the Second World War.

WOLFE Yes, yes, can you get to your point? What's your point today?

CALLER My point, Jim, is that I grew up speaking English. My father grew up speaking English. My grandfather grew up speaking English. Now when I get on the bus or the subway, all I hear is Chinese. And I can't understand any of it. If people want to come to Canada, they should speak English. And that's the trouble with people who come to Canada from Hong Kong. They just don't learn to speak English. If they don't want to speak English, then they should go back to where they came from, Jim.

(Sam turns off the radio.)

SAM   That's the kind of talk you get to those kind of questions, Josh. That's the kind of talk you get. We don't need that kind of talk in our school. We don't need that kind of talk.

(Lights fade on newspaper office.)

SCENE 4

(The stage is dark. The end of the teachers' band performance is heard. It is followed by the sound of people clapping and whistling. Spot light up on Rita, who is standing downstage center. Rita is wearing a tuxedo jacket and holding a microphone. The clapping fades.)

RITA   Let's give one more big hand of applause for that last act, the smartest rock band around, P.E.T.'s very own teacher band, *The P.E.T. School Boys.*

(The sound of clapping and whistling is heard.)

Now P.E.T., I want you to give a big warm welcome to a newcomer to Talent Night. This is her first time on the P.E.T. stage and I know you are going to be impressed. She's a terrific singer and tonight she's here to sing a song made popular by one of Hong Kong's biggest pop stars, the "Hong Kong Diva," Faye Wong.

(Less clapping and a little booing is heard and then fades when Rita, looking angry, puts up her hand for quiet.)

For those of you who haven't heard of Faye Wong, she has millions of fans around the world. Here, to sing one of her most popular songs is Trudeau's own Carol Shen. Give it up for Carol, Trudeau!

(The sound of polite clapping is heard. Carol walks towards Rita from stage left and Rita hands her the mike. Rita leaves the stage. Music

from one of Faye Wong's songs comes on and the clapping fades.
Carol begins singing the song, which is in Cantonese. When Carol has
sung 8 bars, the music and lights fade.)

SCENE 5

(As the lights come up on the entire stage, Ms. Diamond is standing by
the front door. Rita is standing by the intercom in the principal's office.
Joshua is in the newspaper office standing at attention. Sarah, Wendy,
and Carol are in the English class, standing at their desks.)

RITA   And here's your thought for the day, this fine Monday
morning. "All serious daring starts from within." By
writer Eudora Welty. That's all for now Trudeau. Have a
great day!

(Ms. Diamond walks to the English classroom. Carol, Wendy, and Sa-
rah sit down. Rita walks over to the English classroom and sits down.
Lights fade everywhere except the newspaper office and the English
class. In the English classroom, Ms. Diamond is taking attendance. In
the newspaper office, Joshua turns on the radio. The tape-recorded
voice of James Wolfe is heard.)

WOLFE   Good morning Toronto. It's time for the James Wolfe
Show on CRAB AM. Today's topic "Living in Hong Kong,
Canada: Part 2."

(Lights fade on the newspaper office but stay up on the English class-
room. Ms. Diamond walks out from behind her desk and stands in
front of the girls.)

DIAMOND   Okay, let's begin. First, I want to congratulate Rita and
Carol who performed in Friday night's talent show. You
were just terrific! Rita, you did an excellent job as MC.

RITA   Thanks, Ms. Diamond.

DIAMOND   And Carol, you were just wonderful! It takes a lot of
courage to perform in front of everybody when you are
new to the school, and I think you gave everyone a su-
perb performance.

(Carol smiles back at Ms. Diamond in thanks. Sarah is visibly upset.)

Why don't we give a big hand for both Rita and Carol?

(Ms. Diamond and Wendy give the two some applause. Sarah does not applaud.)

DIAMOND   Okay. Let's begin. Earlier this morning Rita read us a quotation by Eudora Welty. Rita, do you remember what she said?

RITA   "All serious daring starts from within" ...

SARAH   *(Interrupting)* Ms. Diamond, could I be excused?

DIAMOND   *(A little annoyed)* Yes, go ahead.

(Sarah leaves the English classroom and walks toward the newspaper office.)

DIAMOND   Right. "All serious daring starts from within." I want you to write a list of 25 things that you would like to do that require "serious daring" from you. Got that? You have 10 minutes. Come up with as many things as you can.

(Carol, Wendy, and Rita take out their notebooks out of their bags and begin writing. Ms. Diamond walks back to her desk, sits down, and begins to do some paperwork. Lights fade out on the English classroom and come up on the newspaper office, where Joshua is sitting on the couch. Sarah stops at the door, walks inside, and perches on the armrest beside him.)

JOSHUA   So whose class are you skipping?

SARAH   I'm not skipping. I'm just taking a little break. *(Pauses)* Hey...were you at the Talent Night on Friday? I didn't see you there.

JOSHUA   No, I couldn't make it. My cousins from Montreal were in for the weekend and my mother wanted me home for dinner. How was it? I heard it was pretty good.

SARAH   Yeah. Some of it was good. Like, the teachers' band, *P.E.T. School Boys,* they were good. And the dance numbers by the Jazz Dance class were great. But, there were so many people who sang songs in Chinese and you couldn't understand a word of them. And all the people who do understand Chinese—most of our school—went crazy. Clapping, whistling. But, like, if you didn't understand any of the words, it was boring. It made me mad.

JOSHUA   What made you mad?

SARAH   All those songs in Chinese. This isn't Hong Kong. This is Canada. In Canada, people should sing in English. You know what I mean? And I'm not the only one who was mad. Some of the girls from Iran were mad too. Nobody performed in Persian. So how come so many people performed in Chinese?

JOSHUA   (Getting excited) Yeah, Sarah, I know what you mean. It's like all those Chinese signs in Chinese shopping malls. That topic came up on Jim Wolfe's program on CRAB. Should people be allowed to build Chinese shopping malls? Does it matter that people who don't speak or read Chinese can't find what they're looking for? Should people who are not Chinese be concerned?

SARAH   Exactly. (Looking at her watch) Well, I better get back to class.

JOSHUA   (Really excited) Sarah, why don't you write an article for the paper about this? Like, a piece for the In My Opinion column.

SARAH   I don't know Josh. I'm pretty busy. I'm not doing so great in calculus and we have another quiz at the end of the week. I really need to work on my math this week.

JOSHUA   Sarah, it won't take long. And it will make you feel better. We need to talk about issues like this in our school. It doesn't have to be long.

SARAH   Well, okay. I'll think about it. No promises, but I'll think about it.

JOSHUA Great, Sarah. You love to write. And you write so well. I remember you wrote some great pieces last year. *(A little flirtatiously)* I'll call you tonight and we'll talk about it some more.

SARAH *(Slightly more interested)* Yeah, call me tonight and we'll talk about it some more.

(Lights fade on the newspaper office and come up on the English classroom as Sarah walks back to Diamond's class.)

DIAMOND Okay, time's up. I want you to get into pairs and share two or three of the items on your list with your partner.

(Sarah walks in and takes her seat.)

DIAMOND Sarah, why don't you take this time to catch up on the assignment. It's based on the quote we heard this morning: "All serious daring starts from within." Write 25 things that you would like to do but that would take "serious daring." The rest of you can share your work—the items that aren't too personal—with a partner.

(Rita and Wendy work together. Carol sits by herself without a partner. Sarah begins writing. Ms. Diamond continues working on her paperwork. When it's clear that she isn't going to be asked to work with Rita and Wendy, Carol takes out a Chinese magazine and begins reading.)

RITA Okay. You first. What were the top three things on your list?

WENDY Number 1. Write my first article for *P.E.T. Tales*.

RITA You're the assistant editor and you haven't written an article for the paper yet?

WENDY Well, I have. But with Josh. Last year, we wrote a few together.

RITA Why don't you write on your own?

WENDY Because my English isn't perfect yet. Josh still has to correct a lot of my work.

RITA You should write on your own. You can always get someone to edit your work if you're worried about making a
grammatical mistake. You don't always have to write
with Josh. What's the second thing on your list?

WENDY Write a second article for *P.E.T. Tales.*

RITA *(Laughs)* And then?

WENDY Write enough articles for *P.E.T. Tales* to become editor
next year.

RITA Wow. You might have a lot of competition. There was a
lot of competition for that job of assistant editor that
you got last year.

WENDY I know. I also know that some people think that the only
reason I got the job was because I'm Josh's girlfriend.

*(At the mention of Joshua's name, Sarah looks up from her work and
glances at Wendy. She then stares straight down at her work, pretend-
ing that she's not listening, but it's clear she's listening intently.)*

RITA Yeah. I heard that too. How long have you guys been
going out?

WENDY Over a year. We met on Mr. Wilson's camping trip. But I
don't like to talk about it very much because his parents
don't know that we're going out.

RITA Why not?

WENDY Because I'm not Jewish and he doesn't think that they
would approve of us going out together.

(Sarah smiles to herself.)

RITA Yeah. Lots of parents are pretty strict about who their kids
date. My parents were. Still are, I guess. But not everyone
thinks it matters if the guys you go out with are from a different race or religion. Rebecca Steinberg is going out
with Kevin Kim. And I'm going out with Sam Tsang.

WENDY *(Surprised)* You're going out with Sam?

RITA Yeah.

WENDY Since when?

RITA Since this summer. We were both working at the same McDonald's™ and started hanging out after work.

WENDY Wow. So have you told your parents?

RITA Yeah. At the beginning they weren't happy about it at all. They told me that they wanted me to stop seeing him. But I told them they if they didn't welcome Sam into our house, then I would see him behind their backs.

WENDY *(Surprised)* You said that?

RITA Yeah. And it scared them. So they told me that he could call and visit when they were home.

WENDY And what about his parents? What do they think of you?

RITA It's kind of hard to know what they think of me because they don't speak much English and I don't speak any Cantonese. So I'm taking a Cantonese class on Saturday mornings. Now I can at least begin to say hello in their language.

WENDY *(Surprised)* You're taking a Cantonese class?

RITA Yeah. The class is mostly filled with Chinese kids who were born here or came here when they were really young. They want to be able to speak Cantonese when they visit Hong Kong. I'm the only Black kid. But there are one or two White kids there too.

WENDY *(Subdued)* That's amazing. Good for you.

(Lights fade on the English classroom.)

SCENE 6

(Lights come up on the newspaper office. Wendy is sitting at the table eating her lunch. Josh is scribbling in a notebook.)

WENDY   So did you know that Rita and Sam are going out?

JOSHUA   *(Looking up at Wendy, but not listening)* What?

WENDY   Rita and Sam are going out with each other. They met this summer working at McDonald's™ and now they're going out.

JOSHUA   *(Still not listening)* Really? Hey, Wen ... I have a great idea for an editorial for our first issue. It's called, "Multi-culturalism: Too Much of a Good Thing?"

WENDY   Too much of a good thing?

JOSHUA   Yeah. It's about Talent Night on Friday.

WENDY   Talent Night?

(Sam walks into the newspaper office and sits down on the couch.)

JOSHUA: Yeah. *(Greeting Sam)* Hey, Sam. Listen to this. Both of you.

              (Reading from his notebook) "On stage was a good-looking Oriental girl singing a song in Chinese. Now—

SAM   *(Interrupting)* Oriental girl?

JOSHUA   *(Ignoring Sam's interruption)* Now some people might have looked at this and thought, 'Wow, what a great way to promote multiculturalism. A multilingual event is a great idea.' However, the problem was that P.E.T's Talent Night was not multilingual, nor was it multicultural. Songs were available only in English and in Chinese. Is this fair to the rest of P.E.T. students and cultures?"

WENDY   You want to write an editorial about how singing in Chinese is a problem?

JOSHUA   Yeah. Just listen. I'm not finished.

(Reading)   "If Chinese songs were performed, then songs from all of our diverse cultures should have been performed. And if it was not possible to perform songs in each and every language, then only English songs should have been performed."

WENDY   Only English songs?

SAM   *(Standing up and walking to the table, with an edge in his voice)*   Why only English songs Joshua?

JOSHUA   *(A little defensively)*   Because this is Canada. In Canada we speak English. English is the official language of our school.

SAM   *(Getting angry)*   When I walk down the halls, I hear a lot of different languages. I don't only hear English. The Iranian guys speak Farsi. Some of the East Indian guys speak Urdu. English is not the only language people speak at this school.

JOSHUA   *(Also getting angry)*   Well, I heard that a lot of people were angry after Talent Night. They thought that Talent Night violated cultural equity.

SAM   I don't believe this.

JOSHUA   Believe it Sam. I've found our controversy. The first issue of our paper is going to be hot. Everybody will want to read it!

(Wendy gets up and paces around the room.)

SAM   But Joshua, what about—

JOSHUA   *(Interrupting)* I've already talked to Sarah about writing an opinion column about her personal reaction to Talent Night and Wendy—

(Realizing that she's not where he thought she was) Wen?

WENDY   *(Quietly)* Yes?

JOSHUA   What I'd like you to do is write your own opinion column about the language controversy at P.E.T.

SAM   Language controversy at P.E.T.? We don't have a "language controversy" at P.E.T.

JOSHUA   We do now. And it's going to save our paper. Wendy, do you know what would be really cool? If you wrote about your own decision to only speak English. So you could get better and better at it.

SAM   *(Looking at Wendy in surprise)* You don't speak in Cantonese? Ever?

WENDY   *(Ignoring Sam, speaking to Joshua)* You want me to write about myself?

JOSHUA   Yeah. Your column would give a personal, human touch to the controversy.

SAM   Joshua, there's no humanity in starting a controversy about using Cantonese at school. Do you know what's going to happen?

JOSHUA   Yeah. I know what's going to happen. We're going to sell lots and lots of newspapers. *(Speaking very quickly)* I gotta go now. I need to see if I can find Sarah. I want to talk to her about her column. It's already Wednesday and we need her to finish her piece by Friday afternoon, so you and Sam can include it in the layout Friday night.

SAM   *(To Wendy)* Just you and I are working Friday night? *(To Joshua)* Where are you going to be?

JOSHUA   At a family Bat Mitzvah. I've got to be there. I have no choice. But I know you both can manage without me. It'll give Wendy some experience in making editorial decisions. I'll call her after the service and see how you made out. I need to go now. See you later Wendy. Think about that column!

(Joshua leaves the newspaper office.)

SAM   *(In Cantonese)* [This is a big mistake.]

WENDY   *(In English)* Maybe it is, maybe it's not. We won't know if it's a mistake until we try.

SAM   *(In Cantonese)* [How can you be so naive? Of course it's a mistake. And why don't you speak to me in Cantonese?]

WENDY   *(In English)* I'm not naive. I just don't agree that this is a mistake. And the reason I don't speak to you in Cantonese is because I always speak to you in English.

SAM   *(In English)* You always speak to me in English because Joshua is always around and you don't want him to feel left out of the conversation. Okay, I can understand that. But right now, it's just us. Speak to me in Cantonese.

WENDY   We're in school. In school I speak English.

SAM   Always?

WENDY   Always.

SAM   Why?

WENDY   To practice.

SAM   To practice. So are you going to write this column for Joshua?

WENDY   Yes.

SAM   But Wendy, don't you see the danger of saying in school everybody should only speak English? You don't have the right to make it difficult for people to speak their own language in school.

WENDY   I'm not going to say, "everybody should only speak English." I am going to say, "In school *(emphasizing)* I only speak English."

SAM   But Wendy, you're Chinese. If you say, "In school I only speak English," people who think that *(emphasizing)* everybody should only speak English, will use what you say to hurt people who want to speak their own language. They'll say, "Even Chinese people think they should only speak English."

WENDY   I don't plan to speak for all people. I plan to speak for myself.

SAM   It's not possible to speak only for yourself. How many other Chinese students from Hong Kong write for the paper? How many other Chinese students can give another point of view? How many?

WENDY   *(Is silent)*

SAM   *(Getting angry)* None. That's how many. None.

WENDY   *(Remains silent)*

SAM   *(Getting angrier)* Do you know what I think? I think that this is more about making Josh happy than it is about you wanting to write about speaking English.

WENDY   *(Remains silent)*

SAM   *(Very angry)* Do you know what else I think? I think you
            want to act White. You only speak English so you can
            act White. You need to act White to be Joshua's girl-
            friend. There's no room in Joshua's life for "an Oriental
            girl" who speaks Cantonese.

WENDY   *(Quietly)* That's enough. I don't want to talk about this
            anymore.

SAM   Well, I do. Why aren't you going to the Bat-Mitzvah as
            Joshua's date, Wendy? Why? I know why. Because you
            wouldn't fit in. You're not Jewish. You're not White.
            That's why.

WENDY   *(Visibly upset)* Stop it. Stop it right now. These are awful
            things you are saying. I won't listen to this.

*(Wendy walks out of the office and off stage. Lights fade on newspa-
per office.)*

SCENE 7

*(Lights come up on the English classroom, which is empty at lunchtime.
Sarah approaches the classroom from stage right, Carol from stage left.
Each is carrying a calculus book with her. Carol enters the classroom first,
takes her usual seat, and props up the calculus book on the desk so it is
visible to the audience. Sarah, seeing Carol is already working in the
classroom, chooses to sit as far away from her as possible. She, too,
props up the calculus book on the desk so it is visible to the audience.
Both girls work on their calculus separately. The tape-recorded voice of
Sarah is heard.)*

SARAH   How do you do this?
            (Pause) Damn.
            (Pause) Maybe I should ask her. Nah.

SCENE 8

*(Wendy's living room. The television is on and Wendy is listening to the
news in Cantonese. On a table beside the television, sits a sculpture of a
woman and a man embracing.)*

(As the lights come up, Wendy enters downstage right with a plate of rice and vegetables and sits down on the couch in front of the television. She begins to eat her dinner while watching TV. The phone on the coffee table rings and Wendy mutes the sound of the television so she can answer the phone.)

WENDY   Hello?

(Pauses, then coldly) Hi Sam. What's up?

(Pauses, a little less coldly) Apology accepted.

(Pauses) Yes, you're right. My relationship with Joshua is none of your business.

(Pauses) No, not yet. I'm watching the news. I'll write the column after the news. Okay. See you tomorrow.

(Pauses) Sam? Are you still there? Good. There's something I want to tell you. It's about my situation here in Toronto. I'm here on my own. My parents are in Hong Kong and I don't have any brothers or sisters here either. You know, the typical "astronaut family"? Parents in Hong Kong. Daughter in Toronto.

(Pauses) My father? He's a journalist in Hong Kong. My mother is a doctor.

(Pauses) Right. There aren't a lot of jobs for Hong Kongese journalists in Toronto. Anyway, because I'm here on my own, my relationship with Josh is very important to me. For me, he's like a second family. My second family in Toronto.

(There is a knock at the door.) Sam, I gotta go. Josh is here. See you tomorrow. Yeah. Fine. Bye.

WENDY   *(Opens the door, pulls Joshua inside and reaches over to hug and kiss Joshua.)* Hi! Nice to see you.

(They kiss warmly.)

JOSHUA   Nice to see you too.

WENDY   Come in. How long can you stay? Would you like some dinner?

JOSHUA   *(Comes into the room and sits down on the couch)* I can't stay long. My mother is expecting me. I just came by to give you something. You watching the news?

(Wendy sits down beside him and takes his hand)

WENDY   Yeah. I always watch the news at the end of the day. I've told you this before, haven't I? It reminds me of home. Back in Hong Kong, we all used to watch the news at the end of the day. My father, my mother and I. My father would make some funny or ironic comment about nearly every story and my mother would laugh.

JOSHUA   *(Squeezes Wendy's hand)* So Wen, are you going to work on the column tonight? If you work on it tonight, I can go over it with you tomorrow. Then you can rewrite and it will be ready for layout on Friday.

WENDY   Okay. I'll begin working on it tonight. After the news. Are you sure I can't give you some dinner?

JOSHUA   I'm sure. I need to go home soon. But I've brought you something.

(Opens his knapsack and pulls out a gift that has been loosely wrapped in tissue paper)

I didn't have time to wrap it properly. But I didn't think you'd care.

WENDY   *(Carefully unwrapping the tissue paper)* No, I don't care at all. Oh,...Josh. A stand for your grandmother's sculpture. Let's see how it looks.

(Wendy carefully places the sculpture on the stand)

Doesn't it look great?

JOSHUA   Yeah. It does look great. I'll tell her how great it looks when I see her.

WENDY   Maybe she'd like to come and see how it looks. I could have her over for tea. I would love to meet her, Josh.

JOSHUA   (*Dropping Wendy's hand, getting up to leave*)
I don't think so, Wen. It will be a pretty busy weekend. Lots of family parties.

There won't be time for her to come over here. Maybe another time.

WENDY   (*Pulling Joshua down on the sofa, taking his hand in hers*) Josh. I want to meet your family. I had a horrible fight with Sam today after you left to find Sarah. He said that there's no room for a Chinese girlfriend who speaks Cantonese in your life. That's not true, is it Josh?

JOSHUA   (*Pulling away, getting up off the sofa, angry*)
Sam should mind his own business. Of course, there's room for you in my life. You are in my life. I'm here visiting you, aren't I? But I just can't introduce you to my family right now. And I can't stay to talk about this because I'm late. I wish I could stay for dinner tonight. But I can't. My grandmother arrived on the 5:00 train and I told my mother that I would be home 20 minutes ago. I'll call you later.

(*Kisses the top of her head*) Bye.

(*Joshua unlocks the front door and walks out of the apartment*)

WENDY   (*Softly*) Bye. Talk to you later.

(*Takes the remote control and presses the mute button so that the sound of the Cantonese news is heard once again. Lights fade slowly until all the audience can see is the blue light of television lighting up the stage.*)

SCENE 9

(*The kitchen at Joshua's house downstage left. Classical Chinese music is playing. Nana is sitting at a table in the kitchen reading a magazine. On the table are a teacup and a CD case. Joshua enters stage left with a teapot. He pours the tea into Nana's cup, picks up the CD case and examines it. Lights fade.*)

SCENE 10

(Lights come up on the newspaper office where Wendy and Sam are working on the large table, laying out the newspaper.)

WENDY Okay. So we have Josh's editorial on page two and Sarah's piece "I Am Canadian and I Speak English" on page three. I'm thinking of putting my own column on the same page as Sarah's piece. What do you think?

SAM What's the headline on your column? "I am Chinese But I Speak English?"

WENDY Very funny. I've decided to call my new weekly column, "On My Mind," and this particular piece "Choices."

SAM "Choices." Okay. Put it on the same page as Sarah's piece.

WENDY Fine. So how many ads were you able to sell for our first issue?

SAM Ten.

WENDY Ten? Wow! That's pretty good! How did you manage to sell ten ads?

SAM I expanded our client base.

WENDY Yeah? Who are our new clients?

SAM People who want to advertise their tutoring services to Hong Kong students at P.E.T.

WENDY Really. Are the ads ready to be printed?

SAM Yeah. They are all on the computer. Here's a hard copy for you to look at.

(Sam hands Wendy a several pieces of paper with the ads on them.)

WENDY   *(Anxiously)* Sam. These ads are all in Chinese.

SAM   *(Grinning)* I know. That's what our clients wanted. It's a changing market. Our new clients are willing to pay us $50 for a Chinese ad that's geared to Chinese students. I've never been able to sell 10 ads before. Isn't it great?

WENDY   *(Very anxiously)* Sam, if we publish these ads, then we'll have a Chinese ad on the same page as Sarah's piece, "I am Canadian and I Speak English."

SAM   Right. It's all about "choices," isn't it? Choosing to speak English, choosing to advertise in Chinese.

WENDY   Sam, publishing those ads is going to create a problem for Josh. Sarah will be angry. Maybe others will be too.

SAM   Wendy, not publishing those ads is going to create a problem. We made $500 on those ads. We can't afford not to publish them if we want *P.E.T. Tales* to survive.

WENDY   We should speak to Josh about this.

SAM   Wendy, the copy shop closes in an hour. We won't make our deadline if we wait to ask Joshua what he thinks. You're the assistant editor. You make the decision.

WENDY   I can't make such a big decision Sam. I'm not the editor. This whole issue was Josh's idea. I'm sure he'll call soon. We'll ask him what he thinks and then bring the paper to the copy shop.

(Wendy starts pacing.)

SAM   Wendy, Joshua is out with his family this evening. He's not going to call before the copy shop closes. If you want to be editor of the paper next year, you have to learn to make tough decisions. We don't have enough time to wait for Joshua to call. In the absence of the editor, the assistant editor makes decisions.

Are you going to pull the Chinese ads because Sarah
doesn't like to hear Chinese at school? Or are you going to give our advertisers the right to choose what
language they want to advertise in? Make a decision
Wendy. Make a decision.

*(There is silence on the stage while Wendy keeps pacing for a few
minutes.)*

WENDY   *(Stops pacing and take a deep breath)*

All right. We'll print the ads. Let's finish the layout and
bring it over to the copy shop.

(Lights fade.)

SCENE 11

*(At the Bat Mitzvah. Klezmer music is playing. Joshua and Nana Naomi
are sitting side by side at a round table with a white tablecloth located
downstage center. Nana Naomi is dressed in a classic suit and is wearing
red lipstick. The music comes to an end. Nana begins to speak.)*

NANA   *(With a slight Yiddish intonation)* So Josh, tell me, how
are you doing?

JOSHUA   Not bad, Nana, not bad.

NANA   You look at little sad tonight.

JOSHUA   Just a little tired Nana. That's all. I was really busy getting the paper ready for layout. And how about you,
Nana? You're the one who looks a little sad tonight.

NANA   Grandpa Harry would have loved to have been here tonight. To hear his youngest granddaughter at her Bat-
Mitzvah.

JOSHUA   *(Quietly)* I know.

(Pause) I'm missing someone tonight too.

NANA   Really? And who's that?

JOSHUA   A friend who I'd really like to introduce you to.

NANA   So why didn't you invite her? Her, right?

JOSHUA   Right. Because mum wouldn't have wanted her here.

NANA   Why not?

JOSHUA   She's not Jewish. She's Chinese. From Hong Kong.

NANA   I see. What's her name?

JOSHUA   Wendy. Wendy Chan. She's the friend who has your "Second Family" sculpture. She would love to meet you Nana. She asked if I would invite you over for tea. She wants to tell you how much she admires your work.

NANA   I'd love to meet her and have tea. I'd also love to see "Second Family" again. It's always been one of my favorites. I made it in honor of our tenth wedding anniversary. I really liked being married to Harry. It was a fine marriage. But Josh, I can't meet her until you've told your parents about her. It would cause too much trouble in the family.

JOSHUA   I understand Nana.

NANA   Why do you think that your mother wouldn't have wanted her here?

JOSHUA   Ever since Susan moved in with Bill, Mum's been worried that neither of her children will marry Jews. There's a lot of pressure on me to date within the community.

NANA Have you met her parents yet?

JOSHUA Just once. They live in Hong Kong and Wendy usually goes back to visit them. They've only been here once since we've started seeing each other.

NANA So she lives all by herself in Toronto?

JOSHUA Yeah.

NANA I see. It can be lonely living on your own. *(Changing the subject)* How's the newspaper work going? You were telling me something about a language controversy at your school?

JOSHUA *(Excitedly)* Yes. The kids from Hong Kong? They usually speak Cantonese with each other. Not only outside school, Nana, inside school too. Even though lots of them know how to speak English. And lots of people who don't speak Cantonese feel left out. They don't understand what's going on. And they think that since we are living Canada, everyone should speak English.

NANA *(Reminiscent)* You know, when I was growing up, Yiddish was Montreal's third language.

JOSHUA *(Surprised)* Yiddish?

NANA Yes, Yiddish. You'd hear it everywhere. There was even a daily Yiddish newspaper in Montreal. Yiddish Theatre, too. I remember we saw a Yiddish play at His Majesty's Theatre when I was a teenager. But in school, we'd always use English. We were embarrassed to use Yiddish. It was a language from the "old country." We didn't want the teachers to think we weren't real Canadians who couldn't speak English. *(Admiringly)* It's amazing to me that the students in your school are not embarrassed to speak Cantonese.

JOSHUA   *(Confused)* Nana, you admire people who speak Cantonese in an English school?

NANA   *(With conviction)* I think it's admirable not to be embarrassed about speaking your first language in school. You don't have to give up your own language to learn English. You know, I remember my mother telling me that in the 1920s, when her older cousins were going to school, the downtown Jews tried to get the government to create a tax-supported, public Jewish school system. Do you know who fought them the most?

JOSHUA   The government who didn't want to spend the money?

NANA   No. By 1930, the Quebec government was actually prepared to give the community their separate school system.

JOSHUA   Wow. The non-Jews who didn't want a Jewish school system?

NANA   No. Not the non-Jews.

JOSHUA   Then, who?

NANA   The uptown Jews, the more established ones. One uptown rabbi said that the Yiddishists, the people who wanted a separate school system, were "the worst enemies of their country." The uptown Jews thought that a Jewish school system would bring back old country ignorance and superstition. Yiddish and the old country embarrassed them and they didn't want to call attention to themselves. They were afraid of being persecuted for being different as they had been in the past. They wanted to fit in, to be thought of as real Canadians. But, tell me, Joshua, who decided real Canadians speak English? You know, if a separate Jewish school system had been developed, your father would have spoken and read Yiddish. You and your sister would have learned Yiddish. The language wouldn't have been lost.

(Lights fade.)

SCENE 12

(Wendy's living room, downstage right. As the lights come up Wendy is re-reading the paper she and Sam have just published. The television is on low and is tuned to a program that features Jackie Cheung singing in Cantonese. Wendy is pacing while she is reading, her body unconsciously swinging slightly to the music. There is a loud knock at the door. Wendy jumps at the sound, mutes the sound of the television and goes to answer the door.)

WENDY   *(Speaking quickly, nervously)* Hi, Josh. Come in. How are you? How was the service? How did your cousin do? Was she nervous? Come sit down.

JOSHUA   *(Laughing on his way to the sofa)* Hey, slow down, Wen. You must be buzzing from the layout session. How did everything go?

(Joshua sits down on the sofa.)

WENDY   *(Pacing, breathing deeply, trying to relax)*

Fine. Everything went well. The paper is in the copy shop. They'll deliver it first thing Monday morning.

JOSHUA   So how does it look?

WENDY   It looks great.

JOSHUA   Well, what about the opinion page? What does that look like?

WENDY   The opinion page?

(Pauses, continues to pace)

JOSHUA   *(Getting a little edgy)* Yeah. The opinion page.

WENDY   Well, it has your editorial on Talent Night, Sarah's piece on speaking English, my new column, and some ads.

JOSHUA   How many ads?

WENDY   *(Stops pacing)*

Three on the opinion page. Sam managed to sell 10 ads in all. (Speaking quickly). Isn't that great? Ten ads, Josh. We made $500 on the first issue. That's half of our debt paid off!

(Pauses and continues pacing again)

JOSHUA   *(Getting a little more edgy)* Ten ads? Who bought them?

WENDY   *(Stops pacing and takes another deep breath)*

Sam sold all ten ads to people who want to tutor students at P.E.T. Chinese students at P.E.T. The (hesitating) interesting thing about the ads is that the clients sent them to us in Chinese.

JOSHUA   *(In disbelief)* Chinese? Why did they send them in Chinese? Did you translate them into English?

WENDY   *(Quietly)* No, Josh, I didn't translate them. We published them exactly as we received them. In Chinese.

(There is a long pause where neither speaks)

JOSHUA   *(Speaking slowly, deliberately, trying to contain his anger)* So that means that there are three Chinese ads under my article on multiculturalism and Sarah's article on speaking English. *(Voice rising in anger, getting up from the sofa)* Do you realize what you've done? You've contradicted everything that Sarah and I wrote. You've made us look stupid. I can't believe that you published the ads in Chinese without consulting me! What were you thinking?

WENDY   *(Voice rising in anger)* Well, I'm sorry you're so upset. And I'm sorry for not discussing this with you. But Joshua, you weren't around. And we had a deadline. If I had translated the ads then Sam would have lost the business of his Chinese clients. We made $500 tonight.

JOSHUA   *(Bitterly, walking toward the door)* There are some things that are more important than money, Wendy. You made me look stupid tonight. You should have talked to me before printing the ads.

WENDY   *(Anxiously)* Josh, don't leave yet. It was not my intention to make you look stupid. But without the money from Sam's ads, we have no paper. You know that as I well as I do. I had no choice. (A little bitterly) Just like you had no choice not to invite me to the Bat Mitzvah.

JOSHUA   *(Unlocking the door, turning to face Wendy)* You did have a choice, Wendy. You could have waited to talk to me and have the paper come out a couple of days late. The two situations are completely different.

WENDY   *(Voice rising in anger)* Are they, Joshua? Are the two situations really so different? You spend most of the weekend here, but you can't invite me home for dinner. You sleep with me and we make plans to go to university together, but you can't introduce me to your family. You bring me a sculpture that your grandmother made called "Second Family," but you tell me she can't come for tea. You say you have no choice, Josh. But you do have choices. We all have choices. Rebecca Steinberg is going out with Kevin Kim. You could choose to talk to your mother about us. But you choose not to because you are afraid. At least I wasn't afraid to make a difficult choice, Josh. At least I wasn't afraid.

(There is a pause where Wendy and Joshua look at each other without saying anything.)

JOSHUA   *(Opening the door)* I need to go now. It's late.

WENDY   *(Quietly)* Okay. Will you give me a call tomorrow? We need to talk about this some more.

JOSHUA   I don't know. I'll be pretty busy with my family.

WENDY   *(Pauses)* Right. Well *(turning her back on him)*, good night.

JOSHUA   Good night.

(Joshua leaves the apartment. Wendy closes the door, takes the remote control and presses the mute button so that the sound of the Cantonese variety show is heard once again. Then she presses the button again so the sound is turned off. She turns the sound back on, back off, back on, back off. Lights fade slowly until all the audience can see is the blue light of television lighting up the stage.)

SCENE 13

(The stage is dark. Lights up on Wendy and Sam, who is carrying a table with some newspapers on it downstage center and on the principal's office where Rita is making the lunchtime announcements. Sam leaves to get more papers and Wendy sets up the table with the papers they have already brought in. She sticks up a sign with the name of the paper, P.E.T. Tales, on the front of the table. When Sam returns with more papers, he helps Wendy set up.)

RITA   Good afternoon, Pierre Elliot Trudeau. This is Rita, your student council president and it's time for your Monday lunchtime announcements. At the top of the list is a reminder to buy the first issue of P.E.T. Tales. It's on sale in front of the cafeteria. Your support of the paper is important. Without it, the paper may fold. Buy your copy today.

(Lights fade on Rita and focus solely on Sam and Wendy. Rita leaves the stage.)

SAM   So have you seen Joshua today? Is he angry about the ads?

WENDY   No, not since Friday night. And yes, he's angry. The ads contradict his editorial and he thinks we've made him look stupid.

SAM   But the whole point of publishing a controversial issue of the paper was to increase readership so we could get more ads. Now we've got ads. Isn't he happy about that?

WENDY I guess it's not only about getting more ads anymore. It's about his editorial being taken seriously. He sees himself as a serious writer.

SAM Well, if he seriously believes that Carol's performance at Talent Night is a problem and that the multiculturalism we have at this school is "too much of a good thing", then I think you have a problem. You are going out with someone who doesn't like to hear your language.

WENDY (*To audience*) Yeah, I have a problem.

(*Sarah walks onto the stage and approaches the table. She is holding a copy of the paper in her hands and looks angry.*)

SAM (*Seeing Sarah approach*) Now, this should be interesting.

SARAH (*Angrily*) Have either of you seen Josh?

WENDY No, not today.

SAM (*Brightly*) Is there something we can help you with?

SARAH Whose idea was it to publish ads in Chinese? Right under my article on speaking English? Were you trying to make me look stupid? Make fun of my argument?

SAM (*Calmly*) It had nothing to do with your article. It had to do with selling as many ads as possible so we could clear the debt we inherited from last year. In case you haven't noticed, there are a lot of Chinese students at this school and we have advertisers who want to reach them.

SARAH Well, as someone who doesn't understand Chinese, I was appalled to see that most of the ads in the paper were in Chinese! What if I am interested in what is being advertised? I'm left out because I can't read Chinese.

Any ad that is put into the paper is meant for everyone in this school. The only language that everyone understands in this school is English.

WENDY   Sarah, the ads are advertising tutorial services by tutors who can work with people in Cantonese.

SARAH   I don't care what the ads are advertising. When I open any issue of my school's newspaper, I want to be able to read every single word in it. If the paper was meant to be written in Chinese, we would find it in a school in the Orient.

SAM   (*Staring hard at Sarah*) The paper wasn't written in Chinese. It was written in English. Only the ads were written in Chinese. Advertisers pay for the space and as long as they stay within the limits of the law and the policies of the School board, they can use the space in whatever way they want to.

SARAH   (*Staring back at Sam*) Well...

(*Pauses, speaking slowly, emphasizing each phrase*)

What we need, then, is a school policy that says the only language people can use in this school is English. (*Speaking at a normal speed*) I'm going to start a petition and lobby the principal for an English-only policy. We'll see how people in this school really feel about all the Chinese that's spoken here.

(*Sarah walks off the stage. Wendy and Sam are silent for a few seconds.*)

SAM   You know, when I read Sarah's article after you left Friday night, I got very angry. So angry that I wanted to hit someone. I wanted to throw one of the chairs against the wall. I wanted to trash the newspaper office. After I dropped off the paper at the copy shop, I went for a long walk. I walked and walked and walked. After a while I felt better. Despite everything. Now I feel even worse than I did Friday night. It was a mistake to come to Canada. A mistake to come to this school. The people here don't want us. We don't belong. We don't speak English. We aren't White. People resent our language. They resent us. They make fun of our accents when we speak English and then are annoyed and angry when we speak Cantonese. Sometimes I hate it here and wish we had never come. Sometimes I think I will never feel comfortable here. Sometimes I think the best thing for me and my whole family would to be return to Hong Kong.

(Wendy reaches out to touch Sam's arm in sympathy. He shakes it off and storms down the hallway past Carol who is holding a paper in her hands and looks angry.)

WENDY   *(Upset, but trying to composing herself)*   Hi Carol. How's it going?

CAROL   *(In Cantonese)* [Not good. I am very upset. This article on speaking English. I can read between the lines. Would there have been such a fuss if the advertisements were in another language, not Chinese? I thought Canada was a free country, not a dictatorship. I am really mad. I am offended and—]

(Rita enters, walking quickly to the table, interrupting Carol.)

RITA   *(Concerned, speaking quickly as she approaches the table)* Hey, Wendy. What's going on? I just passed Sam in the hallway and he didn't even say hello. What's wrong?

WENDY   Sam just stormed out of here. To cool off, I guess. He is so angry, Rita. So angry. *(Looking at Carol)* So is Carol.

(Carol looks at Rita, looks back at Wendy, then shrugs her shoulders and walks off stage.)

RITA   Did you guys have a big fight with Joshua?

WENDY   No, not with Joshua. With Sarah.

RITA   Sarah?

WENDY   Sarah was just furious that we had published Chinese ads in the paper. She's going to start a petition asking the principal to create an English-only policy at school.

RITA   *(In disbelief)* An English-only policy?

WENDY Yes. Rita, do you think a lot of people will sign the petition?

RITA Wow. I don't know. It's hard to say. Do you have any idea where Sam may have gone?

WENDY No. He didn't say. I think he needs to be alone right now. Most people in this school don't have such strong feelings about people speaking Chinese, do they?

RITA What do you mean?

WENDY I mean, you don't think that lots of people would actually sign a petition for an English-only policy, do you?

RITA Well—

WENDY Don't people have the right to choose what language they want to speak? A policy would limit people's choices. (*Looking at Rita*) When Joshua wrote his editorial, he wasn't advocating for an English-only policy. He was simply asking questions about what languages people should use at school. I don't even think he cares much about the language question anyway. He was just trying to create a controversy.

RITA Right.

WENDY I'm sure he doesn't believe that everyone should be forced to speak English at school. I don't think he believes that ... He's not like Sarah. Or is he? I really don't know. I really don't know.

(Rita touches Wendy's arm in sympathy. Lights fade out.)

SCENE 14

(The English classroom. Ms. Diamond is sitting behind her desk. Rita enters, wearing an African or East Indian scarf on her head.)

RITA Good morning, Ms. Diamond. You wanted to see me before the first bell?

DIAMOND Yes, Rita. Thanks for coming in. Sit down.

(Rita sits down in a chair in front of Ms. Diamond's desk.)

The principal received a petition from one of the students yesterday afternoon asking him to implement an English-only policy at Trudeau. Fifty people have signed it. Fifty signatures in a school of 1,200 students is significant enough for him to want to know more about what's going on. So he's asked me to talk to you. You're the president of the student council. What's happening here?

RITA Well, personally I don't think we have a language problem at Trudeau. I mean, yes, there are a lot of students who speak Cantonese to each other, but because I speak another language myself, I understand why they speak Cantonese to each other. I mean, I don't speak English to my grandmother, even though she understands quite a bit of English, because she would think I was being standoffish. If people from Hong Kong speak to other people from Hong Kong in English when they know how to speak Cantonese, they would be considered show-offs.

DIAMOND *(Exasperated)* Show-offs? That's silly. Why would they be considered show-offs for speaking English? English is the language everyone speaks in Canada. And French, I guess.

RITA *(A little defensively)* Well, Sam explains it like this: In Hong Kong, there used to be a lot of competition to get into university. And everyone who got into university had to show that they were very proficient in English since almost all the universities in Hong Kong were English speaking. There was a lot of pressure on everyone to do well in English. Naturally, some people learned English better than others. So speaking in English became a way of showing off.

DIAMOND (*In a bossy manner*) But, it's wrong for people to think that way. It's important for students from Hong Kong to practice speaking English as much as possible. They need English to survive here.

RITA But it's weird to speak English with other people who speak the same language you do. It's even weirder when you're speaking to friends. It's like saying, "I don't want to be close to you." English is more (*searching for the right word*)—more (*pauses*) formal. It's more formal and it's (*with a little embarrassment*)—it's colder.

DIAMOND (*Insulted*) But at school you speak English, don't you? And it's not your first language either. Do you find English cold?

RITA No. But that's because I've been here since I've been 7 years old. I've grown up speaking English to my friends, even the ones who speak my own language. It doesn't sound cold when I speak English with them. But lots of the students in our school have only just arrived from Hong Kong. And speaking English with each other means something different for them than it does for me.

DIAMOND (*Impatiently*) But what about the problem of the non-Chinese-speaking students not understanding what's going on when people speak Chinese?

RITA Well, there are different ways to deal with that issue. Some people just ask somebody to translate. Personally, I don't like having to ask so I'm taking a course in Cantonese.

DIAMOND I see. Well, it seems that I need to hear what other students think about this. Here's what I want to do. I want to hold a school hearing after school today. And I want you to announce it to everyone as soon as the national anthem is over.

(*Lights fade on the English classroom.*)

SCENE 15

(As the lights come up on entire stage, Rita is standing by the intercom in the principal's office. Ms. Diamond is standing by the front door. Joshua and Sarah are in the newspaper office. Carol is in the English class. Wendy and Sam are selling papers at their table downstage center.)

RITA   And here's a special announcement. Ms. Diamond will be conducting a school hearing on the question of whether we need an English-only policy at Trudeau. This school hearing has been assembled in response to a recent petition signed by a number of students.

(In the newspaper office, Sarah has a determined look on her face while Joshua looks uncomfortable. In the English classroom, Carol is looking at the floor. At the table selling newspapers, both Wendy and Sam look grim.)

Students who have an opinion they wish to share with Ms. Diamond and other students and teachers should report to Room 125 after school today. Now here's your thought for the day. It's by writer, Gloria Anzaldúa, "… if you really want to hurt me, talk badly about my language. Ethnic identity is twin skin to linguistic identity—I am my language. Until I can take pride in my language, I cannot take pride in myself."

(Sarah reacts with anger, Joshua with embarrassment, and Wendy and Sam with grateful surprise. Carol looks up from the floor and nods her head.)

That's all for now Trudeau. Have a good day.

(Lights fade out everywhere but the newspaper table.)

SAM   So, do you think Joshua will speak at the hearing?

WENDY   Probably.

SAM   Any idea of what he's going to say?

WENDY   (*Sighing*) Well, we finally talked about the whole situation on the phone last night. He feels badly that the controversy we started in the paper has led to a petition. But he's also afraid if he speaks out against an English-only policy, he'll look stupid. (*Sadly*) And not looking stupid is more important than defeating the policy. (*Sighing and picking up a cardboard carton under the table*) Well, I have to drop something off and then get to class. I'll see you after school.

SAM   Okay. Do you know what you are going to say at the hearing?

WENDY   (*With determination*) Yes.

(*Lights fade out on the newspaper table and come up on the newspaper office where Joshua and Sarah are talking.*)

WENDY   Hi Joshua.

JOSHUA   (*Looking up, sounding uncomfortable*) Hi Wendy.

WENDY   (*Visibly upset, almost in tears*) I'm on my way to English but I just wanted to drop this off before going to class. See you.

(*Wendy walks quickly out of the newspaper office*)

JOSHUA   (*Quietly*) See you.

(*Joshua opens the cardboard carton, carefully unwraps the bubble paper inside and pulls out Nana Naomi's sculpture, "Second Family."*)

(*Lights fade.*)

SCENE 16

(*The hearing in Room 125. A table has been set up downstage right. Ms. Diamond is sitting behind the table on which there is a pad of paper, a pen, and a glass of water. Sarah, Joshua, Wendy, Sam, and Rita stand in a semicircle downstage center. Sarah and Joshua are standing together at the right of the semicircle, close to Ms. Diamond. Wendy, Sam, and Rita are standing together at the left of the semicircle. There is a big space between Sarah and Joshua and the other three. Carol stands outside the semicircle, downstage left. She says nothing in this scene. Sometimes, when Sam or Rita speaks Carol raises her head and looks at Ms. Diamond. When Joshua or Sarah speaks, she lowers her head and looks down on the floor. Ms. Diamond occasionally takes notes as each of the characters speaks.)*

DIAMOND   Please begin.

SARAH   I strongly support the idea of an English-only policy at Trudeau. A lot of people were angry by the amount of Chinese used at Talent Night. As Joshua Greenberg said in his editorial, "If it is not possible to obtain performers in each and every language represented in our school, then only English should be used because it's the language that we all have in common."

RITA   I am Western African. I would have enjoyed hearing a Ewe song performed at Talent Night. But no one volunteered to perform it. We didn't go for it. Why should those who did go for it be stopped from performing what they want to perform?

JOSHUA   But I feel left out when people speak Cantonese and I can't understand them. At Talent Night there were two groups of people: those who understood the Chinese acts and those who didn't. Instead of promoting multiculturalism at our school, the event divided us. This wouldn't have happened if—

SAM   *(Interrupting)* Talent Night did not divide our community. It was Talent Night, not English night. We were there to watch people perform and demonstrate their talent. You can enjoy a performance without understanding every word. It happens at heavy metal concerts all the time.

SARAH   An English-only policy would ensure that when I go to a school event, I would be able to understand every single word that is spoken.

SAM   People who are uncomfortable when they don't understand Chinese are not used to sharing space with people who speak different languages. They want to take away other people's rights so that they don't have to feel uncomfortable, not even for a moment. That's not fair. Toronto—

SARAH   (*Interrupting*) If all acts at Talent Night had been performed in English, it would have assisted those who are learning the language to—

SAM   (*Interrupting*) But Toronto is no longer just an English-speaking city. It is a multilingual city. We all have to share space with people who speak languages we don't understand. We all have to share the discomfort.

JOSHUA   It's good for people to be forced to speak English at school. They'll learn it faster. Look at people like Wendy Chan. She speaks English really well. And that's because she decided—

RITA   (*Interrupting*) Instead of an English-only policy, we should be offering Cantonese classes during the school day and encouraging as many students as possible to take them. There would be a lot less anger if more people could speak Cantonese.

JOSHUA   An English-only policy will benefit our Chinese students in the long run. It's a good thing.

RITA   Maybe we should be thinking of making Cantonese classes compulsory for students in this school.

DIAMOND (*Scribbling a last few notes*) Thank you all for your contributions. Does anyone else want to say anything?

            (*Carol raises her hand, but Ms. Diamond doesn't see her.*) Wendy?

WENDY   (*Stepping forward*) The day after they enrolled me at Trudeau, my father and mother left Toronto to go back to Hong Kong. The last words my mother said to me as she went through the security gate at the airport were,

"I want you to speak English."

(*In Cantonese*) [To do well in this country you must learn to speak English well.]

(*In English*) My mother wanted all the advantages that were available to Canadian-born students to be available to me. To please her, I decided I would only speak English in school. And speaking English all day did open some doors. I had enough confidence to go on Mr. Wilson's camping trip even though I had never gone camping before and didn't know anyone else who had signed up for the trip. On that trip I met people who were born here and one or two became important friends for a while. But choosing to only speak English also closed some doors. I didn't make any friends with people from Hong Kong.

(*In Cantonese*) [I guess they thought I wasn't interested in being friends with them because I always spoke English.]

(*In English*) Maybe they thought I was juk-sin, a banana, White-washed. I miss speaking Cantonese.

(*In Cantonese*) [I would like to be friends with others from Hong Kong. There are many things we share.]

(*In English*) My mother does not know the discomfort of trying to speak English all day, everyday. She is in Hong Kong where she can speak Cantonese. Some days, my mouth, my cheeks, my lips, my throat hurt. When my mother tells me, "I want you to speak English," she thinks only of the doors that might open. Not the doors that close. An English-only policy will close doors for those of us who speak other languages. Unable to say what we would like to say in English, some of us will remain silent. An English-only policy also closes doors for those of us who want to practice speaking other languages with students who already know them well. In the last few weeks, I have learned that the doors we have opened are sometimes slammed shut by an unexpected force. It is prudent to keep as many doors open as possible. Thank you.

DIAMOND   Thank you, Wendy.

(Ms. Diamond stands up and the students who have been facing the audience turn to face her.) I was moved by the argument that many non-Cantonese-speaking students in this school feel left out when they hear Cantonese being spoken in the hallways and classrooms of our school. I must admit, I often feel left out myself.

(Joshua and Sarah nod vigorously. Carol looks at the floor, Sam stares hard at Ms. Diamond and Rita and Wendy glance briefly at each other.)

However, I was also moved by the argument that Toronto is no longer just an English-speaking city and that we all have to share the discomfort of not understanding everything we hear. When I was growing up, the city was largely made up of people of English, Scottish and Irish descent. We were actually a British town, not just an English one. But the Toronto of my childhood and youth is not your Toronto. We have the largest Chinese community in North America. Toronto is the world's newest great Chinese city.

(Sarah opens her eyes wide in surprise and anger. Joshua, Sam, Wendy and Rita stand very still, listening intently. Carol looks up.)

I will report what has been said this afternoon to our principal and vice principals. They will make a decision about a school language policy. Thanks to everyone for your time. Have a safe trip home and enjoy your weekend.

(Ms. Diamond and Carol both leave the stage from their respective exits. Sarah gives Wendy a hostile look and follows Ms. Diamond off the stage calling her name, asking to speak to her before she leaves. Sam and Rita embrace. Joshua and Wendy look at each other for a long time. Finally, Joshua speaks.)

JOSHUA   I didn't know that it hurt your mouth to speak English.

WENDY   Now you know.

JOSHUA (*Nodding slowly*) Now I know. Wendy, I'm sorry. For lots of things.

WENDY Yeah?

(*There is a pause while Joshua thinks of what he wants to say next. Off stage, Sarah calls out Joshua's name.*)

JOSHUA Yeah. Well, I guess I'll see you around.

WENDY (*Quietly*) See you around.

(*Joshua leaves the stage. Wendy watches him go and then turns to join Rita and Sam. Lights fade.*)

Appendix B: Critical Educational Ethnography in Postmodern Times

INTRODUCTION: ON HYBRID TEXTS AND MULTIPLE VOICES

The 4-year (1996–2000) critical ethnography at the center of this book began with an investigation of how immigrant high school students born in Hong Kong used different languages to achieve academic and social success in a Toronto school where English was the language or medium of instruction. The study revealed that although the use of Cantonese was associated with academic success for Cantonese-speaking students, it also created different kinds of linguistic and academic dilemmas for teachers and students in the school. These dilemmas and issues were complex and required skillful negotiation. I believed that educators could learn a lot from reading about the ways that students and teachers at Northside negotiated academic and linguistic dilemmas at school and decided to write this book.

The book is one of several different texts that have been produced to disseminate the results of the study. Other texts include articles in academic journals and books, a videotape of the student playwriting workshop described in chapter 6, and a playscript that appears in Appendix A. Yvonne Lincoln and Laurel Richardson, American writers on qualitative research methodology, have written about the importance of producing multiple texts in our postmodern times. Richardson writes that the core of postmodernism is the *doubt* that any method or theory, discourse or genre, tradition or novelty can claim to present the whole truth. Yet, a postmodern position "does allow us to know 'something' without claiming to know everything. Having a partial, local, historical [situated] knowledge is still knowing."[1] Lincoln works with this idea of partial knowing and suggests that if all texts are only partial and historically and culturally situated, then there is only a limited chance that the multiple understandings that come from an ethnographic project will be presented in a single text. Ethnographers, she believes, need to create multiple texts, each of which speaks to a different audience.[2] My articles in academic books and journals are written for readers interested in issues of multilingualism in schooling and innovative ways of writing and disseminating critical ethnography. The videotape, playscript, and this book have been produced for readers who are negotiating linguistic, cultural, and racial differences in their own classrooms and schools.

On Hybrid Texts and Representing Multiple Voices

There are several reasons why I decided that a major text from the study would be a book that combined insights from the ethnographic study with pedagogical discussions for educators working in multilingual schools. First, although there are many valuable ethnographic studies of second language learners in schools, and there are many useful manuals for educators of these students, there are very few books that combine insights from ethnography with suggestions for teachers, school administrators, and school policy makers. Researcher and scholar Linda Tuhiwai Smith tells us that the critical research must be "useful" and directed toward social transformation.[3] It is my hope that this book's mix of ethnographic description, analysis, and pedagogical discussion will be useful by introducing readers to the everyday dilemmas of one multilingual school and providing opportunities for them to extend what they learn from that multilingual schooling context to their own.[4] Second, a hybrid text that mixes

---

[1]See Richardson (1994, pp. 517–518).

[2]See Lincoln (1997).

[3]See Tuhiwai Smith (1999).

[4]The first hybrid, ethnographic, teacher education text I read and worked with in my own teacher education classes was Sonia Nieto's book, *Affirming Diversity: The Sociopolitical Context of Multicultural Education*, which was first published in 1996 and is now in its third edition (Nieto, 2000). Nieto's work was an important model in the writing of this book.

ethnographic description and analysis with reflection on pedagogy allows me to both represent and write in multiple voices.

As explained in the Preface, each chapter in the book begins with an ethnographic text that provides a space for student and teacher voices to emerge without any commentary from me. Of course, my own voice is not completely absent from these opening ethnographic texts. Like feminist anthropologist Ruth Behar, in preparing these texts for inclusion into the book, I "undid necklaces of words and restrung them" back together. I also "snipped at the flow of talk, stopping it sometimes for dramatic emphasis long before it had really stopped."[5] I also introduced each opening ethnographic text with some background information. Even so, the absence of commentary at the beginning of each chapter makes more space for the participants' voices in the book and invites multiple interpretations of what they have to say from the readers.

In designing, conducting, and writing up the study, I have also tried to create opportunities for research participants to discuss their point of view through their own pen rather than mine. In chapter 5, Evelyn Yeung's perspectives emerge from her art journal entries, and in chapter 6, Timothy Chiu has his say through his play, *No Pain, No Gain*. In the other chapters, the participants' points of view were elicited through formal interviews and informal conversations and then transcribed.

On Writing in Multiple Voices

Yvonne Lincoln writes that ethnographers embody multiple selves and are able to choose from among these selves particular identities for the texts we want to write. In other words, we can choose the voice, range, and register we want to use for different texts. In the Introduction and the commentaries, where I described work that has been written by other researchers and academics, I wrote in an academic voice that, I hope, is accessible to educational practitioners and to the general public. Although I wrote the Introduction and almost all of the commentaries myself, in chapter 4 I shared the commentary space with antiracist writer and educator Gordon Pon, who was one of the research assistants on the project. Here, our different researcher voices were merged together. Sometimes, the voice of one or more of the research participants joined the analytical discussion in the commentaries. However, the participant's voice was typically included as part of an argument that I had already created rather than as part of a collaborative argument that we had developed together. The analysis and argu-

---

[5]See Behar (1993, p. 16).

ments in each chapter, then, have not been written collaboratively by the research participants and me. However, I did ask those participants whose words are used to illustrate the book's central arguments to read and respond to the first draft of the manuscript and I took their feedback into account when writing the final draft. This recycling of the emerging arguments back to the research participants, and the refinement of the analyses that appear in this book worked toward ensuring that the work contained what ethnographers Patti Lather and Yvonne Lincoln have respectively called "face validity" and "internal validity."[6] It also worked toward keeping the work open-ended with respect to the authority, interpretation, reinterpretation, and finality of its findings.[7] An example of the way my analyses were refined by feedback from the research participants is the inclusion of biographical information about each of the teachers from Northside. In their responses to an earlier draft of the book, the teachers at Northside felt that my description of their work was "flat."

What was absent from my commentaries of their teaching strategies, they believed, was a biographical account of who they were as teachers. Such accounts were important to include in the book as they would contextualize the everyday teaching decisions they made in terms of their own life histories of learning.

Although my analyses can be critiqued for not being collaboratively co-constructed by the research participants and me, the process of writing ethnographic texts was of little importance to the teachers and students at Northside. What was important was having the results disseminated in teacher development events at the school and having the team create opportunities for student development. The research team responded to both of these needs, and our teacher and student development work is now discussed.

Contemporary ethnographers are expected to make room for a personal reflective voice, which examines their own position in relation to the research. Lincoln suggests that this examination include some discussion of the researcher's own personal experiences of topic under discussion, her own handling of the educational problems she is analyzing, the ways that contact with particular research participants might have influenced her thinking as a researcher and educator, the difference between writing as an insider or outsider in the research situation, and the limits and possibilities of both positions.[8] I have undertaken this kind of reflective discussion in chapter 3.

---

[6]See Lather (1986) and Lincoln (1997).

[7]See Van Maanen (1988) and Marcus and Fischer (1986).

[8]See Lincoln (1993). For an example of an ethnography in which the writers do an excellent job of reflecting on their own positions in relation to their research, see Lather and Smithies (1997).

In the pedagogical discussions, it is my teacher educator's voice that emerges. As a critical educational ethnographer who is also a teacher educator, I wanted my ethnographic findings and analyses to speak *to* and *with* those who work in and with schools rather than *at* them.[9] As mentioned earlier, I also wanted to disseminate my research in a way that was useful. It is my hope that the pedagogical discussions will engage readers in reflecting on their own practice and provoke new insights. In chapter 4, I shared the pedagogical discussion space with Gordon Pon.

THE RESEARCH TEAM

As explained in chapter 1, over the 4 years of the study, I worked as the principal investigator and leader of a multilingual, multicultural, multiracial research team that was composed of a co-investigator, 10 graduate and undergraduate students from two universities in Toronto, as well as some of the high-school students studying at Northside. One Chinese, Cantonese-speaking parent born in Hong Kong also joined the team as a translator and transcriber for a short period of time.

Working with a multilingual, multiracial team allowed me to solicit and engage with a variety of perspectives on data collection and analysis. In addition to me and its Hong-Kong born, Chinese co-investigator, Cindy Lam, the team included seven Hong Kong-born Chinese women (Tammy Chan, Wing-Yee Chow, Veronica Hsueh, Judith Ngan, Victoria Shen, Noel Tsang, Alice Yeung) and two Chinese men, one born in Canada (Gordon Pon) and the other (Edmund Tang) in Hong Kong. Cindy and seven of the eight Hong Kong-born assistants spoke fluent Cantonese.

The eighth, Victoria Shen, had immigrated to Canada at age 7 and no longer spoke Cantonese fluently. Two of the Hong Kong-born assistants, Alice and Edmund, who were undergraduate students at the University of Toronto, had been high school students at Northside.

The 10 research assistants did not all work together at one time. There were a total of five research teams: one that was put together for the pilot study in the summer of 1994, and four different research teams that were put together over the 4 years of the project. A new team was established every year with at least one team member from a previous year joining a new team.[10] I led the

---

[9]See Ellesworth (1994).

[10]The graduate and undergraduate research assistants who worked on the project in Year 1: Judith Ngan; Year 2: Judith Ngan, Gordon Pon, Victoria Shen; Year 3: Gordon Pon, Victoria Shen, Wing-Yee Chow; Year 4: Gordon Pon, Wing-Yee Chow, Tammy Chan, Edmund Tang, Noel Tsang, Alice Yeung. The Northside parent who participated in the project as a translator was Mrs. Y. Tsiu. Veronica Hsueh, a newly graduated teacher education student, worked on the pilot study during the summer of 1994.

work undertaken by all five teams while Cindy Lam, the co-investigator, participated in the first 2 years of the project. Other work commitments prevented Cindy from participating in the final 2 years of the study. Cindy's role in the project was to help me assess the data that was being gathered in the study and provide me with feedback on the decisions I needed to make about the collection of more data. The principle ways in which Cindy and I worked together were through letter writing and preparing for conference presentations. Some of the insights from this work are discussed in chapter 5.

OUR FIELDWORK

The research teams and I conducted both traditional and innovative ethnographic research. We spent the first 3 years conducting fieldwork at Northside and reading together in study groups. The fourth year was spent transcribing and translating data, discussing different ways of understanding talk by Cantonese-speaking students, and examining both the bilingual and monolingual transcripts for important ideas and discourses.

Participation Observation and Document Analysis Activities

We conducted participant observation activities in a number of different classrooms and at a variety of co-curricular events. We spent time observing interactions in the following classrooms: Art (Enriched Art, Information Design, Interior Design, Photography, and Senior Art), Business Studies, Calculus, Computer Science, Drama, English, ESL, ESL Drama, Finite Math, Geography, Mandarin, Peer Tutoring, and Physical Education. These particular classes were selected as research sites because of their high enrollment of Cantonese-speaking students and their teachers' interest in our project.

The co-curricular school events we observed included an annual exhibition of students' artwork; after-school classes taught by the math department to prepare its senior students for a university-sponsored math contest; Music Night; a lunchtime Halloween Party for new ESL students sponsored by the Newcomers' Group; a campaign assembly for school elections of the student council executive; an antiracist workshop for students in grade 10 and grade 11; and Parents' Night. We also spent time observing interactions in the cafeteria and the library and I disseminated early findings from the study in three Professional Development events for teachers. Two of these events were planned for the teachers at Northside, whereas the third was planned for the local association of Asian Educators.

Our document analysis activities included the examination of important school board policies, the Quality Assurance School Review done the year before the study began, and the school's course calendars, newsletters, newspapers, and yearbooks.

Ethnographic Interviewing, Translation, and Tape Recording Everyday Language Practices

Individual members of the team and I interviewed teachers from all of the classrooms just mentioned. Although most of the interviews can be described as formal interviews, which were tape recorded and transcribed, a few are best described as informal conversations. These informal interviews were not tape recorded, but recorded by hand in our fieldwork notebooks.

We also interviewed students from a variety of language, cultural, and racial backgrounds: Anglo-Canadian; Canadian-born Chinese, Euro-Canadian; Hong Kong-born Chinese; Iranian (born both in Canada and Iran); Taiwan-born Chinese and South Asian, born both in and outside of Canada. Once again, although most of these student interviews were formally conducted, tape recorded, and transcribed, a few were undertaken as informal conversations and recorded by hand. Almost all the student interviews were undertaken in English; one was undertaken in Cantonese. The Cantonese interview was conducted by one of the bilingual research assistants on the team and translated by another. Although I took a 10-week course in Cantonese at the University of Toronto in the first year of the project so I would be able to at least understand a few words in Cantonese and more confidently distinguish the use of Cantonese from Mandarin, I am a non-speaker of Cantonese. The bilingual research assistants on the team sat in on my interviews with Cantonese-speaking students, transcribed the interviews, and provided me with their own interpretations of the students' responses to the interview questions. While working with linguistic and cultural interpretators meant working with multiple layers of interpretation, it also meant that I had access to some of the sociocultural, sociolinguistic background knowledge necessary for understanding talk by Cantonese-speaking students participating in the study. This knowledge, the importance—and complexity—of which has been discussed by sociolinguists interested in intercultural interview situations, was not accessible to me without linguistic and cultural interpreters.[11] It is knowledge that I believe strengthened my analysis. However, researcher Sandra Kouritzin, who conducted life-history

---

[11]See, for example, Belfiore and Heller (1992); Briggs (1986); Gumperz (1992).

interviews with immigrant mothers, makes a compelling argument for not using translators during ethnographic interviews.[12]

She believes that translators can distance participants in an interview, reduce the trust and privacy of an interview, and may not be as careful with the affective dimensions of speech as the researcher. Given that Kouritzin was conducting life-history interviews about how immigration had influenced the women's lives and expectations, her concerns about the use of translators are noteworthy. It is also interesting to note that several of the women interviewed by Kouritzin thanked her for giving them confidence in their ability to make themselves understood, and for giving them an extended period of time in which they could practice English. Although there are many different issues to take into consideration when deciding whether or not to use cultural and linguistic interpreters, I decided that working with interpreters would enhance the goals of the study rather than constrain them.

Moving on to a discussion of the tape recording of everyday language practices, we recorded talk in four different types of classrooms: art, computer science, English, and math. At the same time as we recorded speech in these classrooms, we interviewed the Cantonese-speaking students whose talk had been recorded to see if we could find out why particular language practices were in place. The bilingual research assistants on the project transcribed and translated the Cantonese and bilingual (Cantonese/English) talk that had been recorded. Although there is always the possibility that the presence of a tape recorder in the classrooms might have inhibited talk among the students, we collected enough talk and information from the student interviews to be able to describe and analyze a number of different language practices in place at the school. Discussions of those bilingual Cantonese/English language practices that are relevant to the discussions undertaken in this book appear in the Introduction.

Hybrid Reading: Research Reports, Memoirs, and Plays

At the same time as the fieldwork just described was being conducted, some of the research assistants worked with me in a study group. The study group read both traditional research reports on the education of Chinese immigrant students and teachers as well as a memoir and play by two Asian-American writers.[13] The influence of this hybrid reading can be seen in the

---

[12]See Kouritzin (2000).

[13]The research reports we read included works by McKay and Wong (1996); Lee (1996); and Lam (1996). The memoir and play we read were *The Woman Warrior; Memoirs of a Girlhood Among Ghosts* by Maxine Hong Kingston (1989); and *FOB*, by David Henry Hwang (1990).

ways I have blended findings from ethnographic and educational research with insights from literature in some of the chapters.

A model for this blending of social science and literature came from ethnographer Ruth Behar's *historia* of Esperanza Hernández, which she describes as a *historia,* rather than a "life history" or "life story."[14] The word *historia* does not make any distinction between history and story. Behar tells us that before the development of the discipline of history in the 19th century, the relation between history and fiction was more fluid. Cervantes, for example, claimed that the true author of *Don Quixote de la Mancha* was an Arab historian. He was merely its purveyor. Behar saw her own ethnographic work in this way. The book was produced in collaboration with Esperanza, who agreed to let her *historias* be borne across a variety of borders: the border between Mexico and the United States, the linguistic borders between Spanish-speaking Mexicans and English-speaking Americans, and the class borders between poor Mexicans and wealthy Americans.[15] Like Cervantes, and the contemporary work of other Chicana creative writers in the United States, Behar merged history and fiction in her ethnography, *Translated Woman*, and combined her ethnographic insights with poetry, storytelling, and critique.

As Behar writes, in our postmodern times, the fluid border between reality and fiction and the partiality and packaging of truth has been brought to the attention of many of us: ethnographers, historians, journalists, and fiction writers. In the field of anthropology, interpretative anthropologists such as James Clifford and George Marcus have subjected traditional ethnographic writing to a sophisticated textual analysis and have demonstrated that the writing of ethnography is both a literary and a political act.[16] Reflecting contemporary feminist and postcolonial thinking, Clifford and Marcus have written that researchers cannot presume that their ethnographies are transparent mirrors of culture and have proposed a new agenda for ethnography: an agenda that encourages more innovative, dialogic, reflexive and experimental writing, which can reflect a deeper self-consciousness of the workings of authority, power, and the partialness of truth, both in the text and in the world. My blending of ethnographic findings with insights from literary works is an attempt to respond to this postmodern, literary turn in anthropology and educational ethnography. The strongest use of fiction appears in those pedagogical activities that direct the reader to my

---

[14]See Behar (1993).

[15]See Behar (1993, pp. 16–17).

[16]See James Clifford and George Marcus (1986).

play, *Hong Kong, Canada,* in Appendix A. While the characters and plot in *Hong Kong, Canada* are fictional, the linguistic and racial conflicts dramatized in the play actually occurred and were documented during fieldwork. Because many of the characters' lines have come verbatim from our interview transcriptions, one way of describing *Hong Kong, Canada* is to call it a testimonial play which, like a testimonial novel, "invents within a realistic essence" literature from the words of those who usually don't make literature.[17] Further discussion of my ethnographic playwriting appears now.

Student Playwriting and the Politics of Researching "Other People's Children"

In the third summer of the project (July, 1998), 15 students from Mrs. Yee's English class were hired as student researchers to participate in a 12-session, playwriting workshop. As explained in chapter 6, the goal of the workshop was to provide the students, most of whom did not use English as a first language, with an opportunity to develop their English language skills and write their own ethnographies through the genre of playwriting.

The idea to involve student researchers in ethnographic research through playwriting evolved from the need to negotiate the politics of researching "other people's children."[18] Contemporary educational ethnographers and researchers have inherited a legacy of racism and colonialism that makes our research suspect.[19] Having undertaken an antiracist, ethnographic project concerning the language practices and linguistic dilemmas of immigrant high school students of color, I wanted to represent the experiences of the research participants in a way that did not lead to the reproduction of the policies and practices of colonialism and racism I meant to challenge. One way of working toward representations that facilitated (rather than appropriated) other people's truths was to have them represent themselves.

The student playwriting workshop also allowed the research team to work toward what ethnographer Patti Lather calls "catalytic validity," evidence that the research process has led to insight, and ideally, activism on the part of the research participants.[20] The desire to work toward "catalytic validity" came from my desire to conduct research that Linda Tuhiwai

---

[17]See Behar (1995, p. 13).

[18]The phrase "other people's children" was coined by Lisa Delpit (1995).

[19]See Goldstein (2000) for further discussion.

[20]See Lather (1986).

Smith (1999) describes as "useful." The ways in which the workshop was useful and led to insight is discussed in chapter 6.

Playwriting As Critical Ethnography

Inspired by the student researchers' monologues, dialogues, and short plays on their everyday school experiences, I decided to experiment with the genre of playwriting myself to produce one of the ethnographic texts from the project.[21] This desire to write up ethnographic data in the form of a play was, once again, related to the difficult work of representing other people's children. As I have written elsewhere, there are a number of reasons why ethnographic playwriting and performed ethnography has the potential to facilitate rather than appropriate the telling of other people's truths.[22] First, the performance of ethnographic playwriting can discourage the fixed, unchanging ethnographic representations of the research subjects that have contributed to the construction of our racist ideas of other people. Second, plays give opportunities to other actors whom, in performing the play, can enact and enlarge the identities of the characters that have been created by me. Third, when ethnographers share data in the form of a play, the subjects of their research and other people can view a performance of the ethnographic work and ratify or critique its analysis. Ethnographers can keep rewriting and performing in response to other people's responses. As mentioned earlier, this provides their work with "internal" or "face" validity. Fourth, performed ethnography offers opportunities for both comment and speechlessness.[23] It allows ethnographers to include what was not said as well as what was said into their ethnographic texts. This was extremely important to this particular ethnographic work, which deals with dilemmas of silence as well as speech. Finally, performed ethnography has the power to reach large audiences and encourage public reflexive insight into the experiences of schooling in multilingual/multiracial communities. As ethnographic playwright Jim Mienczakowski writes, when we are "very

---

[21]The project of turning ethnographic data and texts into scripts and dramas that are read and performed before audiences has been taken up by a number of writers and researchers in the disciplines of sociology and anthropology and in the fields of performance studies, theatre studies, and arts-based inquiry in education. My own playwriting work has been informed by the work of playwrights Anna Deveare Smith (1993, 1994); Eve Ensler (1998); Dorinne Kondo (1995); and Jim Mienczakowski (1994, 1995, 1996, 1997).

[22]See Goldstein (2000).

[23]See Diamond and Mullen (1999) for further discussion of the ways arts-based research provides opportunities for comment and speechlessness.

lucky," the audiences and performers of performed ethnography leave the room or the auditorium "changed in some way."[24] There have been times when students have told me that performing or viewing *Hong Kong, Canada* has helped them question or rethink their own professional practices. In these moments, I know that the play has been "persuasive" and has facilitated questioning of social reality.[25]

But Whose Story Is It?

Although I have argued that playwriting allows for the possibility of facilitating rather than appropriating the telling of other people's truths, there will be readers who will ask whether a White, Euro-Canadian ethnographer should be telling the story of *Hong Kong, Canada* (or the story of *Teaching and Learning in a Multilingual School*). Although student playwriting may be an effective way of negotiating the politics of writing about other people's children, *Hong Kong, Canada* is not a personal ethnography of self-representation (although it includes moments of ethnographic self-representation in the dialogues initiated by the character of Nana Naomi). It is a fictional ethnography of other people. What do I personally know about the dilemmas of immigrant students of color? What is it that I cannot see and hear during fieldwork as a result of my White, third-generation, Euro-Canadian background? These are important questions and ones that I have been struggling with throughout the research project.

In answering the question of "Whose story is it?," I begin by returning to the title of my play, which, as was discussed in chapter 5, comes from the title of a local newspaper feature on recent immigration to Toronto from Hong Kong. As was also discussed in chapter 5, the discourse of invasion exemplified in the newspaper feature had made its way into the everyday school lives of the high-school students and teachers participating in my research study. In discussions with my own students after one of their practice teaching sessions, we realized that this discourse of invasion had made its way into many schools in the greater Toronto area. One answer, then, to the question of whether the story of *Hong Kong, Canada* (or the story of *Teaching in a Multilingual School)* is a story a White, Canadian-born, ethnographer should be telling is this: Uncovering, revealing, and challenging the racist discourse of invasion that limits academic, social, and work-related possibilities for immigrant students is every educator's responsibility. Without White, Anglo-Canadian, and Euro-Canadian invest-

---

[24]See Mienczakowski (1997).
[25]See Lincoln (1993, p. 36).

ment in antiracist research and schooling, the advancement of social justice agendas in education is constrained.

Moving to the question of what I cannot see and hear during fieldwork as a result of my background, I learned that multiple perspectives emerged when I worked with a multicultural, multilingual team of research assistants and engaged with the standpoint theories of Chinese, North-American scholars and writers such as King Kok Cheung, Maxine Hong Kingston, David Hwang, and Anne Jew. These perspectives were enriched even further when Evelyn Yeung and the group of students from Mrs. Yee's English class joined the team. Although I have worked hard to highlight and engage with these multiple perspectives in this book, my colleague, critical ethnographer Jasmin Zine, reminds me that people who write about other people take away space for their work in the public and academic domain. No matter how much space I attempt to make for other people's voices, theories, and perspectives in this book, the question of whether the stories of *Hong Kong, Canada,* and *Teaching and Learning in a Multilingual School* are mine to tell remains unresolved for me.

Learning to Write Plays

Disseminating our research findings in the form of a play required learning new playwriting skills. In the spring of 1999, I joined a 10-week, online playwriting course that was being offered from New York City by the Gotham Writers' Workshop. Each week, the course instructor, Larry Carr, provided us with lectures and assignments that were designed to help us learn the craft of playwriting. Twice in the 10-week period, we were invited to submit an excerpt of the play we were working on for critique by both the instructor and our online coursemates. In order to produce a first draft of *Hong Kong, Canada*, I needed to take the online playwriting course a second time in the summer of 1999. Once I had a complete first draft, I was able to work with it in a number of different ways to gain some feedback on the text.

Getting Feedback and Revising

In the 1999–2000 academic year, the play was given several readings. The first "rehearsed reading" performance was by a group of preservice teacher education students enrolled in a course I taught at the Ontario Institute for Studies in Education of the University of Toronto (OISE/UT) called Minority Students and Equity in Education. Tammy Chan directed this first rehearsed reading (December 8, 1999).

The second (unrehearsed) reading was undertaken by graduate students enrolled in my Critical Ethnography course (March 6, 2000). Four scenes from the play were also dramatically performed by a group of preservice, drama education students on February 19, 2000. Feedback from all three readings and performances informed the writing of subsequent drafts of the play. Feedback from high-school teachers and students in Metro Toronto was elicited after a reading and scene performance at OISE/UT's annual Future Teachers' Club Conference on April 7, 2000. Feedback was also solicited from the students and teachers working in the school in which the research took place in the spring of 2000. This round of feedback from students and teachers informed the fourth draft of the play. As mentioned earlier, a full staged performance of *Hong Kong, Canada* premiered in July, 2000. Rehearsals for the production led to the further rewriting of the script as both Tammy and the actors contributed their own understandings of other people's school experiences to the performance of the play.[26] Feedback from members of the audience on the July, 2000 performances led to more rewriting. It is this sixth revision of the script that appears in Appendix A.

CONCLUSION: ON RIGOR, PERSUASIVENESS, AND TRUSTWORTHINESS

In conclusion, I have used the criteria of internal, face and catalytic validity as a way of pursuing rigor and persuasiveness in my research. I have also used multiple data sources, methods, and theories in my research to develop data trustworthiness. The ultimate test of my success at achieving rigor, persuasiveness, and trustworthiness lies in the ways readers who see their own interests and experiences represented in the book respond to and engage with the commentaries and pedagogical discussions presented. I look forward to dialoguing with the readers of the book.

---

[26]For a description of the different kinds of feedback I received from these various readings and performances, see Goldstein (2001a).

Appendix C: Developing Oral Presentation Skills

by Judith Ngan

DEMONSTRATION SPEECH

Introduction:

Good morning/afternoon. I'd like to show you how to use one sheet of paper to make an eight-page booklet from folding and cutting. It is very easy to make and a neat, efficient, little booklet that requires no stapling and can be done in minutes!

Body:

You need the following materials:
- a piece of paper, any size
- a pair of scissors

Fold the paper in half lengthwise.
Make a sharp crease.
Unfold the paper, fold in half in the opposite direction, and fold again in half.
Cut a slit along the folded line just until the point where the two lines intersect.
Unfold the piece of paper; if done correctly, the cut should be in the center of the paper.

Fold lengthwise again, push the paper in towards the center, press down on the folded lines.

Conclusion:

I have just shown you how to make a booklet from folding and cutting. You can try using different sizes of paper to create your own booklet. I hope you've enjoyed my presentation.

OUTLINE OF LECTURE ON DEVELOPING ORAL PRESENTATION (REPRODUCED ON A TRANSPARENCY FOR VIEWING BY STUDENTS)

1. Content

Set limits.
Know your materials well.

2. Organization

Introduction
Body
Conclusion

3. Making an Outline

Why use an outline?
Easier to remember.
Easier to look at during presentation.
Helps you become involved in what you say.
Reduces anxiety.
Gives you confidence.

4. Before Your Presentation

Practice by yourself.
Practice with someone.
Prepare thoroughly.

5. Presentation Style

Eye contact
Body movement
Voice

6. Delivery

Breathe
Stance
Pauses
Fillers

7. Aids

Visual
Action

Remember
You are the authority on the topic.
Your teacher welcomes your questions and wants you to succeed.
Watch how the teacher does it.
Watch how other people do it.
Practice as much as you can.
Leave time for question and answer.

LECTURE ON DEVELOPING ORAL
PRESENTATION SKILLS

1. Content

Set limits.
The key word is "limitation." Avoid trying to cover everything related to
your topic and/or rambling on and on during the presentation.

Choose the most important points and sequence them in a logical order.
If the content itself is limited, its subsequent organization will be easier
and lend itself to a clear presentation with well-defined points.

Know your materials well.

2.   Organization of Content

Introduction
There should be a logical sequence of steps, each of which leads to the next. This involves introducing the topic at hand, defining it, and adding some justification as to why the topic is of interest, before proceeding.

Body
The body of the talk should be presented such that the listener is carried from point to point.

Conclusion
Recap briefly and have a clear-cut ending.

3.   Making an Outline

Why use an outline?
Easier to remember.

Easier to look at during presentation.

Helps you become involved in what you say.

Reduces anxiety because you are not concentrating too much on the audience and/or their reactions.

This gives you confidence.

4.   Before Your Presentation

Practice by yourself.
Try videotaping yourself if you have access to a video camera, practice in front of a mirror.

Practice with someone.
Ask the person to tell you where your mistakes are.
Ask the person if he/she understands your speech.

Prepare thoroughly.
Mentally practice your speech when you are on the bus. Practice until you know your speech well.

5.   Presentation Style

Eye contact is important.
With a large group you can sweep the faces (but not too quickly) and concentrate momentarily on each one.

Never look down.

Eye contact is the biggest confidence booster there is; one can completely win an audience this way.

Body movement
Remember to move naturally and slowly. Do not sway, pace, or rock.

Use your hands to gesture or help emphasize a change in mood or tone.

Voice
Speed is important—not too fast, not too slow. You can ask the audience if they're with you or should you perhaps slow down.

Volume—better to speak too loudly than too softly.

Intonation—your tone should naturally match what you are saying.

Clarity—pronunciation.

6.   Delivery

Breathe
Before speaking breathe deeply and slowly; this will slow your heart rate and eliminate the racy feeling you might otherwise experience.

Stance
Always approach the audience. Retreat only when necessary.

Keep your feet slightly apart; knees slightly bent, much like a volleyball player's stance. This will keep you from stiffening up and will keep your knees from shaking.

Pauses

Keep track of what you've already said and what you would like to say next. You can take a 5-second pause after each sentence or phrase; remember what you have to do.

Fillers

Don't fill the pause with "ums" and "aahhs." Don't connect disjointed sentences. You planned to stop, so stop.

7. Aids

Visual

Use blackboard, diagram, and charts. It inspires the confidence of the audience. They have something to follow and the aids also offer variation.

Action

Think of involving your audience in your presentation.

References

Anzaldúa, G. (1987). *Borderlands/La frontera: The new mestiza*. San Franciso: Aunt Lute Books.

Behar, R. (1993). *Translated woman: Crossing the border with Esperanza's story*. Boston: Beacon Press.

Behar, R. (1995). Introduction: Out of exile. In R. Behar & D. Gordon (Eds.), *Women writing culture* (pp. 1–29). Berkeley: University of California Press.

Belfiore, M. E., & Heller, M. (1992). Cross-cultural interviews: Participation and decision-making. In B. Burnaby & A. Cumming (Eds.), *Sociopolitical Aspects of ESL* (pp. 233–240). Toronto: OISE Press/Stoughton.

Bhabha, H. (1994). *The location of culture*. London: Routledge.

Boal, A. (1979). *Theatre of the oppressed*. London: Pluto Press.

Bourdieu, P. (1991). *Language and symbolic power*. J. B. Thompson (Ed.) & G. Raymond & M. Adamson (Trans.). Cambridge: Polity Press (Original work published 1982).

Bourdieu, P. (1993). *Sociology in question*. London: Sage Publications.

Briggs, C. (1986). *Learning how to ask: A sociolinguistic appraisal of the role of the interview in social science research*. Cambridge, MA: Cambridge University Press.

Butler, J. (1999). Performativity's social magic. In R. Shusterman (Ed.), *Bourdieu: A critical reader* (pp. 113–128). Malden, MA: Blackwell Publishers.

Chan, A. (1983). *Gold mountain: The Chinese in the new world*. Vancouver: New Star Books.

Chan, K., & Hune, S. (1995). Racialization and panethnicity: From Asians in America to Asian Americans. In W. D. Hawlley & A. W. Jackson (Eds.), *Toward a common destiny: Improving race and ethnic relations in American* (pp. 205–233). San Fransciso: Jossey-Bass.

Cheung, K. K. (1993). *Articulate silences: Hisaye Yamamoto, Maxine Hong Kingston, Joy Kogawa*. Ithaca, NY: Cornell University Press.

Chow, R. (1990). The third space: Interview with Homi Bhabba. In J. Rutherford (Ed.), *Identity, community, culture, difference* (pp. 207–221). London: Lawrence & Wishart.

Chow, R. (1993). *Writing diaspora*. Bloomington: Indiana University Press.

Clifford, J., & Marcus G. (Eds.). (1986). *Writing culture: The poetics and politics of ethnography*. Berkeley, CA: University of California Press.

Coelho, E. (1994). *Learning together in the multicultural classroom.* Markham, Ontario: Pippin Publishing.

Coehlo, E. (1998). *Teaching and learning in multicultural schools.* Clevedon: Multilingual Matters.

Corson, D. (2001). *Language diversity and education.* Mahwah, NJ: Lawrence Erlbaum Associates.

Cummins, J. (1996). *Negotiating identities: Education for empowerment in a diverse society.* Ontario, Canada: CABE (California Association for Bilingual Education).

Deavere-Smith, A. (1993). *Fires in the mirror.* New York: Anchor Books/Doubleday.

Deavere-Smith, A. (1994). *Twilight, LA. 1992.* New York: Anchor Books/Doubleday.

Delpit, L. (1995). *Other people's children: Cultural conflict in the classroom.* New York: The New Press.

Delpit, L. (1998). What should teachers do?: Ebonics and culturally responsive instruction. In T. Perry & L. Delpit (Eds.), *The real Ebonics debate: Power, language and the education of African-American children* (pp. 17–26). Boston: Beacon Press.

Diamond, C. T. P., & Mullen, C. (1999). Art is a part of us: From romance to artful story. In C. T. P. Diamond & C. Mullen (Eds.), *The postmodern educator: Arts-based inquiries and teacher development* (pp. 15–36). New York: Peter Lang.

Donmoyer, R., & Yennie-Donmoyer J. (1995). Data as drama: Reflections on the use of readers theater as a mode of qualitative data display. *Qualitative Inquiry, 1*(4), 402–428.

Ellesworth, E. (1994). Representation, self-representation, and the meaning of difference: Questions for educators. In R. Matusewitz & W. Reynolds (Eds.), *Inside/out: Contemporary critical perspectives in education* (pp.99–108). New York: St. Martins.

Ensler, E. (1998). *The vagina monologues.* New York: Villard.

Fanon, F. (1967). *Black skin, White masks.* New York: Grove Press.

Freire, P. (1970). *Pedagogy of the oppressed.* New York: Seabury.

Fong, A. (1992). How come you don't have an accent? In M. Sugiman (Ed.), *Jin Guo: Voices of Chinese Canadian women.* (pp. 163–178). Toronto: Chinese Canadian National Council.

Gee, J. (1996). *Social linguistics and literacies: Ideologies in discourses* (2nd ed.). New York: Falmer Press.

Genesee, F. (1994). *Educating second language children.* New York: Cambridge University Press.

George, K. (1994). *Playwriting: The first workshop.* Boston: Focal Press.

Goldstein, T. (1997). Bilingual life in a multilingual high school classroom: Teaching and learning in Cantonese and English. *Canadian Modern Language Review, 53*(2), 356–372.

Goldstein, T. (2000). *Hong Kong, Canada:* Performed ethnography for anti-racist teacher education. *Teaching Education Journal, 11*(3), 311–326.

Goldstein, T. (2001a). *Hong Kong, Canada:* A one-act play for teacher education. *Journal of Curriculum Theorizing, 17*(2), 1–14.

Goldstein, T. (2001b). "I'm not White": Anti-racist teacher education for early childhood educators. *Contemporary Issues in Early Childhood, 2*(1), 3–13. Available at www.triangle.co.uk/ciec

Goldstein, T. (2002). Performed ethnography for representing other people's children in critical education research. *Applied Theatre Researcher, 3*(5), 1–11.

Goldstein, T., & Lam, C. S. M. (1998, March). Negotiating identity in "Hong Kong, Canada." Paper presented at *TESOL 98*, Seattle, WA.

González, J., & Darling-Hammond, L. (1997). *New concepts for new challenges: Professional development for teachers of immigrant youth.* Washington, DC: Center for Applied Linguistics.

Gougeon, T. (1993). Urban schools and immigrant families: Teacher perspectives. *Urban Review 25*(4), 251–287.

Gumperz, J. (1992). Interviewing in intercultural situations. In P. Drew & J. Heritage (Eds.), *Talk at work: Interaction in institutional settings* (pp. 302-327). Cambridge, England: Cambridge University Press.

Hall, S. (1996). The significance of New Times. In D. Morley & K.-H. Chen (Eds.), *Critical dialogues in cultural Studies* (pp. 223–237). New York: Routledge.

Harklau, L. (1994). ESL versus mainstream classes: Contrasting L2 learning environments. *TESOL Quarterly 28* (2), 241–272.

Heller, M. (1988a). Introduction. In M. Heller (Ed.), *Codeswitching: Anthropological and sociolinguistic perspectives* (pp. 1–24). Berlin and New York: Mouton de Gruyter.

Heller, M. (1988b). Strategic ambiguity: Codeswitching in the management of conflict. In M. Heller (Ed.), *Codeswitching: Anthropological and sociolinguistic perspectives* (pp. 77–96). Berlin and New York: Mouton de Gruyter.

Heller, M. (1994). *Crosswords: Language, education and ethnicity in French Ontario.* Berlin and New York: Mouton de Gruyter.

Heller, M. (1995). Code-switching and the politics of language. In L. Milroy & P. Muysken (Eds.), *One speaker, two languages: Cross-disciplnary perspectives on code-switching* (pp. 158–174). New York: Cambridge University Press.

Heller, M. (1999). *Linguistic minorities and modernity: A sociolinguistic ethnography.* New York: Longman.

Heller, M. (2001). Legitmate language in a multilingual school. In M. Heller & M. Martin-Jones (Eds.), *Voices of authority: Education and linguistic differences* (pp. 381–402). Westport, CT: Ablex.

Heller, M., & Martin-Jones, M. (2001). Introduction: Symbolic domination, education and linguistic differences. In M. Heller & M. Martin-Jones (Eds.), *Voices of authority: Education and linguistic differences* (pp. 1–28). Westport, CT: Ablex.

Hernández, H. (1997). *Teaching in multilingual classrooms: A teacher's guide to context, process, and content.* Upper Saddle River, NJ: Prentice Hall.

Hogue, W. L. (1996). *Race, modernity, postmodernity: A look at the history of the literatures of people of color since the 1960s.* New York: State University of New York Press.

Hwang, D. H. (1990). *FOB and other plays.* New York: Plume.

Igoa, C. (1995). *The inner world of the immigrant child.* New York: St. Martin's Press.

Jaramillo, A., & Olsen, L. (1999). *Turning the tides of exclusion: Advocacy skills for educators and advocates for immigrant and ESL students.* Oakland: CA: Tomorrow. Available at www.californiatomorrow.org

Jew, A. (1992). Everyone talks loud in Chinatown. In T. Watada (Ed.), *Asian voices* (pp. 47–53). Toronto: North York Board of Education.

Kagan, S. (1986). Cooperative learning and sociocultural factors in schooling. In Bilingual Education Office, *Beyond language: Social and cultural factors in schooling language minority students* (pp. 231–298). Los Angeles: Evaluation, Dissemination and Assessment Center, California State University, Los Angeles.

Kim, E. H. (1982). *Asian American literature: An introduction to the writings and their social context.* Philadelphia: Temple University.

Kingston, M. H. (1989). *Woman warrior: Memoirs of a girlhood among ghosts.* New York: Vintage International.

Kogawa, J. (1981). *Obasan.* Markham, Ontario: Penguin Books Canada.

Kouritzin, S. (2000). Immigrant mothers redefine access to ESL classes: Contradiction and ambivalence. *Journal of Multilingual and Multicultural Development, 21*(1), 14–32.

Kondo, D. (1995). Bad girls: Theater, women of color, and the politics of representation. In R. Behar & D. Gordon (Eds.), *Women writing culture* (pp. 49–82). Berkeley: University of California Press.

Lam, C. S. M. (1996). The green teacher. In D. Thiessen, N. Bascia, & I. Goodson (Eds.), *Making a difference about difference: The lives and careers of racial minority immigrant teachers* (pp. 15–50). Toronto: Garamond Press.

Lather, P. (1986). Issues of validity in openly ideological research: Between a rock and a soft place. *Interchange, 17*(4), 63–84.

Lather, P. (1986b). Research as Praxis. *Harvard Educational Review, 56,* 257–277.

Lather, P., & Smithies, C. (1997). *Troubling the angels: Women living with HIV/AIDS.* Boulder, CO: Westview Press.

Lawrence, S. M., & Tatum, B. D. (1999). White racial identity and anti-racist education: A catalyst for change. In E. Lee, D. Menkart, & M. Okazawa-Rey (Eds.), *Beyond heroes and holidays: A practical guide to K-12 anti-racist, multicultural education and staff development* (pp. 45–51). Washington, DC: Network of Educators on the Americas. (Available from NECA, P.O. Box 73038, Washington, DC 20056-3038. Also at necadc@aol.com)

Lee, S. J. (1996). *Unraveling the "model minority" stereotype: Listening to Asian American youth.* New York: Teachers College Press.

Lepage, R. (1968). Problems of description in multilingual communities. *Transactions of the Philological Society,* 189–212.

Lin, A. (1988). Pedagogical and para-pedagogical levels of interaction in the classroom: A social interactional approach to the analysis of the code-switching behaviour of a bilingual teacher in an English language lesson. *Working Papers in Linguistics and Language Teaching, 11,* 69–87.

Lin, A. (1997a). Analyzing the "language problem" discourses in Hong Kong: How official, academic, and media discourses construct and perpetuate dominant models of language, learning and education. *Journal of Pragmatics, 28,* 427–440.

Lin, A. (1997b). Bilingual education in Hong Kong. In J. Cummins & D. Corson (Eds.), *Encyclopedia of language and education—Volume 5: Bilingual education* (pp. 281–289). Dordrecht/Boston: Kluwer.

Lin, A. (2001). Symbolic domination and bilingual classroom practices in Hong Kong schools. In M. Heller & M. Martin Jones (Eds.),*Voices of authority: Education and linguistic differences* (pp. 139–168). Westport, CT: Ablex.

Lin, A., Wang, W., Akamatsu, N., & Riazi, M. (in press). Absent voices: Appropriated language, expanded identities, and re-imagined storylines. *Journal of Language, Identity and Education.*

Lincoln, Y. S. (1993). I and thou: Method, voice and roles in research with the silenced. In D. McLaughlin & W.G. Tierney (Eds.), *Naming silenced lives* (pp. 29–47). New York: Routledge.

Lincoln, Y. S. (1997). Self, subject, audience, text: Living on the edge, writing in the margin. In W. Tierney & Y. S. Lincoln (Eds.), *Representation and the text* (pp. 37–55). New York: SUNY Press.

Lippi-Green, R. (1997). *English with an accent: Language, ideology and discrimination in the United States.* New York: Routledge.

Lu, V. (1996, November 10). "Hong Kong, Canada." *Toronto Star,* p. B1.

Luke, A. (1997). Critical approaches to literacy. In V. Edwards & D. Corson (Eds.), *Encyclopedia of language and education, Volume 2: Literacy* (pp. 143–151). Dordrecht/Boston: Kluwer.

Luke, A. (1999, March). *New times, new identities, and new literacies.* Plenary address, TESOL '99, New York.

Luke, C., & Luke, A. (1999). Theorizing interracial families and hybrid identity: An Australian perspective. *Educational Theory, 49*(2), 223–249.

Ma, S. M. (1998). *Immigrant subjectivities in Asian American and Asian diaspora literatures.* New York: State University of New York Press.

Maclear, K. (1994). The myth of the "model minority": Rethinking the education of Asian Canadians. *Our Schools/Our Selves, 5*(3), 54–76.

Marcus, G., & Fischer, M. (1986). *Anthropology as cultural critique: An experimental moment in the human sciences.* Chicago: University of Chicago Press.

Martin-Jones, M. (1995). Codeswitching in the classroom: Two decades of research. In L. Milroy & P. Muysken (Eds.), *One speaker, two languages: Cross-disciplinary perspectives on code-switching* (pp. 90–111). Cambridge, England: Cambridge University Press.

Martin-Jones, M., & Saxena, M. (2001). Turn-taking and the positioning of bilingual participants in classroom discourse: Insights from primary schools in England. In M. Heller & M. Martin-Jones (Eds.), *Voices of authority: Education and linguistic differences* (pp. 117–138). Westport, CT: Ablex.

McGroarty, M. E., & Faltis, C. J. (Eds.). (1991). *Languages in school and society: Policy and pedagogy.* Berlin/New York: Mouton de Gruyter.

McKay, S. L., & Wong, S. C. (1996). Multiple discourses, multiple identities: Investment and agency in second-language learning among Chinese adolescent immigrant students. *Harvard Educational Review, 6*(3), 577–608.

Mienczakowski, J. (1994). Theatrical and theoretical experimentation in ethnography. *ND DRAMA, Journal of National Drama, U.K., 2/2,* 16–23.

Mienczakowski, J. (1995). Reading and writing research: Ethnographic theatre. *ND DRAMA, Journal of National Drama, U.K., 3/3,* 8–12.

Mienczakowski, J. (1996). An ethnographic act: The construction of consensual theatre. In C. Ellis & A. P. Bochner (Eds.), *Composing ethnography: Alternative forms of qualitative writing.* (pp. 244–264). New York: Altamira Press.

Mienczakowski, J. (1997). Theatre of change. *Research In Drama Education, 2*(2), 159–171.

Miller, J. (1999). *Speaking English and social identity: Migrant students in Queensland high schools.* Unpublished thesis, University of Queensland, St. Lucia, Queensland, Australia.

Miner, B. (1998). Embracing Ebonics and teaching Standard English: An interview with Oakland teacher Carrie Secret. In T. Perry & L. Delpit (Eds.), *The real Ebonics debate: Power, language and the education of African-American children* (pp. 79–88). Boston: Beacon Press.

Mullen, C. (1999). Whiteness, cracks and ink-stains: Making cultural identity with Euroamerican preservice teachers. In C. T. P. Diamond & C. Mullen (Eds.), *The postmodern educator: Arts-based inquiries and teacher development* (pp. 147–190). New York: Peter Lang.

Nakanishi, D., & Nishida, T. (Eds.). (1996). *The Asian American educational experience: A sourcebook for teachers and students.* New York: Routledge.

Nieto, S. (2000). *Affirming diversity: The sociopolitical context of multicultural education* (3rd ed.). New York: Longman.

North York Board of Education. (1996). *Northside: 1995–1996. Quality assurance school review.* Toronto: North York Board of Education.

North York Board of Education. (1995). *Language for learning policy.* Toronto: North York Board of Education.

Norton Peirce, B. (1995). Social identity, investment and language learning. *TESOL Quarterly, 29*(1), 9–31.

Norton, B. (2000). *Identity and language learning: Gender, ethnicity and educational change.* New York: Longman.

Olson, R. A. (1999). White privilege in schools. In E. Lee, D. Menkart, & M. Okazawa-Rey (Eds.), *Beyond heroes and holidays: A practical guide to K-12 anti-racist, multicultural education and staff development* (pp. 83–84). Washington, DC: Network of Educators in the Americas.

Pennycook, A. (2001). *Critical applied linguistics: A critical introduction.* Mahwah, NJ: Lawrence Erlbaum Associates.

Perry, T. (1998). "I 'on know why they be trippin'" : Reflections on the Ebonics debate. In T. Perry & L. Delpit (Eds.), *The real Ebonics debate: Power, language and the education of African-American children* (pp. 3–15). Boston: Beacon Press.

Perry, T., & Delpit, L. (Eds.). (1998). *The real Ebonics debate: Power, language and the education of African-American children.* Boston: Beacon Press.

Piller, I., & Pavlenko, A. (2001). Introduction: Multilingualism, second language learning, and gender. In A. Pavlenko, A. Blackledge, I. Piller, & M. Teutsch-Dwyer (Eds.), *Multilingualism, second language learning, and gender.* New York/Berlin: Mouton de Gruyter.

Pon, G., Goldstein, T., & Schecter, S. (in press). Interrupted by silence: The contemporary education of Hong Kong-born Chinese-Canadian adolescents. In R. Bayley & S. Schecter (Eds.), *Language socialization and bilingualism.* New York/Berlin: Mouton de Gruyter.

Rampton, B. (1995). *Crossing: Language and ethnicity among adolescents.* London: Longman.

Reid, M. (Producer/Director). (1995). *Skin deep: College students confront racism* [Video]. San Fransciso, CA: Resolution/California Newsreel.

Richardson, L. (2000). Writing: A method of inquiry. In N. K. Denzin & Y. S. Lincoln (Eds.), *Handbook of qualitative research* (2nd ed.) (pp. 516–529). Thousand Oaks: CA: Sage.

Rodriguez, R. (1982). *Hunger of memory: The education of Richard Rodriguez—An autobiography.* Boston: David Godine.

Rubin, D. L. (1992). Nonlanguage factor affecting undergraduates' judgements of nonnative English-speaking teaching assistants. *Research in Higher Education, 33*(4), 511–531.

Said, E. (1994). *Orientalism* (2nd ed.). New York: Vintage Books.

Scott, J. H. (1998). Official language; unofficial reality: Acquiring bilingual/bicultural fluency in a segregated southern community. In T. Perry & L. Delpit (Eds.), *The real Ebonics debate: Power, language and the education of African-American children* (pp. 189–195). Boston: Beacon Press.

Slavin, R. (1983). *Cooperative learning.* New York: Longman.

Slavin, R. (1990). *Cooperative learning: Theory, research, and practice.* Englewood Cliffs, NJ: Prentice Hall.

Sleeter, C. (1999). Teaching Whites about racism. In E. Lee, D. Menkart, & M. Okazawa-Rey (Eds.), *Beyond heroes and holidays: A practical guide to K-12 anti-racist, multicultural education and staff development* (pp. 36–44). Washington, DC: Network of Educators in the Americas.

Smitherman, G. (1998). Black English/Ebonics: What it be like? In T. Perry & L. Delpit (Eds.), *The real Ebonics debate: Power, language and the education of African-American children* (pp. 29–47). Boston: Beacon Press.

Suárez-Orozco, C., & Suárez-Orozco, M. (1995). *Transformations: Immigration, family life, and achievement motivation among Latino adolescents.* Stanford, CA: Stanford University Press.

Tatum, B. D. (1997). *"Why are all the Black kids sitting together in the cafeteria?" and other conversations about race.* New York: Basic Books.

Taylor, C. (1994). *Multiculturalism: Examining the politics of recognition.* Princeton, NJ: Princeton University Press.

Toronto District School Board. (1998). *Literacy foundation policy of the Toronto district school board*. Number B.01. Toronto: Author.

Tuhiwai Smith, L. (1999). *Decolonizing methodologies: Research and indigenous peoples*. London: Zed Books.

Tung, P., Lam, R., & Tsang, W. K. (1997). English as a medium of instruction in post-1997 Hong Kong: What students, teachers, and parents think. *Journal of Pragmatics, 28,* 441–459.

Van Maanen, J. (1988). *Tales of the field: On writing ethnography*. Chicago: University of Chicago Press.

Williams, R. L. (Ed.). (1975). *Ebonics: The true language of Black folks*. St. Louis: Institute of Black Studies.

Wong, C. S. L. (1993). *Reading Asian American literature: From necessity to extravagance*. Princeton, NJ: Princeton University Press.

Yang, J., Gan, D., & Hong, T. (1997). *Eastern standard time: A guide to Asian influences on American culture: From Astro Boy to Zen Buddisim*. Boston: Houghton Mifflin Company.

Yee, M. (1993). Finding the way home through issues of gender, race, and class. In H. Bannerji (Ed.), *Returning the gaze: Essays on racism, feminism, and politics* (pp. 3–37). Toronto: Sister Vision Press.

Yee, P. (1996). *Struggle and hope: The Story of Chinese Canadians*. Toronto, Ontario: Umbrella Press.

Yon, D. (2000). *Elusive culture: Schooling, race and identity in global times*. Albany, NY: SUNY Press.

Yule, G. (1996). *The study of language* (2nd ed.). Cambridge, England: Cambridge University Press.

Zavala, M. (2000). Puerto Rican identity: What's language got to do with it? In S. Nieto (Ed.), *Puerto Rican students in U.S. schools* (pp. 115–136). Mahwah, NJ: Lawrence Erlbaum Associates.

Author Index

211

Subject Index

Note: Page numbers with *n* indicate footnotes.